EVANGELIZING YOUTH

EVANGELIZING YOUTH

GLENN · C · SMITH · EDITOR

P A U L I S T
NATIONAL CATHOLIC
EVANGELIZATION ASSOCIATION
WASHINGTON, D.C.

TYNDALE HOUSE
PUBLISHERS, INC.
WHEATON, ILLINOIS

Cover photo by James M. Weber

First printing, July 1985

Library of Congress Catalog Card Number 85-50216
ISBN 0-8423-0791-5
Printed in the United States of America

CONTENTS

WHO SAID YOUNG PEOPLE HATE CHURCH?

Do you recall the statement made in the 1970s: "We must write
off the teenaged generation—they simply don't like religion"?
What a mistake that was—at least if you poll the vast numbers
of teens and young adults who flock to such parachurch
organizations as Young Life, Youth For Christ, Campus Crusade,
Inter-Varsity, Teen Challenge, Sonlife, The Awana Clubs, and the
dozen or so other Christian youth organizations that are literally
booming with success.

One organizer of just such a parachurch youth fellowship
recently said, "If the church had read the signs correctly, we
would have no reason to exist. As it is, we have had to bring
America's youth back to the church." It's true, too! Whoever
thought you'd see the day when every room on the University of
Illinois campus in Urbana would be rented and filled with
thousands of young college students who would spend their entire
Christmas vacation in an intensive spiritual retreat? From
Christmas to New Year's Eve, they listen to the likes of Josh
McDowell, James McLeish, Jay Kesler, and Billy Graham.

Who would have predicted that we would see the day when every campus in the nation would have an active interest in sound Bible study and teaching—not in the classroom, but in the dorm? Youth For Christ now has some 800 full-time staff persons (many of their top brass are practicing Catholics) throughout the United States with another 4,000 trained volunteers reaching out to our high school-aged kids.

Inter-Varsity is even larger, and on every campus you will find young men and women working within this organization to reach their peers for Jesus Christ and the church. Representatives—who number in the thousands—must seek their own sponsorship, depending on friends and churches for their support.

When asked the secret of their success on the campus, one worker said, "We reach the students where they are. We operate in the world they live in, not where we wish they were." These parachurch organizations have added a professionalism to their efforts that few denominations could afford to do. They have the best in Christian psychiatrists, psychologists, sociologists, and medical doctors cooperating in the development of outreach, to not only the healthy kids on campus, but the troubled as well.

Word of Life Fellowship was established by Jack Wyrtzen in New York state, and through it he has reached out to millions of our American youth. In 1982 alone he led some 33,000 of them to accept Jesus Christ into their lives. Around 400 students per year graduate from his Bible institute; and 86,520 young people attended his spiritual "Round-Ups" last year on his ninety-acre ranch located on an island in Schroon Lake, New York. When President Ronald Reagan asked Jack, "How do you do it?" Jack answered, "We introduce our youth to the Book our country was founded on, the Bible!"

Even if the ranch does have excellent accommodations and programs, "It's the *Bible* that draws the results," Jack insists. "America's youth is in search for God, not gold. Since God, the source of all knowledge, has been expelled from the classroom, we need to fill the gap."

On the other side of the nation you'll find Rich Wilkerson. Based in Tocoma, Washington, Rich reaches out to America's teens. He claims that they have been abandoned by the church, and that some 22 million of them "have become alienated from their peers, their families, and the church." In the past several years he has made presentations in over 700 public schools, and he carries a list of recommendations from principals, senators, law officers, and clergy.

"Think of it," he told a recent gathering of clergy, "1½ million teens between thirteen and seventeen are alcoholics; 1.8 million kids run away from home every year; there are over 10 million single-parent homes and some one in ten Americans are admitted homosexuals. What a time to raise up kids without God." When preacher Wilkerson speaks, kids listen. The casually dressed twenty-nine-year-old minister strides up and down the gym floor, trailing his microphone cord behind, and tosses anecdotes sprinkled with teenage jargon. "He cuts through to their hearts," one principal said in praise of Rich's talk.

Not only do these parachurch ministers reach out in places the church cannot go—the public schools and campuses of our nation—but they have taken to the airwaves as well. Take Mel Johnson and his program "Tips for Teens." For the past thirty years Mel has been broadcasting his program every day from Minnesota, and today he has some 100 radio stations across the nation carrying his fifteen-minute program to kids. On one of his programs he hit right at the heart of our teens, taking on their idol, Randy Newman, and his hit record, "Born Again." He criticized him in his talk entitled, "Rock to Ruin." He quoted Newman's song in which he says that Jesus "never done a thing for me."

The kids love Mel, and Mel loves the kids. Daily, hundreds of thousands listen to such talks as "Spark Plugs"; "Sit Tall in the Saddle"; "Hang in There Partner"; "Me and My Big Mouth" and the like. They are all Bible based, God honoring, and Christ centered. Are the kids listening? If those thousands of letters pouring in every afternoon are any indication, they are not only listening, but getting some sound spiritual direction as well.

Dr. Jay Kesler, director of Youth For Chist, International, with a following in the millions, hits right at the core of the problem. He states, "Most young people have not established a relationship with God in which they can feel forgiven for their sins and clean before God. They need to become a new person in Jesus Christ. The young person in trouble is weighted down by moral guilt and has not had a legitimate spiritual experience that enables him to deal with his spiritual needs." Jesus Christ is the answer, and the Bible the way of instruction. Jay's plan for recovering America's young is fourfold: 1) A gradual development of a healthy self-concept; 2) development of positive peer relationships; 3) establishment of a meaningful relationship with a caring adult; and 4) a transformation through a spiritual rebirth experience.

Jay goes on to tell us that Christianity—the church—has something distinct to offer young people when they commit their lives to Christ. These include: 1) A sense of mission; 2) freedom to love; 3) a healthy self-concept; 4) Bible-based values; 5) a message of forgiveness and redemption; and 6) a Person to share, Jesus Christ.

Down in Texas where everything is big, you find Campus Crusade has one of its greatest youth reachers. Josh McDowell speaks at more than 500 universities in some fifty-two countries, heralding the claims of Jesus Christ and the reliability of the Bible. In the last three years he has spoken to more than three-and-a-half million college students—who came to heckle, and left with a new appreciation of Jesus and his Word.

Josh's lecture series on campus, featuring such titles as "Christianity—Hoax or History," are always jam packed. One university graduate student said of him, "If I had had this material last year, I could have intelligently answered almost every negative assertion made by my Old Testament professor."

Sceptics look down on these parachurch organizations. One denominational report complained to *Time* magazine last year that "they are draining off millions of dollars from the church's social welfare programs." A ten-thousand-dollar giver to these organizations told me last week, "That's the reason we give—the church has left the spiritual for the social, and we put our money where it counts."

Whatever the case, if these exploding and successful parachurch organizations have anything to teach us, it is that America's young people want spiritual—not social—answers to life's perplexing questions. There must be a life-changing experience that leads to an action-filled commitment.

An example of the kind of commitment that follows such Bible-based knowledge is found in Intercristo, for example. Director Dick Staub and his staff operate a Christian job service located in Seattle, Washington. They list some 23,000 available jobs in various Christian organizations around the world. To date they have placed over 100,000 applicants through Intermatch. This service will match up your vocational skills with a Christian organization seeking persons with such qualifications. Here's a job placement center established to place God's people in God's work.

How are Catholics to view such organizations? Are they competitors with the church? Father Alvin Illig, Director of the National Catholic Evangelization Center in Washington, D.C., believes they are exactly what they claim to be: parachurch. Alongside the church. They are not in competition but are specialists in their fields. There are some 6,500 of them in number, including Youth For Christ, Young Life, and Word of Life for high schoolers; Campus Crusade, Inter-Varsity, and Navigators for collegians; Christian Business Men's Committee for men; Christian Women's Club for women; Christian Medical Society for doctors; and on and on.

The problem doesn't lie with the existence of the parachurch organizations and their skills, it comes when the church fails to properly recognize these outstanding organizations that are designed to *serve the church.*

With the ever-increasing shortage of clergy and the continual growth of lay ministries, we need to recognize and use to the fullest these specialists in youth ministry. If they appear to exist "outside the church" structures, whose fault is that? Perhaps it is time for us to acknowledge their skills, their specialties, their growth to maturity. It appears to us that their time has come. When so many pastors complain that these parachurch organizations are stealing their members away from active church participation, perhaps it is because they are offering the youth an exciting place to serve, a spiritual direction for their lives, and most of all, an opportunity for a personal relationship with Jesus Christ.

Under the direction of the Paulist Fathers and the National Catholic Evangelization Association, we have conducted a two-year survey into the many excellent organizations within the United States that have centered their interest and skills on the evangelization of youth. We have concentrated on what Christians can learn from one another about the evangelization of American youth.

We trust that this book will contain, not only stories of great people and programs, but more especially models for you to duplicate in your own denominational churches. It is to be a *trans*-denominational sharing of professional ideas on how to best reach America's young people for Jesus Christ and his church.

As editor, I was recently asked why so many churches succeed with youth, while so many others fail. After this research, it has become obvious to me that there are three basic answers to that question. First, the successful church (or program) holds high a personal relationship with Jesus Christ; second, it bases its information upon the Holy Scriptures and trains people how to effectively use the Bible; and, third, its leaders are not afraid to ask for deep personal commitment.

One Catholic pastor thought that sounded rather Protestant, to which I suggested, "Remember, it was Pope John Paul II who told the seminarians at North American College on February 22, 1980, 'Nothing in life can take precedence over proclaiming Jesus Christ to all nations, to speak of his power to save, and to assure every man and woman that whoever believes in Christ will not die, but will have eternal life.' " As for the Bible, I added, "The Pope also mentioned in that same talk to the students that 'the first priority is the Word of God. God's Word is the center of all theological study; it is the chief instrument for handing down Christian doctrine and it is the perpetual source of spiritual life.' "

Concerning the total commitment that these parachurch organizations seem to demand of their followers, Catholics are reminded of Pope Paul VI's Bicentennial Message to the American Bishops given in Rome on June 6, 1976. The Pope said, "The world says to us today precisely what a group of individuals recorded in the Gospel once said to the Apostle Philip: 'we wish to see Jesus' (John 12:21). And it is Jesus that we must show to the world—Jesus and no substitute. Hence, Venerable Brothers, we exhort you to the utmost vigilance in the matter of catechetical content, as you endeavor to point out to children and to adults the Way, the Truth, and the Life, who is Christ."

What are the youth of America asking of the church today? "We would see Jesus." How can we best serve and reach the youth of America today? Show them Jesus.

—Glenn C. Smith

Dr. Glenn C. Smith is a graduate of Loyola University in Chicago and The Catholic University of America, and has his doctorate from Trinity Evangelical Divinity School, Deerfield, Illinois. He is a staff member of the National Catholic Evangelization Association.

THE NATIONAL FEDERATION FOR CATHOLIC YOUTH MINISTRY: WHAT IS IT AND WHAT DOES IT HAVE TO OFFER?

In 1982, after the U.S. Catholic Conference had made the decision to cut back services to the field, the Advisory Board for Catholic Youth Ministry was presented with a dilemma over what to do about the services provided by the National CYO Federation. On January 20, 1982, the board voted unanimously to establish an independent corporation, the National Federation for Catholic Youth Ministry (NFCYM).

The National Federation for Catholic Youth Ministry replaced and expanded upon the services of the National CYO Federation and the U.S. Catholic Conference. The Federation works through a network of diocesan, provincial, regional, and national structures. The goals, as written in the Articles of Incorporation, are: "In light of the Gospel message, the Federation will foster the development of youth ministry in the United States through the Catholic Youth Organization (CYO) and other expressions of ministry to, with, by and for youth." The purposes are to:

- Provide national leadership support, and direction for adults and youth in youth ministry
- Advocate for the needs of youth (social, spiritual, cultural, and physical) and provide a forum for addressing issues pertinent to youth
- Promote the multicultural development of youth ministry and collaborate with such efforts whenever possible
- Promote the faith formation and skills development of youth ministry personnel
- Promote and enable peer leadership among youth
- Provide a national forum for the voice of Catholic youth
- Foster collaboration with other youth-serving and church-related agencies.

The Federation sponsors two regular conferences on youth ministry-related issues: the National Catholic Youth Conference, a biennial youth gathering held in the odd numbered years; and the National Conference on Catholic Youth Ministry, an adult gathering held in the even numbered years. The locations vary to enable different regions easy accessibility.

A variety of youth ministry-related publications are handled by the national office as well as religious recognition medals for Catholic youth in Girl Scouts, U.S.A., and Camp Fire, Inc. The Federation also publishes *Emmaus Letter,* a quarterly newsletter of resources, national news, and reflective articles geared to the diocesan and parish youth minister.

Membership is through a system of diocesan affiliation dues based on Catholic population. Membership is renewed at the beginning of each calendar year. Besides receiving significant discounts at Federation sponsored events, Federation members are tied into a national communications network for the sharing of youth ministry ideas and resources.

The Federation is governed by a board of directors with one voting member from each of the affiliated dioceses along with the regional youth and adult voting positions. The board meets annually to set policy and direction. Between meetings, the executive committee and officers oversee the operations of the national staff.

THE HISTORY OF CATHOLIC YOUTH WORK IN THE UNITED STATES

Today's present form of organized Catholic youth work was initiated in 1980 in Chicago. In an attempt to give youth another role model, rather than Al Capone and other popular gangsters, Bishop Bernard J. Sheil established the CYO (Catholic Youth Organization) with a boxing program in 1930. This organization was created "to promote among Catholic youth a recreational, educational, and religious program that will adequately meet their physical, mental, and spiritual needs in their after-school hours; and without regard to race, creed, or color, to assist those people who are in need; to inspire, direct, and guide the natural creative instincts of young people into those worthwhile channels, which permit the widest expression of personality, individually or in groups, while instilling in their minds and hearts a true love of God and Country."[1] With this beginning, Catholic youth work in the United States has evolved and expanded to where it now consists of many diversified and networking programs throughout the country.

After the boxing program was initiated, it was several more

years before the National Catholic Welfare Conference (predecessor of the National Conference of Catholic Bishops/U.S. Catholic Conference) became involved and the organization gained recognition. In 1940 His Eminence Giuseppe Cardinal Pizzardo and Archbishop Amleto Giovanni Cicognani created the National Council of Catholic Youth, composed of a college/university section and a diocesan section. The college/university section provided for the unification of Catholic youth on both Catholic and secular college campuses. The diocesan section consisted of parish youth councils affiliated through their respective dioceses with the National Council. There were to be two distinct councils: the teenage council for young people fourteen to eighteen years old, and the young adult council for members eighteen to thirty years of age. At this point, however, the organization was still lacking in any real participation or interest.[2]

Several years later, in 1951, under the leadership of Richard Cardinal Cushing of Boston, the first national convention of Catholic youth was held in Cincinnati. With this event, the National Council came into full existence as a real working organization. This national youth organization developed a handbook in the mid-1950s highlighting National Catholic Youth Week, founded in 1951 by the Rt. Rev. Msgr. Joseph E. Schieder, Director of the NCWC Youth Department. "Its purpose was 'to emphasize the potential of youth by pointing out their capacity and willingness to assume responsibility' and 'to encourage youth by making them aware of their opportunity for good.' The organization also promoted Communion Sunday and the annual National Catholic Youth Communion Crusade. Competitions, such as the national oratorical contest and the national short story contest, were sponsored annually."[3]

During the 1950s and 1960s, while growing and developing in the United States, Catholic youth work acquired various titles, but the most popular was the "Catholic Youth Organization" (CYO). In the early 1960s the name was adopted nationally as the official title. "CYO continued to offer parish youth a diversified program of religious, cultural, social, and athletic activities and attempted to bring them closer to their parish community. In 1965 the advisory board to the National Director of the Catholic Youth Department defined the goals and purpose of CYO as follows: 'The ultimate goal of the Catholic Youth Organization is to assist

youth and all others in this Apostolate—laity, religious, clergy—
to seek the kingdom of God by engaging in temporal affairs by
ordering them to the plan of God. The Catholic Youth Apostolate
then is a participation in the salvific mission of the Church itself
. . . thus the immediate goal of the CYO Apostolate is the
consecration to God of the leisure hours of youth and the
sanctification of youth through a well-balanced leisure time
program.' "[4]

The Impact program, which was initiated in 1967, began entry
into group process in leadership training both for youth and
adults working with youth. The Spero program, another program
related to leadership training, followed in 1975.

Emphasis on defining the role of the diocesan youth director
paralleled this growth in youth work. The U.S. Catholic
Conference published *The Diocesan Youth Director* in 1972 "to
assist diocesan youth directors in clarifying objectives and to help
them determine specific programs for youth in their dioceses."
The diocesan youth directors were directed to integrate their own
programs with programs of other diocesan officials as well as
those of community organizations and government.[5]

Goals in youth ministry were becoming more unified nationally
and, for the first time, a common vision was developing. The
term "youth ministry" became generally accepted. In his keynote
address in 1974 to the New England Conference on Youth
Ministry, Rev. Msgr. Thomas J. Leonard, USCC National Youth
Director, stated, "We have passed through a period of time when
many people were looking for the one single easy solution to the
problem of youth and the Church." He felt that the answer could
not be found by looking at just one program. Only when
programs are integrated and applied as part of a total ministry to
young people can maximum effectiveness be achieved.[6]

This emphasis on a unified approach to youth work led to the
Advisory Board for Youth Activities commissioning a paper on
total youth ministry in 1975. In 1976 *A Vision of Youth Ministry*
was published by the USCC Department of Education as an in-
depth study of the field. (A copy of this publication is contained
later in this introduction.) The USCC followed up on the *Vision*
paper with a series of publications designed to offer practical
assistance to youth ministers.

Following the publication of the *Vision of Youth Ministry*, individuals involved in different aspects of youth work began to come together to discuss common goals. Collaboration in youth ministry was becoming a reality at various levels: "Dioceses opened youth ministry offices; young adults were hired to coordinate parish youth ministry programs; colleges offered workshops and courses in youth ministry; and adults who worked with parish youth began searching for more effective ways to reach out to them."[7]

The Northeast Center for Youth Ministry was opened in 1978. John Roberto opened this center to share his vision and knowledge of the philosophy of total youth ministry. "In 1980 the Northeast Center and the USCC Department of Education organized the National Symposium on Catholic Youth Ministry in the '80s to study the present situation and future trends in church, ministry, youth research, youth development and youth ministry; and to give direction to youth ministry by developing concrete action plans based on the research and expertise of youth ministry leaders from across the country."[8]

Thirty five individuals—all leaders in various facets of youth ministry—gathered for this symposium. Together they exchanged their expertise in the field of youth ministry, and position papers were prepared and compiled into the publication, *Hope for the Decade: A Look at the Issues Facing Catholic Youth Ministry*. This publication offered an overview of the state of youth ministry. It pulled together, as much as possible, the essence of all that had been accomplished to bring Catholic Youth ministry into existence, its present status, and what possible hopes the decade of the 1980s can and will bring.

A new publication, based upon a similar symposium in 1983, is being published. It will deal with how adolescents mature in faith.

NOTES

1. National CYO Federation, *Hope for the Decade: A Look at the Issues Facing Catholic Youth Ministry* (Washington, D.C.: NCYOF, 1980), p. 2.
2. *Ibid.*, p. 3.
3. *Ibid.*, p. 3.
4. *Ibid.*, pp. 3, 4.
5. *Ibid.*, p. 4.
6. *Ibid.*, p. 5.
7. *Ibid.*, p. 6.
8. *Ibid.*, p. 6.

A VISION OF YOUTH MINISTRY

A *Vision of Youth Ministry* is a paper presenting total youth ministry from an in-depth study of the field. Published by the United States Catholic Conference Department of Education in 1976, it remains the guiding philosophical paper used by Catholics in youth work today.

PREFACE

In May 1975, the Advisory Board for Youth Activities, USCC, commissioned a paper on total youth ministry in response to a need for in-depth study of this developing field of ministry. The process designed for producing the paper was based on the belief that any description of youth ministry must grow out of and be confirmed by the lived experience of the persons who exercise this ministry on a daily basis.

Consequently, the paper was developed over fifteen months, in three separate stages of writing and consultation. Hundreds of individuals contributed to this process, and their detailed comments substantially refined the paper at each stage. The final version printed here reflects the beginnings of a national consensus on a vision of total youth ministry as it is understood by youth directors, youth, school superintendents, catechists, coaches, members of the academic community, retreat leaders, young adult youth ministers, scouting personnel and others. In the future, this document will be supplemented with materials describing working models of youth ministry and with resources pertaining to the many practical concerns of those involved in youth ministry.

The Department of Education, USCC, is indebted to the many persons who shared their insights and expertise with us out of a common commitment to youth ministry. We gratefully acknowledge their invaluable assistance, and hope for a continuing dialogue as we continue to clarify and strengthen the Church's ministry with youth.

INTRODUCTION

From people involved in youth work across the country comes the realization that the Church's ministry with youth is entering a new day. Many young people and adults on the grassroots level are experimenting with and creating new forms of pastoral ministry with youth. They have had the imagination and courage to venture down new roads in their attempt to respond to the needs of young people. Today's youth clearly call the Church to ministry, affirming their right to recognition and responsibility in the faith community and declaring that when the Church fails to respond to their needs and gifts, their right of becoming is denied.[1] The leadership of these adults and youth has given rise to the need for all those involved with young people to give thoughtful consideration to the common foundations of their ministry.

This paper presents a vision that reaffirms and recasts the Church's ministry with youth. It offers a focus for the work of youth ministry, and sets forth an outline of its major components. The paper pays respect to the living reality of youth ministry by avoiding a delineation so rigid or detailed as to limit further development. On the contrary, by identifying some of the key concepts related to youth ministry, this paper will serve to stimulate further reflection and creative growth in the ministry of the Church with youth.

I. THE MISSION AND MINISTRY OF THE CHURCH

As one among many ministries of the Church, youth ministry must be understood in terms of the mission and ministry of the whole Church, the community of persons who believe in Jesus Christ and continue his saving work through the action of the Holy Spirit. The Church's mission is threefold: to proclaim the good news of salvation, to offer itself as a group of people transformed by the Spirit into a community of faith, hope, and love, and to bring God's justice and love to others through service in its individual, social, and political dimensions.[2]

The ministry of the Church is the means through which the Church fulfills its threefold mission. As it is used in the earliest sources, the word "ministry" implies "the work that is done by those who believe, the service to each other and the world around them that members of the Christian community perform in the name of Christ."[3]

This ministry of the Church is a common endeavor that unites all Christians in shared responsibility. In the broadest sense, there is no Christian who is not a minister of the Gospel. Each person, however, experiences a particular calling to ministry based on his or her unique gifts. In St. Paul's words, "We have gifts that differ according to the form bestowed on each of us. One's gift may be prophecy; its use should be in proportion to his faith. It may be the gift of ministry; it should be used for service. One who is a teacher should use his gift for teaching; one with the power of exhortation should exhort. He who gives alms should do so generously; he who rules should exercise his authority with care; he who performs works of mercy should do so cheerfully" (Romans 12:6-8).

Paul emphasizes, however, that all of these different qualities are one in their source and in their ultimate goal. "There are many gifts but the same Spirit; there are different ministries but the same Lord; there are different works but the same God who accomplishes all of them in everyone. To each person the manifestation of the Spirit is given for the common good . . . it is one and the same Spirit who produces all these gifts, distributing them to each as he wills" (1 Corinthians 12:4, 5, 11).

Each Christian has a responsibility to use his or her gift for the good of the community and to minister as Jesus did—healing, teaching, guiding, preaching, celebrating, worshiping, enabling, and serving. Ministry is at the very core of Christian life and its essence is expressed with challenging simplicity in the words "A man can have no greater love than to lay down his life for his friends" (John 15:13).

As Henri Nouwen expressed the concept in his book, *Creative Ministry,* "Ministry means the ongoing attempt to put one's own search for God, with all the moments of pain and joy, despair and hope, at the disposal of those who want to join this search but do not know how . . . we lay down our life to give new life . . . we realize that young people call for Christians who are willing to develop their sensitivity to God's presence in their own lives, as well as the lives of others, and to offer their experience as a way of recognition and liberation to their fellow people."[4]

Because ministry involves the giving of self in relationship to another, the Church's youth ministry must be founded in the radical commitment to lay down one's life in service to the young people whose lives are touched. The primacy of this loving gift of self ensures fidelity to the ministry of Jesus and guides the work of youth ministry in fulfilling the Church's threefold mission of Word, Community, and Service.

II. A VISION OF YOUTH MINISTRY

As a manifestation of the Church's mission, youth ministry has many characteristics in common with other ministries of the Church. However, youth ministry has its own particular history and process, its own "story" which guides those who exercise this ministry. A gospel account that especially captures the dynamics of youth ministry is the story of the disciples on the road to Emmaus (Luke 24:13-35).

When Jesus first met these disciples on the road after his death and resurrection, he asked them what it was that they were so deeply involved in discussing. He listened carefully to their reply as they told him of the events in Jerusalem that had troubled and confused them. When they finished, he responded by beginning to interpret the meaning of the events they had witnessed. Their sharing continued until they reached Emmaus, where the disciples persuaded Jesus to join them for supper. Their encounter culminated in the breaking of the bread, in which the disciples recognized their friend as Jesus.

In the same way, youth ministry begins with a presence to the young which engenders the confidence and hope to ask questions. Attentive listening to the concerns of the young person enables the youth minister to understand more deeply the youth's needs and stage of growth. At that point, the youth minister is able to respond, sharing with the young person the help, insights, or values that are the fruit of a life rooted in faith. By drawing out of the youth reflections on the action of God in the events of his or her own life, this sharing enables the young person to begin formulating answers in the light of witnessed tradition and gospel values. The bond created in this relationship is celebrated in community, most fully in the Eucharistic celebration of the Christian community.

If we follow the Emmaus model, youth ministry "is the Church's mission of reaching into the daily lives of modern young people and showing them the presence of God. . . . It is a return to the way Jesus taught, putting ministry before teaching and people over institutions. In this ministry, religious content is a way of life for the person ministering and the young person touched, through a sequential development of faith, dependent on the readiness and need of the adolescent."[5]

The Emmaus story is not the only model for youth ministry

that is provided by the Scripture narratives. Regardless of the specific gospel story used, however, what is most important is that the vision of youth ministry be understood and carried out in a manner that is grounded in Scripture and gospel values and oriented to persons as fundamentally as Jesus' ministry was.

Dimensions of youth ministry. Youth ministry is the response of the Christian community to the needs of young people, and the sharing of the unique gifts of youth with the larger community.

Youth ministry is *to* youth when the Christian community exercises its pastoral role in meeting young people's needs. Ministry to youth draws on the resources and gifts of the adult community to provide opportunities for growth that young people need but cannot always attain on their own. Some ways in which the ministry to youth is currently being carried out include guidance counseling, catechetical programs, organized sports activities, leadership training and job placement for disadvantaged youth, parish youth centers, family life programs, camping opportunities, Catholic schools, etc.

Youth ministry is *with* youth because young people share with adults a common responsibility to carry out the Church's mission. When youth have the opportunity to exercise this responsibility jointly with adults, recognition is given to the particular gifts and insights which these young people bring to their family, parish, or neighborhood. Ministry with youth occurs when they participate as members of parish councils, serve as catechists, lectors, and extraordinary ministers of the Eucharist, and share with adults a responsibility for retreats, community service, or action for justice.

Youth ministry is *by* youth when young people exercise their own ministry to others, particularly to their peers. The operation of peer counseling programs for drug abuse and other problems, tutoring, and many forms of community service are all parts of ministry by youth. Youth also minister to others when they serve as team members for youth retreats, teachers in catechetical programs, and leaders of youth activities.

Youth ministry is *for* youth in that adult youth ministers attempt to interpret the needs of youth and act as advocates in articulating youth's legitimate concerns to the wider community. The adult involved in youth ministry has special access to the views of youth, and ordinarily has a degree of credibility, influence, and resources unavailable to young people. This places a responsibility on the adult to speak for youth and to sensitize and motivate other adults where youth needs are concerned. Ministers for youth might alert parish or diocesan councils to a desire for youth liturgies, work with community leaders to resolve gang problems, or help parents and children to work out misunderstandings and communication difficulties.

The great diversity in youth ministry is reflected in the above examples, and owes its existence to the importance of each distinct dimension of the ministry to, with, by, and for youth.

Goals of youth ministry. Youth ministry is a multidimensional reality, but all of its varied facets are brought into focus by a common dedication to the following goals.

1. Youth ministry works to foster the total personal and spiritual growth of each young person.
2. Youth ministry seeks to draw young people to responsible participation in the life, mission, and work of the faith community.

The Church in ministry with youth is committed to the fullest personal development of young people, particularly those who face the greatest barriers in achieving this goal by reason of material poverty, loneliness, racial discrimination, social injustice, or physical or mental handicaps. This personal development encompasses relationship to self, others, and God, particularly within the context of supportive community.

Many youth experience themselves as alienated from or out of place within the life and work of the whole parish community. Youth ministry seeks to draw young people into the supportive experience of Christian community, and to assist the parish community to welcome the young and share its ministry with them.

In these respects youth ministry is both a ministry *within* the Church, ministering to believers, and a ministry *of* the Church that reaches out to serve others with the love and humility of Christ.

Principles of youth ministry. The living dynamics of youth ministry, through which these goals are achieved, may be best articulated in several key principles of ministry. These assumptions give youth ministry its particular character and underlie its effectiveness.

1. *Youth is a unique time of personal development.* The teenage years represent the critical period of transit from childhood to adulthood, during which physical, psychological, and social growth is more concentrated than at any comparable time span in life. Since the development of faith is tied directly to the interpretation of meaning in one's life and experiences, the teenage years are an important juncture for the individual's spiritual development. The youth begins to forge a personal sense of meaning and set of values, and becomes capable of a deeper personal relationship with Christ and responsible Christian action. To help young people as they struggle with this effort, youth ministry must involve the understanding of parents, the guidance and example of peers and significant adults, and the ongoing maturing of the faith community which accepts the responsibility to share in the youth's search for meaning and a language of faith.

2. *Youth ministry is concerned with the total person.* Youth ministers should take seriously their responsibility to help young people grow as total persons, socially, spiritually, culturally, etc.

   The total young person has many important concerns which must be understood in the context of daily living, including family situations, relationships with peers, academic and extracurricular involvement, response to religion, and moral value questions. In the life of each young person, different needs express themselves at various times during the process of maturing, and one of the hallmarks of youth ministry should be sensitivity to the young person's readiness for new steps.

3. *Youth ministry is rooted in relationships.* Youth ministry involves first and foremost, not programs, but relationships. Within accepting relationships, young people are enabled to face and to accept themselves and others, to clarify their goals and values, and to dare to become the persons they are called to be. Relationships that form youth ministry are those that form community and mediate the grace of Christ, challenging young people to greater growth and openness to God.

The relationship of persons in a ministerial situation involves a mutual openness to change and willingness to grow. Both youth and adults are enriched by this bond, in such a way that the faith community is vitalized and the risen Christ witnessed to.

4. *Youth ministry is a call to community.* God calls youth and adults alike to be members of his people, the Church, to join in pilgrimage to the Father and share insights into the meaning and value of life. As the Body of Christ, the community brings to youth the life-giving presence of Jesus in Word and Sacrament. Absolutely essential to effective youth ministry is the support and lived example of the surrounding faith community, particularly the parish. Without this, youth ministry exists in a vacuum that cuts short fuller growth and maturity in faith. Because the young person is involved most fully in the local communities of family, parish, and school, youth ministry is most effectively carried out in these settings. Youth ministry serves to support and enhance the basic faith commitment of youth in each of these community contexts. Youth ministry also exerts a force for healing and reconciliation in those communities which suffer from the strain of youth's need to reject and then reintegrate their roots.

5. *Youth ministry proceeds as an affirmation of gifts.* The recognition and development of individual gifts and the building of a positive sense of personal worth and ability are an important aspect of the process of youth ministry. To effectively call the young person toward maturity, affirmation must be united to genuine trust of the young person's integrity and ability. By awakening a young person's potential and accepting his or her gifts, the community enriches its life and its own ability to minister to others.

6. *True ministry duplicates itself.* It is essential that youth ministry evoke in each person the willingness to offer ministry to others. Youth ministry should call youth not only to join programs, but also to join with others in living out the Church's mission to share the good news, live in community, and serve others in love and justice.

The interrelated principles outlined above serve as a foundation for the concept of youth ministry, but this listing is not necessarily exhaustive. With the maturity of the ministry, others will be able to identify additional principles to complement those described here.

Context of youth ministry. In all places, youth ministry occurs within a given social, cultural, and religious context which shapes the specific form of the ministry. Youth culture, secular society, family, and the local Church community are some of the institutions which form the context within which youth ministry must be carried out. Each of these environments exerts an important influence on young people, a consideration which should be reflected appropriately in balanced youth ministry programs.

The influence of youth culture varies in specifics but remains constant in its high degree of pressure for peer conformity. In some respects the young person's milieu contributes many creative opportunities for ministry, such as the interpretation of popular music in terms of gospel values, or the formation of youth movements organized to serve others in love and justice. On the other hand, the environment of youth can present strong pressures toward behaviors that are destructive of self or others and contrary to Christian values, such as drug or alcohol abuse, irresponsible sexual activity, and violence. In today's America, there are few effective efforts to reverse the negative influences that are a part of the youth scene; the tendencies of society, Church, and family toward material success, prejudice, and dehumanized social interactions run counter to the beatitudes, and overshadow the development of the genuine community and justice envisoned by our nation's founders. In our society, too, many young people experience oppression and injustice because of age, economic need, racial discrimination, unemployment, or disability. Youth ministry involves the whole faith community speaking out on behalf of these youth, and working for the resolution of the conflicts they face. In this, youth ministry involves the struggle to present to youth a prophetic witness to Christian life against the predominant value orientation of the general culture, a struggle that renders supportive community all the more important.

The context of the family for the work of youth ministry is crucial, because the young person's relationships with family members are such clear determinants of his or her religious behavior and values.[6] Most young people enter a time of ostensible alienation from the family, a period during which youth attempt to discover their own unique identities by wholesale repudiation of the values of family and childhood. The influence of peers becomes very significant at this point, and often gives rise to tension regarding the relative importance of family and friends. Whether accepted or rejected, however, the family is a concern of great importance for young people; for many, a sign of growth into adulthood is the gradual reintegration of family relationships and traditions into the life of the young person. During the more rebellious periods, many families experience difficult tensions and painful lack of communication; they have a special need for the reconciliation and healing to which youth ministers and family life ministers should address themselves. The building of community among groups of youth and their parents eases many of these tensions and leads to healing dialogue. Many families experience important growth as a loving community during this time as they exercise a mutual ministry of patience, communication, trust, and support of one another. In all aspects of youth ministry, the needs and situation of the family remain a paramount concern.

A final consideration regarding the context of youth ministry relates to the local faith community, most especially the parish. As emphasized in the preceding section, the whole parish community is the life-sustaining backdrop for effective youth ministry.

Programs or activity in the name of youth ministry are sterile in the absence of adults who witness the values communicated by those who minister to youth. Young people need the example, fellowship, and acceptance of clergy, religious, and lay adults to choose love, to choose community, and to choose faith.

A sensitive program of ministry with youth should give careful consideration to the effects of these four important aspects of the youth environment: youth culture, secular society, family, and local faith community.

Components of youth ministry. The preceding sections of this paper set down a broad foundation for parish or diocesan youth ministry programs. To examine the concrete dimensions of such programs, seven components of youth ministry can be identified which describe distinct aspects of youth ministry work: Word, Worship, Creating Community, Guidance and Healing, Justice and Service, Enablement, and Advocacy. Each of these is an expression of the ministry of the Christian community and acts to fulfill the Church's mission. The number and order of these components are not absolutes; however, they represent a consensus on the part of persons involved with youth ministry and are useful as a working description of the most important elements of youth ministry.

1. *Word.* Although the ministry of the Word in the Church touches more than youth ministry, it is a very important component of the ministry with young people. The ministry of the Word is the sharing with others of the gospel message, the good news of God's love and salvation as shown to us in Jesus Christ. This sharing involves elements of what are commonly known as evangelization and catechesis.

Many rich and fruitful insights into the ministry of the Word are provided by Pope Paul VI when he writes, "For the Church, evangelizing means bringing the good news into all strata of humanity from within and making it new." In the same message he makes the point that the Church evangelizes when it seeks, through the power of God's Word, to convert "both the personal and collective consciences of people, the activities in which they engage, and the lives and concrete milieux which are theirs."[7] As it is described above by Pope Paul, evangelization is a complex process that could involve many aspects of the Church's ministry. In some cases, the ministry of the Word involves the initial proclamation of the faith, preceded by "the first means of evangelization . . . the witness of an authentically Christian life,"[8] and followed by the communication of the gospel message.

However, the ministry of the Word in relation to youth involves not only evangelization, but also catechesis in order to render faith "living, conscious, and active."[9] The ministry of the Word is associated most often with formal catechetical approaches, whether in Catholic schools or parish schools of religion. However, as in the story of the road to Emmaus, catechesis is also effectively carried out informally in small groups where there is a genuine concern to join with young people in reflecting on their lives and experiences in the light of Christian faith. A creative diversity of catechetical approaches could be considered in determining the precise model that might be most beneficial at any given point. In every case, however, the approach used should be based on the needs of the persons involved, and should affirm young people as responsible participants in their own growth in faith.[10]

A particularly successful model in the ministry of the Word is the youth retreat, for which young people come together for a day or a weekend of intensive Christian living and peer witness to faith. Catechesis, healing, enabling, worship, and many other aspects of youth ministry occur during these retreats in many forms. However, retreats are most effective as part of an ongoing program that will provide both preparation and adequate follow-through. As an integral part of a parish or school catechetical program, a youth retreat enables young people to experience Christian faith at a level and in a way that is seldom possible within the limitations of the more academic framework.

The fullest effectiveness of the ministry of the Word requires sensitivity to many other aspects of youth ministry because youth need to experience the Christian message in terms of the realities most important in their daily lives: love, family, life values, justice, etc.[11] For this reason, every catechist working with youth is a youth minister, and sometimes will be a healer, enabler, or advocate. In the same sense, all persons involved in other aspects of youth ministry may exercise on occasion the ministry of the Word.

If ministry, in a sense, is making Christ present to people, then the ministry of the Word for both adults and youth is making him present through the message of the gospel as we live it and share it.

2. *Worship.* Worship builds and celebrates the relationship between God and his people; it is a response to God's Word, and a moment of personal and communal encounter with God. For youth ministry, the aspect of worship includes the celebration of the Eucharist, the sacraments, paraliturgical services, prayer sessions, Scripture study groups, and similar expressions of the faith life of youth. It is the focal point of an effective youth ministry program.

One way in which worship fulfills the vision of youth ministry is in building and celebrating a community of youth. If properly approached, youth liturgies can evoke authentic involvement and can strengthen the youth group. Proper celebration implies a sensitivity to the needs of the worshiping community; for this reason youth liturgies should be celebrated respectfully and tastefully so that all participants have a tangible awareness of the presence of God. The priest has a responsibility "to make the celebration festive, fraternal, and meditative." As the presiding minister he is called forth to share his faith life with the gathered community of people by word, gesture, and presence.[12]

Youth worship must be taken seriously by the young people as well as by the adult leadership of the parish. Youth ministers should celebrate what youth celebrate, and invite them to help in the planning of the liturgies. In the framework of youth worship, young people can celebrate the spectrum of their feelings, concerns, and joys, using signs and symbols that have special meaning for them.

Worship also fulfills the goals of youth ministry by providing one of the richest settings for intergenerational sharing. In the context of the whole faith community, young people experience the faith and prayerfulness of a celebrating community.

Many occasions of worship need not involve Eucharistic liturgy; paraliturgical services should be encouraged, especially in areas where clergy are few and heavily burdened. It is important for the spiritual formation of youth that the priest or youth ministers in a parish spend considerable time sharing prayer with them, leading them toward personal as well as group prayer and facilitating penance services, Scripture services, and other celebrations of life, seasons, and sorrows.

Incorporation into a parish faith community means involvement on a communal level in prayer and worship. A sense of prayer and involvement in liturgy may be promoted in parishes by small group prayer, days of reflection, special liturgies for youth (penance services, Eucharistic celebrations), development of good parish liturgies, involvement of young people as lectors, extraordinary ministers of the Eucharist, and musicians, special prayer services that are youth oriented, and spiritual formation programs that promote an understanding of prayer and the ability to pray.

Youth worship must be a living interaction between God and young people, an event that remembers the personal and religious events of the past and initiates even deeper involvement for future becoming, but always celebrates the present relationships as the young person praises, sings, shouts, or whispers "Amen."

3. *Creating Community.* The creation of youth community is a component of youth ministry through which youth grow personally and spiritually. In the life of a community, young people and a few significant adults learn to listen to one another, and in doing so, to hear God speak. As they try to help each other express in words the truths they experience, they learn a living theology. In this kind of community youth have a mutual ministry to each other. They share themselves, their convictions, their faith with each other. That the gospel is communicated and lived in this climate is the premise which underlies experiences such as the youth retreat programs which have been developed around the country.

The creation of community in the family and parish settings is also fruitful for youth ministry. Building new paths of communication and providing opportunities for deeper levels of sharing are part of the ministry of creating intergenerational community; they lead to a situation in which each generation learns to listen and respond to the other. As young people and adults open their lives to each other and realize their common membership in the community of faith, they establish a new basis for identity—the family of God.

The ministry of creating community is also, in a sense, a ministry of celebration. In community, young people are provided with opportunities to celebrate the joys of life in thanksgiving, and to share the suffering and struggles of life with the support of others. Activities such as outings and parties, camping and outdoor experiences, sports, music, and dance are natural expressions of the young person's involvement with life. The occasion of a community celebration nurtures the constructive self-concepts and fruitful relationships that motivate youth ministry.

4. *Guidance and Healing.* Through the work of guidance and

healing, youth ministry responds to the profound needs of modern youth for spiritual and personal counseling, for vocational guidance, and for the reconciliation that heals the wounds of alienation.

The youth minister exercises these aspects of ministry under many conditions, from highly structured situations such as high school guidance counseling to very unstructured moments of sharing that arise as a natural product of a relationship of trust. Frequently, the atmosphere of an evening coffeehouse or the informality of a youth drop-in center are conducive to counseling on a deep personal level; often, the growth and learning that a retreat produces can stimulate a prayerful and meaningful celebration of reconciliation.

As a counselor and guide, the youth minister needs to be aware of the resources and opportunities available in the community because there are frequent occasions when a good referral is the most appropriate response to a young person's needs. Good communication and cooperation among the many agencies established to serve youth are vital aspects of an effective ministry of guidance.

Youth and adults involved in youth ministry are called to be healers and reconcilers in various ways. Family life in many instances is strained by the conflict of needs that may occur during the teenage years; often youth feel alienated from the societal structures and authority figures that influence their lives; in addition, many young people experience a deep alienation from their peers because they are "different"— racially, economically, physically, or socially.

These divisions and wounds in the young person's world can be healed in Christ through the reconciling efforts of peers, family members, or a youth minister who has the confidence of the young person. Peer counseling is an especially effective avenue of healing that should be encouraged. Whenever implemented, however, it should provide necessary training and support groups for the counselors. There are many ways in which youth ministry involves the role of healing, but the fullest expression of this calling is in the prayerful and sacramental reconciliation of the Christian community with God in the New Rite of Penance.

5. *Justice and Service.* One of the principles underlying youth

ministry is that it calls young people themselves to minister to others. Young people have the idealism and sympathy which are requisites for genuine service, and they are generous with their time, energy, and talents.

The justice and service aspect of youth ministry is based on the responsibility of the Church to extend the kingdom of God in the world through service and action on behalf of justice. As the bishops affirmed in the landmark statement, "Justice in the World," "action on behalf of justice and participation in the transformation of the world fully appear to us as a constitutive dimension of the preaching of the Gospel."

As a natural outflowing of the community experience of faith, service and action on behalf of justice should be constitutive dimensions of the Church's youth ministry. First of all, by exercising moral leadership and sharing its material and human resources, the Church in ministry with youth must live out a commitment to young people and communities who suffer discrimination, poverty, handicaps, and injustice. Secondly, by providing models, experiences, and programs, the faith community of the Church should fulfill its responsibility to educate youth for justice and to call young people themselves to action on behalf of others. Both of these responsibilities are important; together, they balance the social and individual aspects of Christian action.

A consciousness of the demands of justice and willingness to serve should characterize the overall stance of youth ministry—not confined to specific programs, but penetrating prayer, recreation, creativity, and Christian witness. Both youth and adults engaged in youth ministry should strive to deepen their sensitivity to the innate dignity of all persons and to the right of each individual to fulfill his or her fullest potential.

In an especially urgent way, the demands of Christian justice today call youth and the faith community-at-large to join with Spanish-speaking, Black, and Native American youth and their communities in dealing with prejudice, and to share with other young people the struggle against hunger, unemployment, and injustice. Youth and adult ministers should also demonstrate sensitivity to the innate dignity of all persons and to the right of each individual to fulfill his or her fullest potential.

Young people have many gifts to share with the aged and

lonely, the disadvantaged, children and the poor. It is critical
that youth ministers create opportunities through which young
persons can share these gifts.[13]

Well-balanced programs that involve action, reflection, and
education enable young people to develop into responsible
Christians who incorporate into their mature faith a
commitment to justice and self-giving love of others.

6. *Enablement.* The concept of enablement is expressed in various
ways throughout this paper; in essence, it involves a
relationship of trust and challenge in which one is led to new
growth and self-confidence. Enablement in youth ministry has
a dual focus: the enablement of both *youth* and *adults* to grow,
lead, and minister.

a. *Enablement of Youth.* The document *To Teach As Jesus Did*
affirms that "Youth have a right and duty to be active
participants in the work of the Church in the world.
Obviously, however, they face certain obstacles because they
are young and lack experience, organizational skills, and
other necessary abilities. Adults engaged in youth ministry
therefore should function mainly as guides and helpers by
giving young people direction and support."[14]

A critical task before youth ministers today is to
recognize the value of peer ministry among youth and to
help young people to develop their gifts to be used in the
wider community. Young people should be welcomed as co-
workers in youth ministry, and programs which develop
their leadership talents should have a central place.

Every young person or team of youth who pursue an
active ministry should be counseled by a qualified adult
who can offer wisdom and support. Such an adult will not
dominate and suppress the leadership of the youth ministers
but will challenge and release it, aware of the ever-amazing
new ways by which young people reach one another.

The mark of effective youth ministry is that it will
involve young people in ministry. A real and active role for
youth must be opened in the Church. In the past,
regretfully, the Church has not communicated the central
fact that young people are important and needed in its real
work. Young people are willing to take their place in the
ministry of the Church and work long hours to share the

presence of God they are discovering. They need training and support from the whole Christian community. With constructive, enthusiastic involvement of people who care, these young persons will bring the healing touch of Christ and his Word to youth who are lonely, frightened, and waiting for someone who understands.

b. *Enablement of Adults.* Christian adults should be with the young people co-seeking, co-helping, co-working. Such a shared cooperation affords all involved an opportunity to grow in Christian love, a chance to share interests and concerns, the possibility to broaden and communicate vision, as well as the opportunity present for each individual to grow in self-esteem.

Adults, faith-filled Christians, are the very center of ministry with youth—adults who are in touch with their faith, living the gospel in all aspects of their lives. Young people look for models, persons they can look up to, and not simply persons with whom they can build a peer relationship. Some of the qualities that should characterize an adult involved in youth ministry are: the quality of presence that a person brings to time spent with the young, the ability to listen deeply to others, the ability to be comfortable in a variety of different settings and the ability to speak credibly of one's own faith experience. What the young need today are not adults who will hand over information, but adults who will hand over themselves and the secret of their own faith.[15]

This personal growth on the part of the youth minister, and the skills and techniques that improve his or her effectiveness should be provided to adults in youth ministry as a way of fulfilling the call to enable adults to minister.

If ministry to youth is to be taken seriously, dioceses and parishes should target key adults for training and budget a significant portion of their funds to underwrite the development and maintenance of such a program. Training an adult for youth ministry is a process of enabling the person to further his or her spiritual growth, increasing an awareness of doctrinal content and of a philosophy of youth ministry, and developing personal skills of communicating and teamwork. Training adults will require a review of their own spiritual lives and creative strength as well as an understanding of the young person's environment and spirituality. This training should be comprehensive, practical, and ongoing, and allow for the sharing of experiences and techniques with other ministry teams.

A well-run and well-financed adult training program can launch a strong youth ministry effort, which in turn has the potential to affect and vitalize every level of parish and diocesan life.

7. *Advocacy.* Advocacy in youth ministry means listening, caring, interpreting. An advocate for youth shows dedication by interpreting and speaking for youth before the Church and secular community. Advocacy "gets down" to the everyday practicality of being a buffer, an intermediary, a broker. It is a call to be a true listener who can then accurately represent the position of youth in the public forum.

In many respects, the advocate acts as a bridge builder because he or she reflects on the attitudes and opinions of the young, determines what they are saying and what they want from Church and society, and transmits these insights to the appropriate persons.

The advocate promotes among young people a sense of being both wanted and needed, and facilitates the ministry of youth by treating them as responsible persons whose views are important.

III. IMPLICATIONS FOR THE FUTURE

Administrative support and leadership.

> "It is the consensus that the Church is neglecting its responsibilities to youth and young adults. There is a lack of interest and involvement on the part of the priests with the youth of their parishes. It is our feeling that parishes have set a priority on money instead of ministry."
> (Youth Position Paper, Bicentennial Hearing, NCYO Federation Convention, San Antonio, Texas)

If the Church is to take youth ministry seriously, then youth and clergy must reach out and respond to one another.

Administrative support and leadership involve spiritual, emotional, and financial backing from bishops, pastors, and other administrators. No program can be effective or ongoing without appropriate support.

Several suggestions which were made by youth representatives participating in the NCYO Federation Convention Bicentennial Hearing and which have widespread validity are:

1. Youth needs should be incorporated into the parish budget. Youth should participate on the parish council, liturgy committees, and other parish organizations. Through this mutual sharing, the parishes would be more unified.
2. Existing youth agencies should be given a broader financial base in order to reach those groups or individuals who have been neglected in the past, e.g., minorities.
3. Youth and clergy, especially bishops, should cooperate in a joint effort to communicate through such methods as dialogue, workshops, and youth conventions.
4. Seminarians should be trained in youth ministry as a regular course of study.
5. Parishes should recognize the leadership abilities of their youth and initiate training programs for them.[16]

If the Church is seriously ready to pursue vital youth ministry, then funds, planning, and both full-time and part-time trained personnel must be committed to the effort. In particular, full-time lay ministers should be utilized, with adequate pay and security for their needs.

Collaboration. No one aspect of youth ministry is independent of others; they are all interdependent elements of a unified total vision. The multifaceted nature of youth ministry requires a process of collaboration among all persons involved in it, rather than fragmentation or competition. In responding to the total young person, youth ministry touches on educational, psychological, social, and spiritual needs, and requires the complementary skills of catechists, liturgists, coaches, young people, counselors, parents, adult advisors, and others. Part of the vision of youth ministry is to present to youth the richness of the person of Christ, which perhaps exceeds the ability of one person to capture, but which might be effected by the collective ministry of the many persons who make up the Church. No single diocesan structure can be proposed that will suit the needs for collaboration in every diocese, nor can any one structure for parish organization serve as a definitive model. A variety of organizational models have been and will be developed to meet the varying needs of different localities and communities, be they urban, rural, industralized, Spanish-speaking, predominantly non-Catholic, economically disadvantaged, or otherwise characterized.

In all of these developing models, however, the process of dialogue, collaboration and joint planning is the key to ending fragmentation and restoring a sense of balance to the ministry with youth. The source of this renewal will be the Christian community's serious response to St. Paul's call to share with one another the gifts of the Spirit for the fulfillment of Jesus' mission.

Call to action. On May 9, 1975, Pope Paul VI said:

". . . we think that we have every reason to have confidence in Christian youth: youth will not fail the Church if within the Church there are enough older people able to understand it, love it, guide it and to open up to it a future by passing on to it with complete fidelity the truth which endures. . . . And this is why we are pleased to dedicate more expressly to you, the young Christians of the present day, the promise of the Church of Tomorrow, this celebration of spiritual joy."[17]

Youth ministry today presents us with the challenge to help reveal the Christ of the gospel and to exhibit our faith in community and in our personal relationships. This is a time of hope and building for the future. More than ever, it is evident today that youth genuinely hunger for the good news of Jesus Christ, and that faith communities are equipped to share it with them if their vision is broad and creative. Many youth ministers have already accepted this challenge. They are examining traditional structures and programs to determine how the objectives of youth ministry are being fulfilled in an attempt to forge a ministry that will meet the real needs of youth today. Now is the time for each person involved with youth to accept the same challenge. The situation is reminiscent of the scene in the

Acts of the Apostles as the apostles gazed up into the heavens when Jesus returned to his Father. For a few moments the apostles were lost in bewilderment and felt like orphans, not knowing what to do. Only the two mysterious men that appeared brought them back to reality by asking, "Men of Galilee, why do you stand here looking up at the skies? This Jesus who has been taken from you will return, just as you saw him go up into the heavens" (Acts 1:10, 11).

For us, as for the apostles, now is the time for action. The vision has been presented. There are many possibilities. It remains to be made a living reality. May the Spirit guide each youth minister in this work together.

NOTES

1. *Minutes of the Bicentennial Hearing,* 1975 National Catholic Youth Organization Federation Convention, p. 18.
2. *Church: The Continuing Quest.* Richard P. McBrien (New Jersey: Newman Press, 1970), p. 73.
3. "Ministry/The Work of Every Believer." Richard Colby and Charity Weymouth, *Origins,* February 12, 1976, Vol. 5, #34, p. 535.
4. *Creative Ministry.* Henri Nouwen (New York: Doubleday, 1971), p. 116.
5. Written intervention of Archbishop John R. Quinn of Oklahoma City at the 1974 Synod of Bishops in Rome.
6. *Religion and American Youth: With Emphasis on Catholic Adolescents and Young Adults.* Raymond H. Potvin, Dean R. Hoge, Hart M. Nelson. (The Boys' Town Center for the Study of Youth Development, Washington, D.C., 1976).
7. "Apostolic Exhortation on Evangelization." Pope Paul VI, *Origins,* January 8, 1976, Vol. 5, #29, p. 459.
8. *Ibid.,* p. 460.
9. *The Documents of Vatican II.* ed., Walter M. Abbott, S.J. (New York: The American Press, 1976), p. 406.
10. *General Catechetical Directory.* Sacred Congregation for the Clergy (Washington, D.C.: U.S. Catholic Conference, 1971), p. 67.
11. *Ibid.,* p. 67.
12. *Directory for Masses with Children.* Sacred Congregation for Divine Worship (Washington, D.C.: U.S. Catholic Conference, 1974), p. 5.
13. *To Teach As Jesus Did,* p. 37, para. #133.
14. *To Teach As Jesus Did,* pp. 36, 37, para. #132.
15. *A Future for Youth Catechesis.* Michael Warren, C.F.X. (New York: Paulist Press, 1975), pp. 29-39.
16. *Minutes of the Bicentennial Hearing.* 1975 National Catholic Youth Organization Federation Convention, p. 33.
17. *On Christian Joy: Apostolic Exhortation.* Pope Paul VI (Washington, D.C.: U.S. Catholic Conference, 1975), pp. 30, 31.

HOW TO MINISTER TO CATHOLIC YOUTH

The Rev. Don Kimball developed an approach which embodies our theory of "How to minister to Catholic Youth." He calls his process the "Youth Ministry Process Chart" (see illustration) and he uses it to: "Help youth ministers expand their attitude toward youth programs beyond the educational or recreational model to a process model of facilitating human growth and faith development; demonstrate that the ministries of community-building, word (evangelization-catechesis), and justice and service occur in the sequence, Community-Word-Service; and remind people that all ministry starts with relationships that build trust."[1]

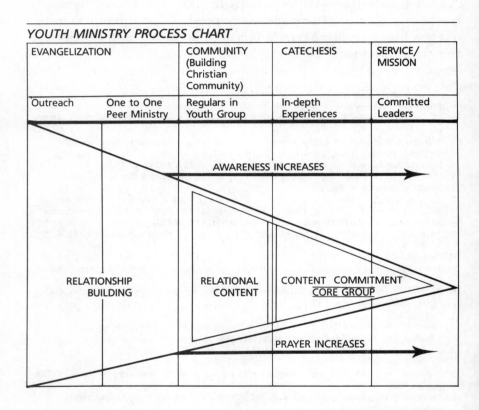

YOUTH MINISTRY PROCESS CHART

EVANGELIZATION		COMMUNITY (Building Christian Community)	CATECHESIS	SERVICE/ MISSION
Outreach	One to One Peer Ministry	Regulars in Youth Group	In-depth Experiences	Committed Leaders

AWARENESS INCREASES →

RELATIONSHIP BUILDING   RELATIONAL CONTENT   CONTENT COMMITMENT
<u>CORE GROUP</u>

PRAYER INCREASES →

The chart, as shown from the arrow, flows from left to right. The first category, Relationship Building, is also the largest in terms of numbers in the program. It consists of those individuals who are in need of outreach and peer ministry "to" them. Relationship Building includes "those outside our faith community (Evangelization) and then those within our faith community who are not quite ready for catechesis (Community)."[2]

The second category, "Catechesis," is not approachable until the firm relationships in category one have been established. This step features a more formal faith development of the individual. "At that point, the listener knows you care, and knows you well enough to observe whether you live what you preach or not. The *content* of catechesis is delivered first relationally, with Jesus and the catechist as *models*. There will follow a more logical presentation (usually with very little resistance) of the content themes in Christianity."[3]

After the first two categories are passed—after solid relationships have been built and a deeper understanding of Jesus and his message has been established—the "listener" can then enter into the Service/Mission category. "This category highlights the person as part of the believing community ministering to the real needs of others." "It's the point at which one accepts God's love so deeply, he or she chooses to be a vehicle for that love to be shared with others."[4]

It must be remembered that those belonging to the Evangelization category outnumber those belonging to the Catechesis category. An even smaller number fit into the Service/ Mission category. Only this smaller group includes those ready to make a real commitment. This core group does not form a clique; it is open-ended to build more relationships and catechesis and, in turn, becomes the key in maintaining the whole process.

"It's important to see this chart not as a technique, but as a measurement of the way Jesus worked in the Gospel stories. He related, revealed, and then called people to commit. He taught, but always while relating to someone. He worked through a few to touch many. And He always modeled what He called others to do. In Jesus, we have the perfect model of a minister."[5]

NOTES
1. National CYO Federation, *Hope for the Decade: A Look at the Issues Facing Catholic Youth Ministry* (Washington, D.C.: NCYOF, 1980), p. 2.
2. *Youth Ministry Resources, Volume III* (Washington, D.C.: U.S. Catholic Conference, Department of Education, 1979), Section: Theory of Youth Ministry.
3. *Ibid.*
4. *Ibid.*
5. *Ibid.*

PART ONE

Outstanding Evangelizers of American Youth

BRINGING YOUTH TO CHRIST
DR. JAY KESLER, PRESIDENT
YOUTH FOR CHRIST, INTERNATIONAL

CHAPTER

1

SIXTY percent of all American teens are claimed to be
unchurched, and yet the American teen is the world's most
"religious of all the world's children." When polled by a national
research agency, American teens claimed a desire to know God
and an interest in becoming churched where spiritual answers
can be found.

Youth For Christ now has some 800 full-time staff persons
throughout the United States, with another 4,000 trained
volunteers reaching out to high school and junior high school
youth across the nation.

Youth For Christ has touched the hearts, minds, and lives of
millions of American youth who never would have been reached
by the local church. YFC has added a professionalism to its
outreach that includes the best of all worlds. You will find
Christian psychiatrists, psychologists, social workers, and
medical doctors cooperating in the development of outreach, not
only to healthy youth, but to the troubled as well.

They reach youth "where they are"—they operate in the world
youth live in, not where we wish they lived.

Here is an outline of how to reach American youth that works. It is interdenominational; it is for Catholic and non-Catholic alike.

Jay Kesler is not only YFC's president, but an effective evangelizer of youth. They listen to him. Not only do youth listen, but pastors, parents, and educators all across the nation find answers to their troubled questions: "How can we reach our kids for Jesus Christ?"

Youth For Christ (YFC) is the name of a large group of full-time staff and volunteers who are committed to the task of reaching young people for Jesus Christ. With programs in 200 cities in the U.S. and over sixty nations around the world, YFC is significant in the worldwide movement for youth evangelism. The mission of YFC is:

To participate in the body of Christ, in the responsible evangelism of youth, presenting them with the person, work, and teachings of Christ, and discipling them into the church.

I. EVANGELISM IN YOUTH FOR CHRIST

Although evangelism has always been central to the purpose of YFC, the methods of evangelism have changed several times to meet the needs of the day.

YFC's roots reach back into the late 1930s and early 1940s when young men, most of them ministers and evangelists, with some laymen, were holding large rallies in the United States, Canada, and England. They were called by various names: Singspiration (Kansas City), Victory Rally (San Diego), Voice of Christian Youth (Detroit), Word of Life (New York), Youth For Christ (Chicago), and Victorious Christian Youth (Tacoma).

YFC in its early years was not as specialized in its ministry to youth as it is today. Crowds were a mixture of young people, middle-aged parents, and a scattering of elderly people. The YFC rally was the Christian's place to be on Saturday.

From 1945 until the early 1950s, YFC was essentially large Saturday night evangelistic rallies. It was the heyday of nationally known evangelists and personalities, converted movie stars, song writers, musicians, and gospel teams. Large cities regularly saw auditoriums seating from 2,000 to 10,000 filled to capacity. A Soldier Field meeting in Chicago drew over 70,000 people.

YFC's development can be divided into three historical periods. The philosophies overlap to some degree: hence, the time periods are approximate.

THE FIRST PERIOD: THE MID-40s TO THE MID-50s
From its organizational birth in 1945 to the middle of the 1950s, YFC experienced fantastic expansion as well as organizational spinoffs. Youth For Christ rallies were formed all over America and in dozens of foreign countries. Organizationally, YFC was a very loosely knit federation. There was little or no control over personnel or the use (or abuse) of the organizational name. This period made YFC both famous and infamous.

A few of the organizations sparked by YFC during those years included The Billy Graham Evangelistic Association, World Vision International, Greater Europe Mission, Overseas Crusades, and Gospel Films.

THE SECOND PERIOD: THE MID-50s TO THE MID-60s
The second era was the beginning of specialization in the adolescent scene. Youth For Christ became YOUTH For Christ through:

1. The birth and spread of the high school Bible Clubs, later to be called YFC Clubs (now Campus Life). In just a few years, 3,600 clubs were functioning.
2. The birth of Lifeline, a summer camping ministry to delinquent teens (now Youth Guidance).
3. The birth and spread of local, regional, and national Teen Talent contests and Bible quizzing.
4. A new emphasis of personal teen evangelism on the high school campus.
5. *Youth For Christ* magazine, now *Campus Life* magazine.
6. Specialized camping programs, High Adventure Teen Trips, and other special ministries to the high school crowd.
7. The birth, development, and spread of Teen Teams sent overseas (now Project Serve).

Clubs were not leader centered; they were teen centered. Clubs existed for the purpose of fellowship, leadership, and evangelism, *in that order.* The good club director was the man who got his kids to produce the club meeting in total—the skit, the singing, even the speaking if possible.

But the honest evaluation of YFC staff was that the YFC ministry was almost exclusively with Christian teens and the religiously oriented. In order to more effectively reach the unchurched teens—those who had dropped out of church, those who had never attended, and kids who could only be described as pagan—the methodologies of Campus Life and Youth Guidance were developed.

THE THIRD PERIOD: THE MID-60s TO TODAY

It is necessary to understand four basic trends which were at work to bring about the new thing called Campus Life.

A. The change in teenagers themselves
   1. Educational impact—the post-Sputnik acceleration
   2. Technological impact
   3. Pseudosophistication
   4. Preference for dialogue over monologue; they began to ask "Why?" much more often
   5. Rapid change
B. Organizational changes within YFC's structure
   1. Tightening up of personnel qualifications
   2. Tightening up of chartering requirements
   3. Strengthening of geographical areas
C. A hard analysis of the scope and effectiveness of the YFC ministry by the "second generation" men
D. A new understanding of the religious makeup of teenage America
   1. Christian teens (converted)—5 percent
   2. Religiously oriented teens—35 percent
   3. Unchurched teens—60 percent

Several staff people met in Salt Lake City in 1962 for what turned out to be a decisive two-day meeting. They conceptualized the new shape of the campus ministry in terms of "teen-to-teen: the Christian teenager properly and successfully communicating in action and word his personal faith in Jesus Christ to his friends, his campus, and his world."

Campus Life meetings were developed as tools for evangelism. The new format allowed us to start spending *significant amounts of time* with students. We took the pressure off Christian kids to produce more and better meetings, which some of them had come to see as their primary spiritual role. At the same time, we ourselves became more person centered even while leading meetings. We had to stop preaching and lecturing and begin discussing and listening to students in order to win the right to be heard by them.

While Campus Life evolved over the years from high school Bible Clubs geared for Christian teens, into an evangelistic outreach to unchurched teenagers, Youth Guidance also began to evolve.

In the early 1950s YFC staff began to work with young boys in juvenile institutions. The courts were also faced with a backlog of cases and were quite open to referring kids to YFC for help during the summer months.

Initially, the main emphasis was summer camping. In 1963 the state of Indiana and then-Governor Matthew Welsh donated Camp Muscatatuck to YFC/Lifeline. Lifeline camps became an exciting trend in YFC and it became a popular program emphasis to hold a YFC Lifeline camp every summer.

Around the mid-60s, a small group of staff began to feel that a summer ministry with delinquents was good, but that the long-term effectiveness of such a ministry was questionable. As a result, full-time Youth Guidance/Lifeline directors began to start with a summer camp and then personally became involved with the young people during the school year on a one-to-one, year-round counseling basis.

Youth Guidance continued to grow and define this specialized ministry with troubled youth. In 1968 several cities began experimenting with group home ministries and a number of staff began ministering with court referrals in small groups.

Campus Life is presently active in 200 cities across the U.S. Over 800 full-time staff and 4,000 volunteers are involved in evangelism to high school and junior high youth. Youth Guidance is presently active in seventy cities across the U.S. Over 150 full-time staff and 1,000 volunteers are involved in evangelism to troubled youth. A description of the methodology and principles of evangelism for Campus Life and Youth Guidance follow.

II. THE CAMPUS LIFE STRATEGY

WHAT IS A HIGH SCHOOL?

There are more than 27,000 high schools in the United States, and they range from Farmersville Consolidated to Park Forest Estates High to Downtown Tech to St. Patrick's Parochial. Each has its own traditions, its own unique personality, its own set of problems. Each has a spectrum all its own: the students themselves. When you've seen one high school, you *haven't* seen them all—and the same can be said of the individual adolescents who populate them.

At present, Campus Life is ministering on no more than 7 percent of these high school campuses. We are confident, however, that the strategy is working and will continue to prove effective as we expand to touch more and more schools. It is responsive to personal needs and at the same time gives thought to influencing the total student body.

Part of its success is based upon a serious analysis of the high school community. One convenient method is to label the students on the basis of social groups: the "rah-rahs," the "greasers," the "hairs," the "jocks," the "eggheads," the "nobodies." Students themselves often think in such terms. Such categories are sometimes misleading, however, since they are based on impressions rather than hard data. Perhaps a social psychologist, after a major amount of testing and interviewing, could divide the student body accurately along those lines.

We in Campus Life opt for a simpler and more reliable analysis based on interest groups. Interest groups are quite easily determined by what students volunteer to do, i.e., what extracurricular activities they are in. The larger interest groups are usually:

> Athletes (male and female)
> Cheerleaders and pep club members
> Musicians

Smaller interest groups include:

> Publication staff members (newspaper, yearbook,
>   underground newspaper)

Drama participants
Officeholders (class government and student association)

In addition, some schools have significant minority group organizations (Black, Chicano, Puerto Rican, Cuban, Native American).

THE DYNAMICS OF A CLUB YEAR
These groups are often at the center of activities and their leaders are often the most influential and socially capable students. Therefore, Campus Life staff people analyze their own interests ("What was *my* bag throughout high school and college?") and attempt to make contact with those interest groups on the campus. *Contacting* thus becomes the foundation of the Campus Life strategy. It continues year-round: without it as a base, the formal Campus Life meetings crumble.

Out of these personal contacts with both leaders and followers in the student body grows the formation of the actual club. Early in the school year, plans are laid for the *Burger Bash,* the first public appearance for Campus Life in the school's activity calendar.

Preliminary meetings let a core group of students know something of the flair of Campus Life and get them committed to making it happen on their own campus. Then the Burger Bash is an evening of food and fun for as many kids as possible, plus a sales pitch for the future excitement of Campus Life and a tipoff that Jesus Christ will not be a stranger to the club.

A week later comes the first Campus Life meeting, known to the staff as *Impact.* It is a mass meeting, again in the evening, at a student's home or some other off-campus location, which attempts to involve as many non-Christian students as possible. It has three main parts:

Crowdbreakers—the unique Campus Life brand of fun
Discussion—an open forum for an issue meaningful to
    student life, moderated by a staff member
Wrapup—conclusions and applications of the gospel by the
    club director

Other occasional ingredients are announcements, social games, short service projects, media presentations, etc. Most often the real goal is to get non-Christian kids to think seriously enough about their lives and their needs that they seek help from staff people or Christian club kids on an individual basis.

The expectations for an Impact meeting are reflected in the following questions:

1. Were there some first-timers?
2. Was at least half the crowd non-Christian?
3. Were there enough kids present to create the Campus Life spirit (usually at least forty)?
4. Was there student response (appointments made, comments offered, etc.)?
5. Were the mechanics smooth?
6. Did the kids get some solid information about Jesus?

Impact meetings continue at two-week intervals throughout the school year. They are the showcase of Campus Life, the expression of our balanced philosophy of life or whole-person concept in active, visual form.

On alternating weeks comes Insight. This smaller meeting is less publicized, since it is designed for new and growing Christians. It is not a clique; it is a cross-section of the school's Christian community interested in spiritual growth. The staff person leads the group in an experience of self-discovery and God-discovery that aims toward Christian maturity. Students encounter Scripture in depth to find guidelines for their lives. And again, personal ministry is a result. Insight has several parts, and tends not to be as programmed as Impact:

Feedback—student descriptions of how previous concepts are working

Discovery—devices that open up student minds to themselves and/or the Bible

Discussion—working out biblical meanings and concepts in an open forum

Wrapup—conclusions from the leader

Action Lab—an individual assignment to be done as the meeting closes or in the following days

Insight may become too large for dealing with some of the specific problems kids face. When this happens small groups are formed by staff and volunteers who contact five or six students of common sex and interest. On the basis of this natural affinity, they are asked if they would be interested in meeting together one hour a week for six weeks to work through a particular problem or explore a particular topic. The intimate dynamics of small groups are often very productive.

Our ministry reaches the ultimate in personal attention through appointments with both non-Christians and Christians. Students are encouraged at both Impact and Insight to fill out a card requesting a chance "to talk with one of the Campus Life staff." These are often times when non-Christians make their commitments to Christ and when Christians work out major spiritual difficulties.

Evangelism occasionally comes through different formats: weekend retreats, overnight parties for girls, summer backpacking or other adventure trips, etc.

This is the overview, the skeleton, of the strategy which God has seemed pleased to bless over the past few years. It is constantly open to change and revision (as hinted by the looseleaf format of this). Youth For Christ has long been known (and criticized) for its premise that while the message is timeless, methods need constant reevaluation and updating.

OUR UNDERSTANDING OF EVANGELISM

Campus Life men and women believe that high school ministry is crucial. High school is the last chance for touching a total cross-section of the community; it is the last time a generation is together. Once high school graduation is over, the generation splits forever.

At the same time, high school is the first time a teenager can make mature decisions. Thus, it is the crucial time to introduce him to Jesus Christ.

The high school is actually the funnel of the community; nearly everybody goes through it. Scan the pages of any neighborhood newspaper and you will see that the high school is a focus of community interest. Parents who may be impregnable to almost everything else have this one chink in their armor; they are concerned about teenagers, especially their own.

And those teenagers happen to be people for whom God's only Son died 2,000 years ago. The problem is that there is a great gap between the death of Christ for them and the modern teenager. It happens to be our privilege to stand in the gap, to hold in one hand the hand of the Lord Jesus and in the other the hand of the teenager for whom he died. That's called evangelism.

Shortly before his death, Jesus stated the twofold purpose of evangelism: "I have chosen you, and ordained you, that ye should go and (1) bring forth fruit, and (2) that your fruit should remain" (John 15:16). We have often been more successful at number one than number two. We are trying in Campus Life to open the pages of the New Testament and find out how God's people rocked their world. We believe that they succeeded so spectacularly because of at least six characteristics: maximum influence, person-centeredness, Spirit-led boldness, multiplication, long-term patience, and follow-through care.

(These will work only in synergism with each other. Any one, taken alone and pushed out of proportion, will result in imbalanced evangelism.)

1. *Maximum Influence.* In Matthew 5:14-16, Jesus said, "You are the world's light—a city on a hill glowing in the night for all to see. Don't hide your light! Let it shine for all; let your good deeds glow for all to see, so that they will praise your heavenly Father." If you get within twenty or thirty miles of New York City, regardless of direction, it is a little hard to miss seeing it. There it sits. You come over the crest of a hill, and there's the Empire State Building. People feel differently about New York. Some people hate it. Some love it (they've got to be a little crazy, but . . .). Others are neutral about it. But there's one thing about New York; you can't ignore it. It won't go away. There it is; it dominates everything. And it's not even on a hill.

Jesus said that his gospel and his people should be unignorable. In their own town or wherever they are, they should be talked about. They are to penetrate every level: they are to be the most noticeable thing around.

If our ministry puts us into a little corner where we're unnoticed, doing a neat little thing with a few people, it isn't New Testament. Jesus said, "If you do it as I want it done, you will be like the city on the hill. Some people will hate you; some will love you. Some will be unsure. But no one will be able to ignore you. You will be an undeniable influence."

Jesus approached his world in such a way as to penetrate every level and influence as many people as he could. Maximum-influence evangelism is finding the *fastest way to influence the most people the most effectively.* Each word is important. *The fastest way to reach the most people* might be a gospel blimp or a bumper sticker or neon sign on the campus lawn that says "God Loves You." But that would not be doing the job *most effectively.* The most effective way often hasn't been thought of yet, which means we must use all our creativity to find it rather than just trying harder and harder at the old standbys.

Campus Life has attempted to shape its methods for maximum influence. Three points are evident from the strategy of the New Testament:

(a) *Mass exposure to the gospel.* We attempt to get together large groups of young people and let them hear the Good News. Various kinds of meetings, Big Five events, even Haunted Houses can pull together a lot of people for an initial exposure to the gospel. Peter and Paul stood up and preached for mass exposure; they planted the seed in thousands of hearts. The fruit of this sowing does not always come up quickly, but the germination process has begun.

(b) *Going for strategic people.* This is not the same as "big-shot" evangelism. Campus Life is not the place for only the student council president and the football team captain, to the exclusion of the 85 percent who are nothing except ordinary teenage people.

It often happens, though, that some of those ordinary kids are reached through a Lydia or an Ethiopian eunuch or a Cornelius. The VIPs coming to Christ may help the cause of Christ in a high school grow faster than it would have if we had ignored them and didn't know who they were.

(c) *Getting the gospel to diverse groups within the school.* Christians came from more than one mold in the New Testament. Campus Life evangelism takes us to kids with long hair and short hair; student leaders and student losers. We try to affect the athlete, the greaser, the kid who's fun to be with, the kid who's no fun to be with, the rich, the poor, the white, and the black. We must aim for maximum influence in all groups. If Campus Life becomes a clique of one kind of kids (usually the leader's favorite kind), we have failed in the first characteristic of New Testament evangelism.

2. *Person-centeredness.* We're familiar with how Jesus began evangelizing Sychar in John 4. He spent time getting through to one woman. The same God who believes in maximum influence also believes in approaching one person at a time and slanting the gospel to their individuality.

In Luke 15 Jesus said he would worry more over one lost sheep than ninety-nine safe ones.

Person-centeredness means three things:

(a) *We operate in their world, not ours.* How did Jesus get through to us? He "became a human being and lived here on earth among us" (John 1:14). He didn't throw down a message tied to a brick; he didn't shout from a megaphone in the sky. He got down here and lived in our world. He risked catching leprosy. He became like us. The only thing he didn't do was sin.

Like Jesus, we must risk everything to invade the world where non-Christian kids are. We go to their campuses, football practices, drive-ins, school plays, etc.; we don't expect them to come to us. And we are misunderstood at times for doing so.

(b) *We speak to their needs.* We don't always jump right off with "God loves you" or "Man is a sinner." We instead relate to students as whole persons. We find out where they're hurting so that we know where to apply the medicine. We want to see healing take place, not just administer a certain number of shots.

(c) *We begin at their starting point.* Paul said in 1 Corinthians 9:20-22, "When I am with the Jews I seem as one of them so that they will listen to the Gospel and I can win them to Christ. When I am with Gentiles who follow Jewish customs and ceremonies I don't argue, even though I don't agree, because I want to help them. When with the heathen I agree with them as much as I can, except of course that I must always do what is right as a Christian. And so, by agreeing, I can win their confidence and help them too. When I am with those whose consciences bother them easily, I don't act as though I know it all and don't say they are foolish; the result is that they are willing to let me help them. Yes, whatever a person is like, I try to find common ground with him so that he will let me tell him about Christ and let Christ save him."

Does that sound like the hardnosed, dogmatic Paul? It is. Paul's gospel stayed constant, but his approach changed with every person he met.

Teenagers never determine *what* our message should be, but they always determine *how* we say it. There is no one perfect way to communicate the gospel; it depends on the individual, for whom Christ died. That's why Campus Life is not a *plan-centered* strategy. We don't have a spiel which we preface with, "Now listen—you need to know these things." We try to be *person-centered* in our strategy. Kids are not *customers;* they are *people.* The only thing that matters about customers is whether they buy or not; their name, feelings, etc., are irrelevant. Kids are people—and after we get to know them as people, we may well indeed use a "plan of salvation" to explain the gospel. But at that point we are sure that this person is interested in finding out the gospel.

3. *Spirit-led Boldness.* Paul described his approach in 1 Thessalonians 2:3, 4, "So you can see that we were not preaching with any false motives or evil purposes in mind; we were perfectly straightforward and sincere. For we speak as messengers from God, trusted by him to tell the truth; we change his message not one bit to suit the taste of those who hear it; for we serve God alone, who examines our hearts' deepest thoughts."

This agrees with the constant use of the word "boldness" in Acts, as the early church hit hard and was "not ashamed of the Gospel of Christ." In 1 Corinthians 1:21-24, Paul says "His message . . . seems foolish to the Jews because they want a sign from heaven as proof that what is preached is true; and it is foolish to the Gentiles because they believe only what agrees with their philosophy and seems wise to them." (Campus Life men might paraphrase thus: "I have two kinds of kids in my club. Some of them want a big dramatic superzap. Then, they say, they'll believe in Christ. The others want a different approach; they want a logical treatise on the existence of God because they're very intellectual.")

Paul continues, "So when we preach about Christ dying to save them, the Jews are offended and the Gentiles say it's all nonsense. But God has opened the eyes of those called to salvation, both Jews and Gentiles, to see that Christ is the mighty power of God to save them." (Again, to paraphrase: "You know what I do? I don't cater to either one. I tell them that Jesus died for them, and that's all I have to say.") Paul defines "my gospel" in 1 Corinthians 15:1-4; it is that Jesus died and rose again, and that that amounts to a cure for the basic human problem. That message, he claimed and practiced, was worth being bold about. He was simply following his Lord, who "taught . . . with great authority" (Matthew 7:29).

So, are the buttonholers right after all? Now let's talk about *Spirit-led* boldness. We are almost dismayed in reading the four Gospels to notice how many people Jesus *didn't* touch. He walked into the Bethesda health spa, healed one man, and left again. Huge crowds in Jericho wanted to see him, but he was preoccupied with one blind man named Bartimaeus.

Paul had great plans for a crusade in Bithynia, but "the Spirit of Jesus said no" (Acts 16:7). The people of the New Testament were not quite mindless fanatics trying to club everybody in sight. They were Spirit-led, and the Spirit didn't lead them to everyone. But the ones he *did* point out got the full dose. There was no compromising or watering down of the message; the believers were bold and unashamed.

We in Campus Life are not above being tempted to pull our punches. "These inner city kids are tough; I just can't come on too strong like the storefront preachers they know. . . ." "These suburban kids are so cool, so sophisticated; I just can't come right out and. . . ." *Our* rationalizations must be junked. *No* kid dare make us back off from the gospel.

We must always guard against the following substitutes for presenting the gospel. They sound good but they are inadequate by themselves.

(a) *Student excitement about Campus Life is not enough.* The Lord has given us some understanding of the high school scene and some great tools for maximum influence. And when we've made a big splash and the student body president is saying, "Wow, Campus Life is the neatest thing in the school," we can be tempted into thinking we've arrived. But the means are not the end.

(b) *Rapport is not enough.* The Lord helps us to win the friendship and confidence of a number of students . . . why? So we can present Christ to them. But if we suddenly turn chicken and start to fear that the kid might not like us anymore if we come on too strong, we betray Jesus. We trade off evangelism to preserve rapport.

(c) *Spiritual generalities are not enough.* This is the "God is great, God is good" speech. "Jesus is cool." "Jesus is your Friend." "We believe in the balanced life—that the spiritual area ought to relate to the mental and social areas." "We want you kids to think tonight about how God fits into your life."

All those lines are very nice and true and serve a good purpose in certain situations—but we have to get more specific than that. We have to communicate the full-fledged gospel before we're through.

Actually, Spirit-led boldness does not fear rejection. The ultimate failure in our ministry is not for a kid to reject Jesus. Many have done so in the past; many, unfortunately, will in the future. If rejection equals failure, then Jesus failed badly many times.

Ultimate failure in evangelism is when we don't really give kids anything to reject. Our methods must always implement Spirit-led boldness.

4. *Multiplication.* Paul, sitting in prison, knew that he personally wasn't going to get to do much more evangelizing. He wrote to Timothy, "You must teach others those things you and many others have heard me speak about. Teach these great truths to trustworthy men who will, in turn, pass them on to others" (2 Timothy 2:2).

He may have gotten that concept from thinking about Jesus' parable of the sower in Matthew 13. A lot of the seeds didn't make it. But the ones that hit good soil were soon producing thirty, sixty, even a hundred plants.

There are two approaches to evangelism: addition and

multiplication. Addition says, "I will go to a high school and set up my imaginary booth, so to speak, and be the evangelist at this school. I will try to run as many kids through my booth as I can. I will tell them what they need to know, check them off as a yes or a no, and keep the line flowing." A lot of kids could find Christ that way.

But multiplication says, "I will set up my booth and lead a kid to Christ. Then I will spend some time with him to make sure he understands what has happened to him. I will show him how to run a booth of his own in the high school. It will take longer than just telling him how to witness; I will show him how witnessing in the New Testament is a by-product of a growing relationship with Christ. I will cause him to become a disciple."

At the beginning, teen-to-teen sharing is less effective. The addition method racks up faster totals. But multiplication eventually catches up and takes the lead.

How did there get to be 3.6 billion people on this earth? Adam and Eve did not set out to have that many babies! They had only a few, but those began reproducing. What if Adam and Eve had set a goal of 3.6 million, but all their babies turned out to be sterile? None of us would be here.

Campus Life conducts Insight meetings because we believe in multiplication. True, it takes time and energy away from Impact. We aren't involved in bringing pagan kids to Christ. But we are building multipliers out of Christian kids. We split our appointments half and half between Christians and non-Christians for the same reason. Leading kids to Christ through appointments is important; discipling Christian kids to do the same is just as important.

5. *Long-term Concern.* We already mentioned, in talking about multiplication, that the producing of new life takes time. The Lord "is waiting," according to 2 Peter 3:9, "for the good reason that he is not willing that any should perish, and he is giving more time for sinners to repent." God is willing to wait.

Now that does *not* mean that he wants us to wait to make the presentation. We dare not do that; we must get the message spelled out as quickly as possible. But we are to be willing to wait all day for a response. The Spirit of God sometimes takes a long time to work internally, and so long as the chemistry is bubbling we cannot afford to get impatient.

One of the reasons is that when we're talking about a whole faith, a new style of life, kids are not impulse buyers. They are too smart. They've been snowed by ad men and politicians before. So when somebody says, "You should become a Christian," the most common response is "Oh, really? Why? Where can I watch you for a while?"

And they may think it over for a very long time. If they eventually decide yes, there is an interesting side benefit. They are born into the kingdom of God a year old! They already know all kinds of things about being a Christian; they're suddenly a lot further down the road of maturity than the kid who just heard a convincing speaker, jumped up, and headed for the counseling room. The ones who take a little longer often turn out to be best results.

We will be credible and authentic over the long haul. We will be there when the kid is ready to make his decision.

6. *Follow-through Care.* Here is where we get down to talking about "fruit that will remain." Paul and Timothy said to the Colossians that "Everywhere we go we talk about Christ to all who will listen, warning them" (but it doesn't stop there) "and teaching them as well as we know how. We want to be able to present each one to God, perfect because of what Christ has done for each of them" (1:28).

The man who has only spiritual dwarfs or stillborns to present to God will be ashamed. The Great Commission asked for more than just going and telling; it also said, "Make disciples." This requires a ministry on several levels. It would appear that Jesus touched at least three. He made disciples of only twelve men, working intensely night and day with them.

He had a relational ministry with a slightly larger circle: Mary Magdalene, Lazarus, Martha, and Mary, the Emmaus people, possibly the seventy. They all knew him; they got the advantage of personal contact with him.

And he touched the third group—the masses—in an even more limited way. About all he could do was stand up in front of them and say, "Here's my message; I hope some of you will accept it."

We each have our favorite areas. Some of us are very good at discipling, and we'd like to do that all the time and avoid the seed-scattering. Others of us are good at touching crowds of kids, but get nervous at one-to-one. We cannot afford the luxury of doing only what we like. To be responsible, we must minister on all three levels.

And then we must be concerned about "working out the new salvation" in the lives of kids who find Christ. We must show that we understand that pediatrics is as important as obstetrics. We have historically been better at delivering spiritual babies than in caring for them afterward. That is irresponsible. We should stop bringing new babies into the kingdom rather than abandoning them on the delivery table.

As we understand more about the characteristics of New Testament evangelism, we must make Campus Life conform to it. After all, the results in the New Testament are fairly impressive.

The temptation will be to concentrate on whichever of these six happens to be our favorite to the exclusion of the others. If we like buttonholing, we can distort the proper role of boldness. If we are by nature low-pressure, we can intentionally misunderstand long-term concern. Only by carefully following the full scope of New Testament evangelism does Campus Life become an effective representative of Jesus on a high school campus.

III. THE YOUTH GUIDANCE STRATEGY

The Youth Guidance Division presently sponsors five types of programs: 1) referral services, 2) residential care centers, 3) institutional services, 4) neighborhood ministries, and 5) creative options.

Referral services are especially designed for delinquent and predelinquent youth. In 1969, the YFCI Board of Directors accepted the following definition:

Youth Guidance is designed to serve the juvenile court, law enforcement agencies, schools, and other public and private agencies by providing a structured program for delinquent and predelinquent teenagers that will result in socially acceptable behavior revolving around implementation of the "balanced life" concept of Youth For Christ.

Youth Guidance cooperates with community agencies in accepting referrals and assisting in the overall program of established agencies. It is not intended to be an isolated agency.

Youth Guidance is designed to provide, over an extended period of time, a plan of counseling and behavior adjustment for each individual that will assist in developing mature attitudes toward self, a motivational framework, *reward systems,* and social standards.

The term "predelinquent" refers to those teenagers who have exhibited antisocial behavior and/or a strong tendency toward delinquent acts. Recognizing a thin line and a high degree of coincidence between delinquency and neglect, the local Youth Guidance director will make the final decision on acceptance of referrals. His general criterion is that the program is specifically intended as a behavior-adjustment agency, not primarily a poverty-fighting or neglect-compensating program. These aspects of social work may, however, be a part of the program in promoting behavior change for antisocial or asocial teenagers.

YFC's approach to the delinquent concentrates on four basic life areas: social, mental, physical, and spiritual. Corrective attention is given to antisocial attitudes and behavior patterns that contribute to delinquency and make the implementation of new life in Christ difficult. The ultimate goal is to see the image of Jesus Christ formed in the teenager through his rebirth and growth. (These goals are basically true for all four Youth Guidance program structures.)

RESIDENTIAL CARE

Closely related to the thrust of referral services is the in-depth ministry of group homes. Every community has teenagers who either have no home or have a home which is tragically deficient in its ability to provide a healthy atmosphere for the child's growth. Because of unstable home environments, teenagers often develop behavior patterns which make it difficult for them to live with relatives or in a foster home. These teenagers usually become wards of the court because of delinquency or neglect.

Group homes and foster homes provide a "new home" for the

troubled young person when his own is unable to cope with him. Placing him in a Christian home for a period of several months gives him the opportunity to experience all the dynamics of the Christian life in an atmosphere which not only understands his troubled background, but is conducive to rehabilitation and new life. Presently, group homes and foster care are increasing emphases in a number of Youth Guidance cities.

INSTITUTIONAL SERVICES

A large number of troubled youth are institutionalized. These teenagers need the ministry of YFC to complement the program of the institution. The vast majority of juvenile institutions are government-operated and usually unable to provide in-depth spiritual guidance.

Institutional Services is designed to bring the gospel and related assistance to the incarcerated teenager and is presently related to the community-based small group ministry. As Youth Guidance staff members provide worship and counseling services to the institution, they build relationships which are then channeled into the community-based small group when the teenagers are released from the juvenile institutions.

NEIGHBORHOOD MINISTRIES

This area of Youth Guidance deals with inner-city young people whose world is their neighborhood and whose options in life are limited by seriously crowded and disadvantaged living conditions. These environments often limit the options for personal development by youth. By involvement in street work, neighborhood recreation activities, and drop-in centers, Youth Guidance staff persons develop helping, caring relationships with many young people who are potential delinquents and "failures." This emphasis on prevention is a hopeful alternative for youth in housing projects and inner-city neighborhoods.

Youth Guidance Neighborhood Ministries is designed to involve urban teenagers in a program leading to an encounter with Jesus Christ and breaking the environmental bindings which hinder the possibility of fulfillment, personal growth, and stability.

Often storefront neighborhood youth centers are used as a positive presence in the community. These centers provide a place for youth to relate to the staff and volunteer workers.

CREATIVE OPTIONS

Several specialized programs have been designed to meet specific needs among youth already involved in one of the four major Youth Guidance ministry programs. These include programs for young girls who are pregnant or have a child, programs to teach basic employment skills, and leadership development programs for older youths in a YG program who have demonstrated leadership potential.

Youth Guidance has focused on four basic causal roots that seem generally to characterize troubled youth. These are the four assumptions:

1. Among young people in trouble there is extensive low self-esteem. The youth see themselves as failures and as having no future.
2. Alienated young people have a peer group that does not produce caring relationships and often produces behavior which is labeled deviant or delinquent.
3. Troubled youth lack a relationship with a caring adult model. There has been little trust developed between the child and an adult who loves unconditionally and who disciplines fairly.
4. The young person has not established a relationship with God in which he feels forgiven for his sin and clean before God as a new person in Christ. The young person in trouble is weighted down by his moral guilt (not just neurotic guilt) and has not had a legitimate spiritual experience that enables him to deal with his spiritual need. (This is not to say the young person necessarily feels guilty.)

Youth Guidance assumes that the extent to which these conditions exist within a young person is the extent to which he or she can be considered a young person in trouble. Youth Guidance does not consider it necessary that a deviant act be committed and a young person subsequently placed into the juvenile justice system before he is considered "troubled" and therefore the object of this ministry. If these conditions exist in a life, there is a need requiring intensive and specialized intervention.

Once the youth worker has assessed the problem, he can develop a philosophy which forms the basis for ministry methodology. The ministry goals flow from this analysis and also form the basis for his evaluation of effectiveness.

MINISTRY GOALS

The primary goal of evangelism and discipleship must be filtered through an understanding of Youth Guidance teenagers. (What are their needs and how can they be reached for Christ and discipled effectively?)

The goal of evangelism interpreted in a ministry with troubled youth has four primary areas:

a. Gradual development of healthy self-concept
b. Development of positive peer group relations
c. Youth's need to establish a meaningful relationship with a caring adult
d. Transformation through spiritual rebirth

Self-concept: The areas relating to an individual's poor self-image are closely connected with his experience in the context of poor or nonexistent relationships.

One of YG's goals is to structure experiences and to create a climate in which the individual is accepted and has opportunities to recognize his or her own worth. Primarily this involves a significant relationship in which an adult accepts, cares for, and pays attention to the youth—no matter what.

Camping experiences and initiative tests are utilized to assist youths in coming to grips with their own unique abilities. For example, a young person who completes a difficult week in a wilderness camping experience, despite all of the physical and emotional fears, will feel good about that accomplishment. This success will begin to change the way he views himself. Small groups can also add to the growth of a young person's self-esteem. Acceptance by group members, trust, and noncompetitiveness are essential elements which contribute to the process of growth.

Positive Peer Relationships: So many troubled youths are familiar with selfishness, manipulation, and hurting others for personal gain. The positive peer group experience can help individuals with socialization problems move from mistrust and gaming to trust and openness. Group experiences become significant growth stimulators if the members in the group can learn to function in more positive ways with each other.

The YG group is designed to facilitate this type of growth. The emphasis is on communication, personal worth, acceptance, trust, openness, and mutual help. New behavior patterns are learned in the context of a safe environment and can be transferred slowly into practice in outside relationships.

Healthy Adult Model: Many of the attitudes, behaviors, and values which troubled young persons exhibit are the result of learning that has occurred through association with negative role models. These models can be parents, other relatives, and friends in the community. Often, though, particularly at an early age, the imprinting of attitudes and behavior patterns occurs in the home through exposure to parents. There is no substitute for a significant relationship with a healthy adult model in facilitating growth and change.

One of YG's major goals is to insure that the young person involved in the YG program experiences good modeling. Since young persons often emulate the attitudes and behaviors of those who are significant to them, modeling can have a profound impact in facilitating behavioral and attitudinal change.

Spiritual Growth Through Personal Redemption: Permeating everything in YG is the spoken and living message of God's love. Basic Christian values are taught as the foundation of growth for the whole person. Jesus Christ, his work, and teachings are presented meaningfully as the way to personal spiritual redemption and growth. The caring relationships and the social concern expressed in YG activities undergird the gospel message.

WHAT CHRISTIANS HAVE TO OFFER

A Christian has some distinct gifts to offer young people because of his faith in Christ. These include:

Sense of mission
Unusual freedom to love unconditionally
Healthy self-concept
Proper commitment to a biblical value system
Message of forgiveness and redemption
Vulnerability and transparency

The Christian, through the quality of his life in Christ, brings to a ministry with troubled youth a distinctive person as well as program.

EVANGELISM AND TROUBLED YOUTH

The process of evangelism involves the communication of the good news—the gospel.

Effective communication exists only where the message and the medium are well integrated and consistent. The medium must be supportive of the message, not distracting or contradictory. The YG staff person's life (the medium) and his relationship with the youth must be supportive of the message being communicated.

Consider the irony of a situation in which the YG staff worker wants to communicate God's love but doesn't take the time to be with and care for a youth who needs his friendship. The YG staffer is called to both proclaim the message (good news) and to become the living extension of the implications of that message. He is called to speak of God's immeasurable love and to let his life be an example of that unconditional love.

Because of the many needs of troubled youths, it is common for them to conform to the YG worker's expectations and beliefs in order to please him. At this stage it is easy for the YG worker to manipulate the youth into a false conversion experience. It is not responsible evangelism if someone takes advantage of a young person's various needs in order to manipulate him into the kingdom.

While confrontation with the reality of Jesus Christ should be a part of our approach, sensitivity is required to avoid violating a youth's personhood as he nears a response based on some knowledge of the gospel and its implications.

A YG youth's response to the gospel is the result of the Holy Spirit in his life; it isn't the result of a clever staff person's technique.

Evangelism in YG essentially consists of a balance of the following:

Proclamation—verbal communication of the gospel

Relationship—real communication with the youth, the process of building a significant relationship

Incarnation—becoming a living extension of the Good News to the needy young person

PROBLEMS

The troubled teenager is a complex package of needs. Unlike the typical teenager, he has needs in the social, physical, and mental areas of his life which are not being met and have little hope of being met in the future.

The typical evangelical approaches to evangelism are inappropriate and ineffective with the troubled teenager. The limitations affecting the delinquent's relationship to society are magnified in his concept of a relationship to God. Relating to the dynamics of troubled youth in the previous chapter, consider the following implications:

1. The teenager who has learned not to trust anybody will find it difficult to trust God.
2. The teenager who models his life after totally selfish parents and family members will not comprehend Jesus giving himself for that teenager's sin.
3. The teenager who believes love is for self-gratification will not understand God's love. This includes the teen who equates "love" with "sex"—a message prevalent in his music and peer group, and probably with his parents, too.
4. The teenager who lives in emotional and material poverty will find it difficult to respond to an offer of "abundant life" from a person he cannot see.
5. The teenager with an underdeveloped or weak conscience will experience little guilt or sorrow for sin.
6. The teenager who does not trust the "establishment" will find it hard to trust the God who is so often associated with the status quo.
7. The teenager who knows only retribution will find it difficult even to consider the significance of God's forgiveness.

These central concepts of God's gift of life are foreign to the majority of troubled teenagers. Couple their emotional makeup with the learned art of superficial response (a form of conning) and the challenge facing the person who works with troubled youth can be readily seen.

A leading Christian adolescent psychiatrist suggests that winning a troubled teenager to Christ involves three steps:

1. Building a friendly relationship, so the teenager begins to accept the worker who has a genuine interest in him. He considers the worker trustworthy and begins to divulge small parts of himself. As the YG staffer proves worthy of the youth's trust and becomes a person who can be profitably modeled, it is time for the next step.

    The first step involves his acceptance of the worker. The conversations with him about God and Christ will be influenced by his evaluation of the YG staffer.

2. The second step of winning the troubled young person to Christ is his acceptance of the worker's ideas. As the delinquent accepts the YG worker, he also begins to accept the worker's message about life and God. Values become sensible as the worker becomes what sociologists call a "significant other." The consistent expression of what makes the YG staffer "tick" and the advice given about life now take on meaning.

3. The third step is a personal decision by the delinquent to relate himself to the Christ he sees in the YG staffer's life. God's Word has been presented to this confused mind and heart through a personal relationship. The encounter of a troubled teen with Christ takes place only after a worker has consistently been an example of a believer.

It is important to recognize that these steps overlap each other and have no sharp beginning and end. Sometimes it is difficult to differentiate the steps as a teenager moves through them. The gospel and the basics of the Christian life are presented throughout the contact with the teenager, but only in the third step will the youth make a genuine response to the Holy Spirit. Until that time, his response tends to be superficial, most likely aimed at gaining the worker's approval, and probably isn't a genuine response to God. Even a teenager's prayer life before step three, while verbally addressed to God, will probably be emotionally related to the worker.

Of course, it is impossible to time schedule these three steps. Total development will likely take many months—even years. For each juvenile offender the time span will vary. For some, the first step might be hurdled in three days; in others, it might take eighteen months. The same is true of the other steps. Each teenager, depending on his background, environment, peer pressure, and his relationship with the YG staffer, will develop at different speeds.

RELATIONAL AND INCARNATIONAL PRINCIPLES
The challenge of working with this segment of today's teenage society is that there is no formula for guaranteed success. The science of human behavior is full of theories, but sorely lacking in fact and proof. A book or a person should not be the source of all the answers. Experts in this field do not give answers; they develop a skill in asking questions.

Youth Guidance staffers should develop their own plans of evangelistic effort and rehabilitation. As long as the procedure has been tested, the worker should have free reign. However, the youth worker should remember that he deals with people having eternal souls. He is not experimenting with rats, mice, or parrots. Prayerful planning for relating to troubled youth should include the following imperatives:

1. Carefully formulate your concept of what leads to normal (not perfect) healthy teenage life. Be aware of the teenage society around you . . . read, read, read . . . observe, observe, observe.
2. Carefully "investigate" every aspect of a teenager's life, but don't become an amateur psychoanalyst. Take advantage of natural situations to learn about the teenager through listening and asking casual questions.
3. Make working hypotheses about what important factors constitute a delinquent's life. What are the basic issues and problems that have led to his antisocial behavior? What, therefore, are his needs? Will you need to concentrate on his poor self-image? His lack of recognition? His home? His friends?
4. Acquaint yourself with a professional social worker, psychologist, psychiatrist, counselor, or educator who can help you. You need someone with whom you can discuss ideas, plans, frustrations, and results.
5. After you have established your evaluation of the basic problems, develop a plan of action that you can initiate casually. This manual is designed to give you the framework for a treatment plan. (See Youth Guidance record forms.) Be sure your plan is practical and deals with the teenager's needs.

Have both short- and long-range goals, so that you can evaluate your progress regularly. Don't work without a plan. Have a goal and a direction to follow, and evaluate continually.

6. Keep an informal record of each contact. Forms in the Youth Guidance records will help you do this. Your records will help you review from time to time. Don't fly by instinct alone. There is a happy balance between the spontaneous leading of the Lord and rigorous record-keeping that will help identify trends and behavior patterns.

7. Be prepared to change your diagnosis and "treatment" plan as your results indicate the need. Saturate your involvement in the teenager's needs with consistent prayer.

PRINCIPLES OF RESPONSIBLE EVANGELISM WITH TROUBLED YOUTH

When sharing Christ's message with troubled youth, be sensitive toward the individuals and their environment. There are three principles which are essential for communicating the gospel meaningfully with troubled adolescents: establish a sincere relationship; present a complete message; and ultilize an effective follow-through plan.

Establish a Sincere Relationship. Troubled adolescents often haven't received the emotional nourishment from their parents that they need. They may not have experienced consistent and unconditional parental love, and they very likely don't know what it feels like to be accepted and loved. If a worker says, "God loves you," it is often difficult for them to comprehend what he means. By demonstrating real love and forming meaningful relationships with individuals, a YG staffer can provide an important basis for sharing God's love and message with them.

A central theme of the gospel is embodied in the words "God loves you." Scripture enlarges this message through parables, examples, exposition, symbolism, and historical accounts that have become very meaningful to traditional Christianity. However, problems often develop when we attempt to communicate this message to alienated young people. The words that are so full of meaning for Christians often communicate quite different ideas to troubled youth.

"God loves *you.*"

We may make a faulty assumption that young people who hear these words have a normal sense of personal identity. Many, if not most, youth workers have been raised in stable homes and have been surrounded by loving parents and friends. They've also been a part of church, school, and a number of other groups that have given them a sense of belonging and worth. Because of their own feeling of self-worth—a largely unconscious feeling—youth workers may assume that the youth to whom they speak have a similar sense of identity. Many youth workers expect the words "God loves *you*" to communicate the same meaning they understand.

But the young person who hears "God loves *you*" may get an entirely different message. For, instead of a positive feeling of self-worth, he may have enormous questions about his own worth.

Such a youth may have been unwanted or "in the way" for as long as he can remember. He may not know who his father is or that his existence is anything more than a liability. He may know that he is worth at least the extra thirty-five dollars a month his mother receives from welfare because of him, but he doubts if his value exceeds that. He has probably never been an active member of any organization or group, with the possible exception of a street gang. He has not been accepted in school, the primary source of social identity for most adolescents. Nor has he received a sense of worth that comes from feeling a part of community programs, church youth groups, and similar enrichment activities. In short, the "you" he hears his youth worker say may have a profoundly different meaning to him than it does for his worker.

"God *loves* you."

People who have grown up in a home where they are loved have a distinct advantage in understanding the meaning of God's limitless love. To realize that their parents still love and accept them in spite of misbehavior is to give some understanding of the nature of unconditional love. Most youth workers have had such a background and find it relatively easy to understand the concept of God's love. But they may be unaware of how much of their own understanding they project onto the young person to whom they are speaking.

The alienated young person who hasn't experienced the

unconditionality of love in his home or personal relationships will have little foundation for comprehending unconditional love. To him "love" may be sexual attraction or at best a fleeting emotional experience, but it is certainly not something to put his trust in. The love that he has experienced has been a manipulative arrangement, an "I'll love you if . . ." kind of relationship which offers its rewards at the cost of freedom. Love becomes a means of control. The "love" that the young person hears often carries a far different meaning from that which the worker intended.

"*God* loves you."

God is our heavenly Father. We have learned that he cares for us in loving and discipling ways, much the same as good earthly fathers do. Many Christians, who have been blessed by loving parents, have a distinct advantage in understanding our heavenly Father. Consider, however, the youth whose mental image of "father" is the man who beats his mom, who drinks the family income, or deserts the family and leaves it destitute. To tell such a young person that God is his heavenly Father will probably not convey the intended meaning.

God is omniscient, holy, and just. To the alienated young person, these concepts may conjure up the image of a super judge in the sky who sees all, knows all, and is ready to pronounce judgment upon failure. And that is what the troubled youth has done the most—failed. He may have the misconception that God makes people do weird things, like telling the man in the city park to holler and preach, or making the people yell and shake at the little church down on the corner. Or he may believe God to be the eternal "Fun Killer" who hates it when people have a good time.

If words are so inadequate to communicate God's truth, how then will these young people ever hear the gospel? Perhaps the word must still become flesh as it did 2,000 years ago. How could mankind ever hear or understand the eternal truths without a living example? Jesus, the Christ, became the living Word, the way, the truth, the life. He lived among mankind, shared human joys, felt human pain, healed wounds, and in so doing gave light to the world. Man learned God's ways by watching Jesus.

His words were powerful—so understandable in his culture— and yet it was his unconditional love that changed people. For

Zacchaeus, it was a meal; for the prostitute, it was acceptance; for the Samaritan woman, it was crossing racial barriers to ask a favor. Jesus participated fully in the love of those to whom he came. He set an example of involvement. At one point he said to his disciples, "I am the light of the world" (John 8:12). He also said to them and to us, "You are the light of the world" (Matthew 5:14). He commissioned us to be his body—not merely a spiritual fellowship but the word of God in flesh.

This word cannot be communicated to troubled youth apart from relationships. Suspicious, untrusting youth cannot be expected to trust in an invisible God when they have never learned to trust God's people—his body. Nor can rejected young people be expected to receive God's acceptance when they have not experienced acceptance from the bearer of the message. Youth who are hungry in body and spirit do not need to hear "be warmed and fed" or that God will take care of them, when the speaker will not put meaning to his words—by providing food for the needy body or nourishment and nurture for the starving spirit.

It is only when youth workers commit themselves to the often thankless task of establishing relationships with these troubled youths that they will begin to comprehend the workers' words. The cost may be sacrificial. The workers may be lied to, stolen from, cursed at, and taken advantage of, but there is no other way. They must give, serve, and love, seldom receiving a "thank you."

Establishing this important relationship often begins with the youth worker who does nothing but listen to the individual. In many cases the youth worker is the first person who has ever cared enough to really listen. The adolescent may be hungry to talk with someone who won't penalize him for his confidences. His hurt is deep, and he wants someone to share it with him. Real listening means trying to see the world through his eyes. It means listening with compassion, not only to words, but to the feelings behind the words. It is not giving advice or portraying a judgmental attitude toward the content of what is being said. It includes loving and accepting someone exactly as he is. This is one important step in demonstrating that God, too, cares enough to listen and feel his pain with him.

Present a Complete Message. When sharing the message of Christ with a troubled youth, the youth worker should be aware that many of these adolescents have experienced deep disappointments and personal rejection. Yet they haven't stopped hoping that love, meaning, and happiness will enter their lives. They will eagerly accept almost anyone or anything whom they feel can provide these elements. Christ should not be presented merely as Savior from sin and from life's problems.

The results are often destructive if the adolescent who "accepts Christ" isn't aware of his own personal responsibility to Christ and is not committed to his life style. When difficulties continue to occur in his life, the adolescent feels rejected by God and his self-image diminishes. He feels God is not working for him, and he doesn't know why. Because the youth feels deceived, he becomes bitter toward God and isn't likely to turn toward him again without a new conversion experience.

The youth worker must share the whole message of salvation—that Christ loves him and desires to be accepted as both Savior and Lord of his life. It is important that the adolescent realizes a decision for Christ involves accepting him as the leader of his life. It means spending time learning to know God and living the way he wants him to live. Keeping Scripture verses such as Luke 14:27-33 and Matthew 10:32, 39 in mind, the YG staffer should encourage the individual to carefully count the cost of a decision to follow Christ. Such an important decision often involves much thought, time, patience, and personal support. If a commitment to Christ is made, the youth worker plays an important role in helping the new Christian mature.

Utilize an Effective Follow-through Plan (Discipleship). Effective follow-through for troubled youth who accept Christ is extremely important. Typically, these individuals have been incapable of forming meaningful relationships and have difficulty, therefore, forming one with God. If the new Christian becomes disappointed, he often feels that the relationship isn't working and gives up. In order to experience lasting change in his life through God's power, he must be taught and shown, by example, God's way of life. It is significant that Christ's command is not only to "go and make disciples" but includes "teaching them to observe all that I have commanded you" (Matthew 28:19, 20).

It is essential to have an effective system so every new Christian may develop into a mature disciple of Christ. The goal of such a system should be that each new Christian is effectively followed through until he can lead another person into mature discipleship.

The most effective means for accomplishing this goal is for each new Christian to have a mature Christian friend to follow. This may be the person who led him to Christ, or someone appointed and supervised by the Youth Guidance director. The YG staffer should give the new Christian a great deal of consistent personal attention, realizing that the new believer is probably extremely lonely and doesn't have many people to turn to for help. The youth worker should be with the new Christian often, praying with him, studying the Bible with him, answering questions, and being available when problems arise.

Most importantly, the new Christian will learn by the worker's example, just as Christ's disciples learned from being with him. It is necessary for the new Christian to develop peer relationships with other Christians as well. Even within an institution, two roommates can read and pray together or seek out another Christian in the unit for fellowship. Most likely the growth of new Christians from such backgrounds will be slow and have many setbacks. You need never be discouraged enough to give up, knowing that God has promised to continue the work he has begun in each Christian.

Most manuals, books, and materials published by Youth For Christ are available through the YFC National Office. To order materials for both the Campus Life and Youth Guidance Ministries, write for a catalog to YFC Sales, Youth For Christ/USA, Box 419, Wheaton, IL 60189.

For assistance in the ministry of your local church, or to begin a YFC program in your community, contact the YFC National Office for more information. The national staff will connect you with the nearest regional or local resource people. For more information you may call or write Ministry Services Division, Youth For Christ/USA, Box 419, Wheaton, IL 60189, or call (312) 668-6600.

HOW YOU CAN TELL OTHERS ABOUT CHRIST
DR. WILLIAM R. BRIGHT, PRESIDENT CAMPUS CRUSADE FOR CHRIST INTERNATIONAL

CHAPTER

2

"But as many as received him, to them he gave the right to become children of God, even to those who believe in his name" (John 1:12).

"You must bring a lot of happiness into the world," a young businessman said to me with tears of joy and gratitude in his eyes. He had just prayed with me and received Christ as his personal Savior. He and his wife had been looking for God for several years, he said. Now he was eager to read the Four Spiritual Laws booklet, which I had shared with him, to his wife. He was confident that she, too, would want to make a personal commitment of her life to our Lord Jesus.

For more than thirty years I have had the exciting privilege of "bringing a lot of happiness into the world" by sharing the Lord Jesus Christ with millions of students and laymen around the world in thousands of situations ranging from personal, one-to-one encounters to extremely large gatherings of people. In almost every case, a large percentage of those who are not believers indicate decisions for Christ.

For example, a sharp-looking young officer of the Royal Air Force of England approached me after a banquet at the Christian Embassy in Washington, D.C., to express his appreciation for my message. I felt strongly impressed to ask him if he had ever received Christ as his Savior. "No," he said, "I haven't."

"Would you like to talk about it?" I asked. He said he would, so I pulled a copy of the Four Spiritual Laws booklet from my pocket and asked him to read it while I greeted others who came to express their desire to receive Christ as a result of my message. He agreed to wait.

After about thirty minutes, I was free to talk with him. By this time he was ready to receive Christ. He believed that Jesus Christ was the Son of God and that he had died on the cross for his sins. We bowed together in prayer, and another name was written in the Lamb's book of life.

While in Atlanta, I stopped at a shopping mall to purchase a tie. The store manager offered his services, and I talked with him while I was choosing a tie to go with the suit I was wearing. I explained that I was in town to meet with a number of Christian leaders to talk about ways to bring our nation back to God. Then I asked, "Are you a Christian?" He said he was not. I asked him if he had ever considered becoming a Christian, and he replied that he had. I asked if he believed that Jesus Christ was the Son of God. "Yes," he said.

"Do you believe that Jesus died for your sins?"

"Yes."

"Do you believe he was raised from the dead?"

"Yes."

"Would you like to receive him as your Savior?"

"Yes, I would."

I read through the Four Spiritual Laws booklet with him. When we came to Law Four, which explains how to become a Christian and ends with a prayer, I asked, "Does this prayer express the desire of your heart?" He assured me that it did, so I suggested that he pray it aloud, which he did. When he finished praying, I prayed for him.

Then I asked him if he knew where Christ was in relation to him. He said that he knew Christ was in his life. I went on to explain how, according to the Word of God, he could have assurance of eternal life (1 John 5:11-13). As is my practice, I wrote down his address so I could send him follow-up material written especially to encourage new Christians in their spiritual growth. He seemed very excited, and I went away rejoicing.

During one of my visits to Boston I was riding an elevator to the tenth floor of the hotel where I was staying. The woman operating the elevator was about seventy years old. "You go up and down hundreds of times each day," I commented. "Do you ever get tired of it?"

"No, I don't," she said. "It's my job."

"One day you'll go up and never come down, if you're ready. Are you ready?"

She seemed to know immediately what I was talking about, and she said, "No, I'm not." I asked if she had ever made a personal commitment of her life to Jesus Christ, and she said she had not. Then I asked if she would like to do so, and she said she would.

I offered to explain the Four Spiritual Laws to her if she were interested. She said she was, but did not want to take time from her job. I agreed with her and suggested that she take the booklet home, read it through, and pray the prayer at the end of the booklet as an expression of her faith in accepting Christ as her personal Savior.

The next day, I asked if she had read the booklet. "Yes," she said. "I read through it and prayed and asked Christ into my life. And then I read it to my ninety-year-old mother, who also accepted Christ. I wanted to thank you for taking the time to give me this information. I'm sure this decision will make a vast difference in my life and my mother's."

People also respond positively to the claims of Christ in group settings. For example, I recently gave a salvation message at a luncheon in Greenville, South Carolina, to 450 executives, many of whom were already Christians. Yet forty-one people indicated salvation decisions for Christ that afternoon as I led them in a prayer of acceptance.

In August 1974 I had the privilege of speaking to an estimated 1.3 million people in Seoul, Korea, at an evening meeting of EXPLO '74, an international congress on evangelism sponsored by Campus Crusade for Christ. In my message, based on Ephesians 2:8, 9, I emphasized that salvation is a gift from God, received through faith.

After I explained the gospel message, I asked for those who wanted to receive Christ—and those who had assurance of their salvation as a result of my message—to stand. All over Yoido Plaza, people stood in response to my invitation. I learned later that about 80 percent of the people there stood to indicate their decisions for Christ.

A few years later, I spoke again at Yoido Plaza for the weeklong 1980 World Evangelization Crusade/Here's Life, Republic of Korea. It was a vast gathering; attendance on the peak night was some 2.7 million people, according to official estimates. Each evening I gave an invitation to receive Christ. As a result, more than one million individuals indicated decisions for Christ, according to estimates.

These experiences are among the thousands that God has graciously given me through the years. I have been privileged to see many lives changed through the power of the Holy Spirit. For example, when I spoke recently in a large church in Dallas, a businessman approached me with a radiant smile. "Do you remember me?" he asked. "I met you in 1966, and you led me to Christ."

My mind raced back through the years to that exciting experience. He had approached me reluctantly and rather skeptically at the insistence of a loved one. As we met, his resistance evaporated, and he responded to the claims of Christ like a thirsty man responds to water. Now God is blessing and using him in a marvelous way.

There was a time when I was very cautious and careful about how I talked with people about Christ. I often used a religious survey, which we taught all of our staff, students, and lay institute trainees to use. But as America became more and more saturated with the gospel, I found that an indirect approach was no longer necessary. I have decided that I can talk about Christ without fear of offense to total strangers on trains, buses, and planes, in offices, on campuses, in a thousand environments.

I simply introduce myself and explain what I am doing as it relates to the ministry of Campus Crusade for Christ. Then I ask the individual if he or she is a Christian. If he or she is not sure, I ask another question: "If you were to die today, are you sure you would go to heaven?" If he claims to be a Christian, I ask, "On what basis are you assured of going to heaven when you die?" If the person is not a Christian, or if his assurance of salvation is unclear, I invite him to read the Four Spiritual Laws booklet and pray with me if he wants to accept Christ.

I have found that a great many people who are not Christians are eager to make decisions for Christ. After reading through the Four Spiritual Laws together, I invite them to pray aloud and ask Christ to enter their lives as Savior and Lord. If they do, I continue through the booklet to give assurance of salvation and simple principles of spiritual growth. I also urge them to join a church where the gospel is preached and where Christ is truly honored and exalted.

I once believed it was necessary to educate a person about Christ over a period of time so he would know enough to make an intelligent decision. I no longer believe this is necessary in most cases. Neither was it true in the first century A.D. Paul writes that both the Colossians and the Thessalonians responded to the gospel the first time they heard it (Colossians 1:5, 6; 1 Thessalonians 1:5).

I am convinced that at least 25 percent of those Americans who are not already Christians would accept Christ if properly approached by a Spirit-filled Christian trained to communicate the gospel. In other parts of the world, the percentage could run as high as 80 to 90 percent. I believe that at least a billion people throughout the world are now ready to place their faith in Christ, though many have not yet heard his name.

An outstanding student from a Buddhist background who was studying for his doctorate at the University of Minnesota became a Christian. Then he returned to his homeland to share the gospel with his family. Within thirty days, thirty of his closest friends found Christ.

Then he asked about his eighty-year-old grandmother and learned that she was at a Buddhist monastery "looking for God." He went to her immediately and told her about Jesus. As she listened, tears streamed down her cheeks. "He is the one I've been looking for all my life," she said, "but I didn't know his name." The head of the monastery had been reading the Gospel of Luke, and with additional information and encouragement he, too, opened his heart to Christ as his Savior and Lord.

John 3:16 reminds us, "For God so loved the world, that he gave his only begotten Son, that whosoever believes in him should not perish, but have eternal life." In 2 Peter 3:9, we are told, "The Lord is not slow about his promise, as some count slowness, but is patient toward you, not wishing for any to perish, but for all to come to repentance."

Christ said he came to seek and to save the lost. When he gave the Great Commission, he said, "All authority has been given to me in heaven and on earth. Go therefore and make disciples of all the nations . . . and, lo, I am with you always, even to the end of the age" (Matthew 28:18-20).

Now if all authority in heaven and earth is given to our Lord Jesus Christ, and if he dwells within us, then we should be like the apostle Paul, as recorded in Colossians 1:28, 29: "So everywhere we go we talk about Christ to all who will listen, warning them and teaching them as well as we know how" (The Living Bible).

In Matthew 4:19, Jesus said, "Follow me, and I will make you fishers of men." It is our responsibility to follow Jesus. It is his responsibility to make us fishers of men. If we are not fishing for men, we are not following Jesus. Frankly, it is that simple.

Some Christians, misunderstanding the scriptural teaching on spiritual gifts, do not witness. They say they do not have the gift of evangelism and therefore do not need to witness. Of course it is quite true that not all Christians have this gift, but nonetheless all Christians are commanded to share their faith in Christ, not just occasionally, but regularly, as a way of life.

You can be sure of this: Since Christ lives within you as a believer, if given the opportunity he will walk around in your body, think with your mind, love with your heart, and go on seeking and saving the lost through you.

You may be asking, "How can I be more fruitful in my witness for Christ?" If so, the following suggestions should help you as you witness for him:

1. Be sure no unconfessed sin is in your life. In Psalm 66:18, we read, "If I regard iniquity in my heart, the Lord will not hear me." The power of God is shortcircuited by our pride, jealousy, dishonesty, immorality, lack of obedience, whatever it may be. God may allow a disobedient Christian to be used on occasion, just as he uses a sign saying, "You must be born again." But do not count on it.

Wait quietly before God. Ask him to reveal any sin that needs to be confessed. Don't be overly introspective; the Holy Spirit will tell you. Remember, too, that Christ died for your sins. In 1 John 1:9 we find God's faithful promise: "If we confess our sins, he is faithful and righteous to forgive us our sins and to cleanse us from all unrighteousness."

2. Be sure you are filled with the Holy Spirit. You will remember that the disciples were with Jesus for three and a half years. But even after their exposure to the most godly life ever lived, after seeing him perform miracles such as no one had ever performed and hearing him teach as no one had ever taught, one disciple, Judas, betrayed him and later committed suicide. The others deserted him. Not until the day of Pentecost, forty days after his crucifixion, were they filled with the Spirit. Then, in his supernatural power, they went forth to preach the gospel of the risen Lord and divided history into B.C. (before Christ) and *Anno Domini* (in the year of our Lord).

The same Holy Spirit is available to us today. He wants to do in and through us in the twentieth century what he did through his children in the first century. His power is available to us today by faith. On the authority of his *command* to be filled with the Spirit (Ephesians 5:18) and his *promise* that he will answer us if we pray according to his will (1 John 5:14, 15), you can pray right now by faith and know the fullness of God's Spirit—provided that you want to be filled, that you turn from all known sin and surrender direction of your life completely to Christ.

3. Pray and take the initiative to share your faith with others. The Bible tells us that we have not because we ask not. We know Christ came to seek and save the lost; we know he'll answer prayers that are according to his will. We can know, therefore, that God will lead us to people hungry to know him—if we ask him.

Don't wait for people to come to you for counsel. Begin each day with a prayer: "Lord, lead me to someone whose heart you have prepared." Then expect the Holy Spirit to lead you.

4. Talk about Jesus. Remember that what is most on your heart will be most on your lips. If you truly love Christ and desire to share his love and forgiveness with others, you will find that witnessing will become a spontaneous experience.

At the same time I must caution that we do not wrestle against flesh and blood, but against the rulers of darkness in this world.

Whenever we witness to nonbelievers, we invade enemy territory. Paul says in Colossians 1:13, 14, "For he has rescued us out of the darkness and gloom of Satan's kingdom and brought us into the kingdom of his dear Son, who bought our freedom with his blood and forgave us all our sins."

Every nonbeliever is a member of Satan's kingdom. I was once a member of that kingdom. So were you. We can expect Satan to do everything he can to prevent us from witnessing. One of his favorite tricks is to try to convince me that the man I am seated next to on a plane, or a businessman or student I am meeting with, is not interested in the gospel. "Don't waste your time talking to him," the devil says. "He won't respond anyway."

It is a battle that never ceases. For several years that whisper of the enemy has been trying to convince me that I have no right to "impose my views" on other people, that "they have a right to their own religion," and so on.

Remember, however, that God works in you to will and to work for his good pleasure, and that no man comes to Christ unless he draws him. God prepares the hearts of people with whom you will be speaking. If we proclaim the gospel, he will draw them to himself as a magnet attracts iron shavings.

God honors faith. When you share Christ, expect God to prepare hearts, and claim the power and wisdom of the Holy Spirit. Expect God to use you. As Christ said, "Be it done to you according to your faith."

5. Successful witnessing is simply taking the initiative to share Christ in the power of the Holy Spirit and leaving the results to God. I find this tremendously liberating because not every unbeliever with whom I share Christ responds positively. In fact, at least 25 percent—and in some cases as many as 50 percent—do not respond positively.

Recently I was seated next to a salesman on a flight from Mexico City to Los Angeles. I began to talk with him about Christ, and he became impatient and told me that he was not interested; he was committed to his own religion.

That was fine with me. It is not my responsibility to lead anyone to Christ. That is the work of the Holy Spirit. It is my responsibility to share the most joyful news ever announced to anyone who listens. But God does not want me to badger, browbeat, or argue to convince men of their need for Christ.

As a new Christian, I was deeply hurt and felt depressed and defeated whenever I saw no response to my witness. I felt there was something wrong with me spiritually. Often I engaged in undue, prolonged introspection, trying to discern why I wasn't "successful."

Then God showed me that I just needed to follow Jesus, love him with all my heart and soul, love my neighbors as myself, and witness as an act of obedience to his command—then leave the results to him. If a person receives Christ, I rejoice. If he does not, I still rejoice that I have obeyed my Lord's command, knowing he can be trusted to honor my act of faith and obedience.

If you have seen little positive response in your recent witnessing, don't get discouraged. Do not give up. Do not admit defeat. Tenacity, perseverance, and continual dependence on the Holy Spirit will ultimately guarantee results.

All around you people are ready to receive Christ as their Savior. I challenge you to perform an experiment for the next thirty days. Each day, on your knees in prayer, ask God to lead you in person or over the telephone to someone whose heart he has prepared for your witness. Go prayerfully and in the power of the Holy Spirit. Present the gospel as contained in the Four Spiritual Laws booklet, or in a similar presentation, and expect God to use you.

At the end of the 30 days, I am sure that you will be convinced that there is no greater adventure than introducing others to our Savior. You, too, can "bring a lot of happiness into the world" by sharing Christ with others.

If you would like further information about Campus Crusade for Christ or about materials to assist you in helping others find a personal relationship with him and growing in their Christian lives, please contact Campus Crusade for Christ, 90-65, Arrowhead Springs, San Bernardino, CA 92414, or call 714/886-5224, Extension 1720.

What kind of impact does Campus Crusade for Christ have upon college students? Perhaps this report can give some insights to those who would question the sincerity and the amount of commitment that flows from their efforts. Over the Christmas vacation, Campus Crusade held their Biannual Celebration in Kansas City and called it KC-83.

It drew some 17,000 college students from all fifty states and several foreign countries as well. It was a historic week of training in evangelism and discipleship. Some of the nation's top leaders spoke to the students: Billy Graham, Howard Hendricks, Elizabeth Elliot, Josh McDowell, Bill Bright, and a host more. Without question, this was one of the most significant events of the twentieth century. Never before have so many college students come together for one single purpose, the evangelization of their fellow students. It may well have been the largest event of its kind in the history of the Christian church.

HAVE YOU HEARD OF THE FOUR SPIRITUAL LAWS?

Just as there are physical laws that govern the physical universe, so are there spiritual laws which govern your relationship with God.

LAW ONE
God loves you, and offers a wonderful plan for your life.

God's love. "For God so loved the world, that He gave His only begotten Son, that whoever believes in Him should not perish, but have eternal life" (John 3:16).

God's plan. (Christ speaking) "I came that they might have life, and might have it abundantly" (that it might be full and meaningful) (John 10:10).
Why is it that most people are not experiencing the abundant life?

LAW TWO
Man is sinful and separated from God. Therefore, he cannot know and experience God's love and plan for his life.

Man is Sinful.
"For all have sinned and fall short of the glory of God" (Romans 3:23). Man was created to have fellowship with God; but, because of his stubborn self-will, he chose to go his own independent way and fellowship with God was broken. This self-will, characterized by an attitude of active rebellion or passive indifference, is evidence of what the Bible calls sin.

Man is separated. "For the wages of sin is death" (spiritual separation from God) (Romans 6:23).

This diagram illustrates that God is holy and man is sinful. A great gulf separates the two. The arrows illustrate that man is continually trying to reach God and the abundant life through his own efforts, such as a good life, philosophy, or religion. *The third law explains the only way to bridge this gulf.*

LAW THREE
Jesus Christ is God's only provision for man's sin. Through Him you can know and experience God's love and plan for your life.

He died in our place. "But God demonstrates His own love toward us, in that while we were yet sinners, Christ died for us" (Romans 5:8).

He rose from the dead. "Christ died for our sins . . . He was buried . . . He was raised on the third day, according to the Scriptures . . . He appeared to Peter, then to the twelve. After that He appeared to more than five hundred . . ." (1 Corinthians 15:3-6).

He is the only way to God. "Jesus said to

During the course of the week, seminars were conducted and students made decisions that were life changing. The goal of the conference was to call the students to a "revolutionary brand of Christianity," a commitment to reach unchurched Americans (all of them) by the end of this century.

One can only imagine the impact this conference will have upon the college campuses across the nation. Thousands of students, inspired to lead, have set forth to reach out to their peers and win them to Jesus Christ and his church.

him, 'I am the way, and the truth, and the life; no one comes to the Father, but through Me' " (John 14:6).

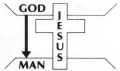

This diagram illustrates that God has bridged the gulf which separates us from Him by sending His Son, Jesus Christ, to die on the cross in our place to pay the penalty for our sins. *It is not enough to just know these three laws.*

LAW FOUR
We must individually receive Jesus Christ as Savior and Lord; then we can know and experience God's love and plan for our lives.

We must receive Christ. "But as many as received Him, to them He gave the right to become children of God, even to those who believe in His name" (John 1:12).

We receive Christ through faith. "For by grace you have been saved through faith; and that not of yourselves, it is the gift of God; not as a result of works, that no one should boast" (Ephesians 2:8, 9).

When we receive Christ, we experience a new birth. (Read John 3:1-8.)

We receive Christ by personal invitation. (Christ is speaking): "Behold, I stand at the door and knock; if any one hears My voice and opens the door, I will come in to him" (Revelation 3:20).
Receiving Christ involves turning to God from self (repentance) and trusting Christ to come into our lives, to forgive our sins

and to make us the kind of people He wants us to be. Just to agree intellectually that Jesus Christ is the Son of God and that He died on the cross for our sins is not enough. Nor is it enough to have an emotional experience. We receive Jesus Christ by faith, as an act of the will. These two circles represent two kinds of lives:

SELF-DIRECTED LIFE
S — Self is on the throne
† — Christ is outside the life
● — Interests are directed
　　by self, often resulting in
　　discord and frustration

CHRIST-DIRECTED LIFE
† — Christ is in the life
　　and on the throne
S — Self is yielding to Christ
● — Interests are directed
　　by Christ, resulting in
　　harmony with God's plan

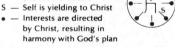

Which circle best represents your life? Which circle would you like to have represent your life? The following explains how you can receive Christ:

You can receive Christ right now by faith through prayer. Prayer is talking with God. God knows your heart and is not so concerned with your words as He is with the attitude of your heart. The following is a suggested prayer: *"Lord Jesus, I need You. Thank You for dying on the cross for my sins. I open the door of my life and receive You as my Savior and Lord. Thank You for forgiving my sins and giving me eternal life. Take control of the throne of my life. Make me the kind of person You want me to be."* Does this prayer express the desire of your heart? If it does, pray this prayer right now and Christ will come into your life, as He promised.

"COME, FOLLOW ME!"
POPE JOHN PAUL II

"THIS IS WHY I HAVE COME TO AMERICA— TO CALL YOU TO CHRIST"

Dear brothers and sisters, dear young people of America, earlier today, I set foot on the soil of the United States of America. In the name of Christ I begin a pastoral journey that will take me to several of your cities. At the beginning of this year, I had the occasion to greet this continent and its people from a place where Christopher Columbus landed; today I stand at this gateway to the United States, and again I greet all of America. For its people, wherever they are, have a special place in the love of the Pope.

I come to the United States of America as Successor of Peter and as a pilgrim of faith. It gives me great joy to be able to make this visit. And so, my esteem and affection go out to all the people of this land. I greet all Americans without distinction; I want to meet you and tell all of you—men and women of all creeds and ethnic origins, children and youth, fathers and mothers, the sick and the elderly—that God loves you, that he has given you a dignity as human beings that is beyond compare. I want to tell everyone that the Pope is your friend and a servant of your humanity. On this first day of my visit, I wish to express my esteem and love for America itself, for the experience that began two centuries ago and that carries the name "United States of America"; for the past achievements of this land and for its dedication to a more just and human future; for the generosity with which this country has offered shelter, freedom, and a chance for betterment to all who have come to its shores; and for the human solidarity that impels you to collaborate with all other nations so that freedom may be safeguarded and full human achievement made possible. I greet you, America the beautiful!

During my first visit in the United States as Pope, on the eve of my first visit to the United Nations Organization, I now wish to speak a special word to the young people that are gathered here.

Tonight, in a very special way, I hold out my hands to the youth of America. In Mexico City and Guadalajara I met the youth of Latin America. In Warsaw and Krakow I met the youth of Poland. In Rome I meet frequently groups of young people from Italy and from all over the world. Yesterday I met the youth of Ireland in Galway. And now with great joy I meet you. For me, each one of these meetings is a new discovery. Again and again I find in young people the joy and enthusiasm of life, a searching for truth and for the deeper meaning of existence that unfolds before them in all its attraction and potential.

Tonight I want to repeat what I keep telling youth: You are the future of the world, and "the day of tomorrow belongs to you." I want to remind you of the encounters Jesus himself had with the youth of his day. The Gospels preserve for us a striking account of a conversation Jesus had with a young man. We read there that the young man put to Christ one of the fundamental questions that youth everywhere ask: "What must I do . . . ?" (Mark 10:17), and he received a precise and penetrating answer. "Then, Jesus looked at him with love and told him, 'Come and follow me' " (Mark 10:21). Yes, he went away, and—as can be deduced from the context—he refused to accept the call of Christ.

This deeply penetrating event, in its concise eloquence, expresses a great lesson in a few words: it touches upon substantial problems and basic questions that have in no way lost their relevance. Everywhere young people are asking questions— questions on the meaning of life, on the right way to live, on the true scale of values: "What must I do . . . ?" "What must I do to share in everlasting life?" This question bears witness to your thoughts, your consciences, your hearts and wills.

This questioning tells the world that you, young people, carry within yourselves a special openness with regard to what is good and what is true. This openness is, in a sense, a "revelation" of the human spirit. And in this openness to truth, to goodness, and to beauty, each one of you can find yourself; indeed, in this openness you can all experience in some measure what the young man in the Gospel experienced: "Jesus looked at him with love" (Mark 10:21).

To each one of you I say therefore: heed the call of Christ when you hear him saying to you, "Follow Me! Walk in my path! Stand by my side! Remain in my love!" There is a choice to be made: a choice for Christ and his way of life, and his commandments of love.

The message of love that Christ brought is always important, always relevant. It is not difficult to see how today's world, despite its beauty and grandeur, despite the conquests of science and technology, despite the refined and abundant material goods that it offers, is yearning for more truth, for more love, for more joy. And all of this is found in Christ and in his way of life.

Do I then make a mistake when I tell you, Catholic youth, that it is part of your task in the world and the church to reveal the true meaning of life where hatred, neglect, or selfishness threaten to take over the world? Faced with problems and disappointments, many people will try to escape from their responsibility: escape in selfishness, escape in sexual pleasure, escape in drugs, escape in violence, escape in indifference and cynical attitudes. But today, I propose to you the option of love, which is the opposite of escape. If you really accept that love from Christ, it will lead you to God. Perhaps in the priesthood or religious life; perhaps in some special service to your brothers and sisters: especially to the needy, the poor, the lonely, the abandoned, those whose basic needs have not been provided for. Whatever you make of your life, let it be something that reflects the love of Christ. The whole people of God will be all the richer because of the diversity of your commitments. In whatever you do, remember that Christ is calling you, in one way or another, to the service of love: the love of God and your neighbor.

And now coming back to the story of the young man in the Gospels, we see that he heard the call—"Follow me"—but that he "went away sad for he had many possessions."

The sadness of the young man makes us reflect. We could be tempted to think that many possessions, many of the goods of this world, can bring happiness. We see instead in the case of the young man in the Gospel that his possessions had become an obstacle to accepting the call of Jesus to follow him. He was not ready to say yes to Jesus, and no to self, to say yes to love and no to escape.

Real love is demanding; I would fail in my mission if I did not clearly tell you so. For it was Jesus—our Jesus himself—who said: "You are my friends if you do what I command you" (John 15:14). Love demands effort and a personal commitment to the will of God. It means discipline and sacrifice, but it also means joy and human fulfillment.

Dear young people: do not be afraid of honest effort and honest work; do not be afraid of the truth. With Christ's help, and through prayer, you can answer his call, resisting temptations and fads, and every form of mass manipulation. Open your hearts to the Christ of the Gospels—to his love and his truth and his joy. Do not go away sad!

And as a last word to all of you who listen to me tonight, I would say this: The reason for my mission, for my journey through the United States, is to tell you, to tell everyone—young and old alike—to say to everyone in the name of Jesus Christ, "Come and follow me!"

Follow Christ! You who are single or who are preparing for marriage. Follow Christ! You who are young or old. Follow Christ! You who are sick or aging; who are suffering or in pain. You who feel the need for healing, the need for love, the need for a friend—follow Christ!

To all of you I extend—in the name of Christ—the call, the invitation, the plea: "Come and follow me!" That is why I have come to Boston tonight: *to call you to Christ*—to call all of you and each of you to live in his love, today and forever. Amen!

WORDS OF LIFE FOR AMERICAN YOUTH
JACK WYRTZEN, DIRECTOR
WORD OF LIFE FELLOWSHIP, INC.

The amazing story of a youth ministry started by Jack Wyrtzen that has touched the hearts of tens of thousands of American teenagers, and growing every year—as told by Barry J. Holohan, staff member of Word of Life, International.

CHAPTER

4

"MORE than forty years ago, I realized that youth who did not know Christ would not come to church because they *wanted* to come to church. However, if we could devise a program of activities that would attract them so that we could win them to Christ and help them grow spiritually, then they *would* become involved in the local church."

This statement from Word of Life's founder and director, Jack Wyrtzen, sums up the phenomenal success story of this youth-oriented organization which has reproduced itself in twenty-one countries around the world.

Wyrtzen is a specialist in evangelizing American youth, and his success shines out from that of his contemporaries with a clear, steady beam of a message aglow with God and with endless enthusiasm and joy. Since 1946, the activities and achievements of Word of Life have been manifold and its influence worldwide. Jack began preaching in churches, prisons, rescue missions, reformatories, hospitals, bars, and night clubs. He was innovative in his methods and used everything from banquets to boat cruises to bring teenagers under the sound of the gospel.

In the 1940s, he was one of the first youth workers to recognize the potential of radio, and his weekly youth meetings grew from a few hundred teens to the great Madison Square Garden rallies during the Second World War, when thousands of young people came to Christ.

In 1948, after great gospel victories in Times Square and overseas, Word of Life purchased a ninety-acre island in Schroon Lake, New York, where Jack expanded his life's work of helping needy teenagers. The island was opened to all teenagers, beyond the distinctions of nationality, race, or religious denomination. For multitudes of youth, Word of Life established the Word of God as the reliable authority for faith and practice. As Jack often says, "We cannot play the game of life without the rule book, the Bible."

Jack determined from the very beginning that Word of Life would be an appropriate name, with emphasis on the "Word" and "Life." When the teenagers were having fun, he encouraged them to "let their hair down" and really become involved. However, when it was time for gospel meetings, they were encouraged to listen and behave, and they did. The messages were straightforward and hard-hitting. Jack pulled no punches. Anyone who has ever heard him speak on "Love, Courtship, and Marriage" has no difficulty in understanding where Jack is coming from. At the beginning of a week at camp, Word of Life feels that it is important to discover where the young people stand in their relationship to Jesus Christ. The opening rally on Saturday night is evangelistic in its fervor. If the young people invite Christ into their lives at the beginning of a week at camp, they will have a greater clarity of mind regarding spiritual things and greater insight into the Word of God that will be taught the rest of the week. Each morning the teenagers are required to attend an hour of Bible study and then to spend thirty minutes alone in prayer and Bible study, known as "quiet time." Their growth is so dependent upon their daily walk that Word of Life publishes a Daily Quiet Time Diary and study guide so that young people will be consistent in the prime time they spend alone with the Lord each day. "Start here at camp and keep going when you get home," Wyrtzen urges.

There are not many rules on Word of Life Island. The young people are not allowed to smoke or indulge in other narcotics, become physically involved, or skip any of the meetings. Time that is not devoted to Bible study in the mornings or the rallies in the evenings is devoted to the unexpected. Pirates may attack the Island, Martians may land in spaceships, or Indians may be found roaming on the camp property. All of the activities are orchestrated by students from the Word of Life Bible Institute. These young people work as counselors during the summer and at Word of Life's Snow Camp in the winter. The counselors are responsible for six young people each week. They live with them in the cabins, canoe, backpack, water ski, play basketball and volleyball with them during the day, and sit with them during the meetings; all this to encourage them to a closer walk with Christ.

One day may be devoted to Sadie Hawkins day, when the girls chase the boys to determine who will accompany whom to the candlelight banquet that evening. During breakfast or lunch the teenagers (divided into teams) will challenge each other to egg-throwing contests, yodeling contests, holding-your-breath-under-water contests, etc.—the unexpected is always happening in the beautiful terraced dining room.

The Saturday night meetings at Word of Life Ranch or Island often resemble a political rally. Pep bands excite the teenager to fever pitch, flags are waved, banners unfurled. After an hour of mayhem that includes skits, music, multimedia programs, and testimonies, Jack speaks to the teenagers with a clear presentation of the old-fashioned gospel. He rarely finishes a meeting without an invitation for the young people to step forward and publicly identify with Jesus Christ.

When the young people leave the Island and return to their homes, they are followed up with Bible study courses which are mailed to them on a continuing basis from the Word of Life International Headquarters in Schroon Lake. Aside from the Bible course, Word of Life has a club program which is now active in forty states across the country, working through the local Bible-believing churches, all to encourage them to move out and on for the Lord. Word of Life Bible Clubs operate with the same Christ-centered vigor that has made the many programs successful on the Island. Word of Life Clubs are operating in local churches in the United States, Canada, and overseas, with literally thousands of young people growing spiritually through this outreach. Using materials and methods developed and printed at the Schroon Lake Headquarters, the clubs are designed for three age groups—Olympians for children ages six to eleven; Teens for those in junior and senior high school, ages twelve to seventeen; and College and Career Fellowship for young adults, ages eighteen to thirty.

Leadership comes from people in the church who are trained and guided by professional Word of Life staff representatives living in the area. The ministry, so vital to today's way of life, is content-centered rather than activity-centered. The lesson materials used in the club program cover the major doctrines of the Bible over a six-year period.

The philosophy of the ministry is to help gospel preaching churches to build a strong and dynamic soul-winning youth ministry. It achieves this by establishing godly ideals in the minds of young Olympians, godly habits in the lives of the teenagers, and godly goals in the lives of the elusive college and career age. These thrusts are achieved through:

1) a meaningful Bible study
2) a daily quiet time
3) Scripture memorization
4) Christian reading
5) personal and mass evangelism
6) Christian service

Young people need incentives to be motivated. Word of Life Scholarship Program whets the spiritual appetite for a closer walk with the Lord by challenging the youth to live up to a standard of excellence in their lives. The program is not used as a measuring stick of success or failure, but is made available to encourage teens to be all that God wants them to be. The teenager may be rewarded for his efforts by being invited as a guest for a week at Word of Life Island. He may also be awarded a gift toward tuition at Word of Life Bible Institute.

Word of Life also conducts periodic roundups all over the world. If there is one common denominator between the Christian and the unconverted teen, it is good fun and laughter. These roundups, although social in nature, are designed to include a solid teen-oriented message of salvation with an invitation to the unconverted teen. They are challenged with the fact that

Christians can have fun, and then with the question, "Where will you spend eternity?" Word of Life uses volleyball marathons, softball marathons, bowlathons (all-night bowling), Operation Nightmares during the Halloween season, basketball marathons, Hub Bubs, etc.

Another facet of Word of Life's ministry is the musical drama tours that criss-cross the country. Led by the Collegians, a 120-voice ensemble of talented young people selected from the student body at the Bible Institute, these tours are on the road for five months every year, presenting the gospel in a different city every night. Written by Harry Bollback, Word of Life's co-director, these productions have included "Let Freedom Ring," a patriotic musical which became a prime-time nationwide television special; "Ring the Bells"; and "God's Portrait of Love." Word of Life's Christmas gifts to America have been "The Passion Play," recognized for its standard of excellence in portraying the final days of our Savior's life on earth in music and drama; and "The Revelation," and "Daniel," based on the two great prophetic books of the Bible.

All of these productions are staged by teenagers who help build and assemble the sets, sing, act, operate the lighting and multimedia on three giant screens, and counsel the multitudes who accept Christ at the conclusion of each program. These productions have been seen by more than one million people.

Although Word of Life is universally recognized as "The Cadillac" of Christian camp programs for youth, it is essentially a family ministry. While especially reaching out to young people, every effort is made to reach the entire family. The Word of Life Inn and Family Campgrounds cater to all ages. The Olympic Center with indoor heated pool, whirlpool, saunas, landscaped gardens, tennis courts, gourmet food, internationally renowned speakers, and talented musicians and singers attract multitudes of people from the U.S. and abroad. This is now called the "ultimate" in Christian camping.

The Bible says, "I will send the Prophet. He will turn the hearts of the fathers to their children" (Malachi 4:5, 6).

Word of Life has been doing that every day, every year for more than forty years. The gospel is also presented on Word of Life's nationwide radio broadcasts. Word of Life staff evangelists tour the country from village to village and city to city, speaking in churches and high school assemblies; the club program continues to expand; the eight Bible institutes produce young missionaries who are now serving around the world; and the total program, conceived in prayer forty years ago, has reproduced itself over and over again in many countries.

As Jack Wyrtzen explained to President Ronald Reagan, "We introduce our youth to the Book our country was founded on, the Bible. We agree with our President who said, 'American society "strayed" from its earliest ideals when it ended prayer in the classroom and to the extent that it has condoned abortion.' America was founded by men and women 'in search of God,' not gold. God, the source of our knowledge, has been expelled from the classroom. He gives us his greatest blessing, life, and yet many would condone the taking of innocent life.

"We have been able to reach thousands of hippies, dope addicts, homosexuals, and those caught up in the sex revolution, as well as spoiled kids from many of the best homes in the land. We also have had as campers cadets and midshipmen from our military academies, high-ranking officers from the Pentagon, and many business and professional people—often more than 2,000 a week.

"Our entire program is geared to produce God-fearing, law-abiding people who are profitable to our society. I believe we have living proof that our program works. Last year more than 20,000 campers came to our U.S. camps from thirty-nine states and thirty-one foreign countries. We are helping thousands of kids of all races and creeds. We give many free scholarships to needy children and young people. This past summer we hosted children and teenagers who came to our shores from Cambodia, Vietnam, Laos, and Mainland China.

"For five ten-day periods in the fall and spring we send thirty of our students to Times Square to work with runaway kids, hippies, alcoholics, dope addicts, prostitutes, and homosexuals.

"We have seen those whose poverty of life and spirit has chased away all hope and ambition. Instead of keeping up the struggle, they have gone under in the fight and the world has trampled them ruthlessly underfoot. They are poor in the possessions of this world, and because of sin they are poor in the possessions of the world that is to come.

"In order to abolish poverty, we believe we must first abolish it from the inside of a man before we can abolish it from the outside, for the outside man is only a reflection of the inside. That is why so often our charities and reforms seem to fail so ingloriously. We get the cart before the horse. We try to fix the outside only. We try to put things in the hand instead of in the heart. We plead for higher wages instead of higher motives.

"Help the inside man to regain self-respect, self-reliance, and self-control. Make him anxious to do a fair day's work. It isn't long before the outside man wears better clothes, has a better home, better food, wants a better government, and wants to live in a better environment.

"Word of Life's results have been very satisfying. In 1982, some 33,000 turned to Jesus Christ through our ministry in the U.S. alone. About 400 graduate from our Bible Institute each year; 86,520 young people attended our roundups in 1982. These were kids from every walk of life imaginable, from the best homes in the land to the worst.

"We believe that many, many young people want to know that the Bible works. We come on with the quiet confidence that Christianity is a superior way of life. We don't try to water down the gospel or use the world's methods, like rock concerts, to attract teenagers. We set their boundaries. The walls hold. Many young people are not rebellious. They are simply pushing the walls to see how far they can go. We make them secure. They don't have to figure it all out by themselves. We've proved it works."

EVANGELIZING TODAY'S YOUTH
RON HUTCHCRAFT,
AREA COORDINATOR, EAST COAST
YOUTH FOR CHRIST, INTERNATIONAL

CHAPTER

5

WORLD WAR II ended with two explosions, and they both changed the course of history. One was the atomic bomb; the other was the birth of the youth culture. That new generation exploded across the world with its own language, its own heroes, its own very different values. With this pulsating new youth culture came a whole new challenge for the church of Jesus Christ.

The four decades since World War II have been costly ones for the growing-up experience. Consider what our young people have lost. In the 1950s teenagers *lost their innocence.* The moral consensus that had held America together for 200 years began to crumble . . . the first tremors of rebellion could be felt. In the 1960s teenagers *lost their authority.* The leadership of parents, of government, of religion were all challenged. There were no leaders left. There were many questions, but no answers. It was in the 1970s that teenagers *lost their love.* It was the "Decade of Me." Love was lost in the wreckage of breaking families.

Teenagers learned all about sex and forgot all about love; virginity became uncommon and teenage pregnancy soared. It had become a very lonely world.

So with innocence and love and authority gone, the teenagers of the 1980s have *lost their hope*. Suicide is becoming a social epidemic, the second greatest killer of our kids. Young people question whether there will *be* a future—and they live as though there won't.

The fallout of four decades rests on today's teenagers. They are very bright—but they are very lost. The young people around us are suffering from a crying hole in their hearts. That hole is so big that it can only be filled by God himself. Religion alone is not enough. The answer lies in a *personal relationship* with God.

Only Jesus Christ can restore what has been lost. He *forgives* people who have lost their *innocence;* he *anchors* people who have lost *authority;* he *embraces* people who have lost *love;* and he gives *life new meaning* for people who have lost *hope*.

God has entrusted to us the mission of bringing together the crying needs of young people with the unlimited resources of Jesus Christ. There are multitudes of young people who *will follow* Jesus Christ if they can just meet him where they live, hear him in their language.

That is what "evangelizing today's youth" is all about. In fact, evangelism is a misused, often misunderstood word in the Christian vocabulary. The New Testament outreach of Christ and the church exposes our modern misconceptions. Evangelizing is *not:*

1. Making people better church members (although that might be a result of evangelism)
2. Getting inactive church members to become active in the church
3. Selling Christian beliefs to spiritual "customers"
4. Just "living the life," hoping people will guess that Christ died for them

Evangelizing young people can, like ice cream, come in many flavors. The *style* will vary; but the *substance* is always the same. Evangelizing is to:

1. *Interest* a person in Jesus Christ
2. *Inform* him clearly about Christ's person and work
3. *Introduce* him to a personal commitment to Christ
4. *Initiate* him into a daily, growing relationship with Christ

That mission has been the "magnificent obsession" of my life for the past twenty years . . . and probably will be for the next twenty. I have spent a lot of time sharing Christ with young people outside the church, and with many inside the church. They both need a personal relationship with Christ.

My perspectives on evangelizing are the product of thousands of opportunities to introduce young people to the Lord, through personal witness, one-on-one conversations, small groups, and large meetings. Also, I have been enriched by the insights and experiences of hundreds of others who have devoted their lives to this mission.

As we explore reaching our young people together, we will look at four strategic areas:

> The message that changes them
> The program that attracts them
> The personal touch that reaches them
> The training that reproduces them

Last summer I watched a dramatic rescue at the Jersey Shore. Three children were drowning in the churning surf. One lifeguard plunged in after them while another cleared all of us out of the water. The one on shore radioed urgently down the beach for more help.

Two more rescuers came running after they had cleared the water they were responsible for. Eventually five lifeguards were needed to row against the tide and bring in those children. With the kids safe, the lifeguards virtually collapsed on the beach, exhausted but successful.

Lifesaving is a serious, urgent business . . . it's the business of those who are willing to "plunge into the surf" after some lost young people. When lives are at stake, you drop everything for the rescue. The spiritual rescue of kids within our reach is worth the *very best* we have.

The "growing-up waters" of the 1980s are turbulent. You and I have been entrusted with a stretch of the beach. The pages that follow are, in a sense, a "Manual for Life-savers." If we each cover our stretch well, we will bring home safe a lot of kids who would otherwise be lost.

THE MESSAGE THAT CHANGES THEM

There were only four people in the room that day, but it was one of the most dramatic days of my life. The room was a hospital delivery room, and I was "coaching" my wife during the natural childbirth of our son. I'm sure the doctor and nurse couldn't have done it without me!

Our obstetrician has delivered thousands of babies, but he has never lost the wonder of it all. After that glorious arrival, he said to me quietly, "This is the greatest miracle known to man." He was almost right . . . birth is the *second* greatest miracle known to man. *Rebirth*—the arrival of a person into *God's* family—is, by far, the greatest. And we are his obstetricians! He allows us the privilege of being the "attending physicians" at rebirth.

The life-giving agent in evangelism is a *message*. Our first responsibility is to be sure that a person understands who Christ is, what he has done for us, and what he expects of us. We have to be sure that the message is clear in our *own* minds . . . and then that we *communicate* it clearly to the young people we know. We have to be prepared to answer the question, "How does a person begin a personal relationship with God?"

It was Jesus himself who told us that "unless a man is born again, he cannot see the kingdom of God" (John 3:3). The Bible describes how to "become children of God . . . born of God" in John 1:12, 13. That birth happens to "all who received him, to those who believed in his name." In other words, a person is not always a Christian; there is a point at which he is *not* God's child and he *becomes* one!

A thinking person might well ask, "Is rebirth a process or an event?" What about physical birth? It is an *event* surrounded by a *process!* Birth is not sudden. There are nine months of growth and preparation for that event. Birth also *begins* a process that takes a lifetime—growing into the fully developed person you were born to be.

The Bible also uses marriage to describe our relationship with Christ. Is marriage an event or a process? Once again, it is an event that is surrounded by a process! There is a period of getting acquainted followed by courtship and engagement. And certainly marriage is more than a wedding . . . but it can't begin without one! There was a day in 1965 when I walked into a church not married, and walked out married. The *process* of my lifelong relationship with Karen began with an *event*.

We cannot present the gospel message properly unless we understand that we are leading people to an *event* that will *begin* their relationship with God. But we must also know that we are introducing them to a *lifelong process* of following Christ.

The message we proclaim is summed up in one word in 2 Corinthians 5:19: "God was reconciling the world to himself in Christ, not counting men's sins against them. And he has committed to us the message of reconciliation." There's the word—*reconciliation*. That is the sound of a relationship *broken*, then *restored*.

This provides a key for explaining the Christian message to young people. The message revolves around a relationship. We need a clear way to express that gospel, one which young people can understand. In fact, one of our first assignments in "Evangelizing School" is to clean up our language! No, profanity is not the problem, but rather it's religious rhetoric. Our witness vocabulary is often filled with "church words" that a young person either misunderstands or doesn't understand at all. Good Bible words such as "saved" or "born again" or "redeemed" can leave a young person in a spiritual haze. "Christian" is a devalued word in today's world. And ask the average man on the street if he "believes in Christ." He will probably say, "Of course, I do." But does he, in the Bible sense of believing? Has he pinned all his hopes on Christ, given him the leadership of his life? Or does he believe in Christ in much the same way he believes in America or George Washington? "Believe" may not say what we mean! We need an organized way to share the Good News—a way to say it without religious "in" words. That is why we begin here with a presentation of the gospel that is clear to a modern young person.

It should not be presented as "five points." It is a way to organize your witness; it should be shared warmly, personally—

not as a religious outline or a prepackaged "plan of salvation."

Remember, the message revolves around this relationship with God, a relationship that

1. Was *intended*
2. Was *ruined*
3. Was *restored*
4. Must be *responded to*
5. *Grows* for a lifetime

I. YOU ARE A UNIQUE CREATION OF GOD, DESIGNED TO ENJOY A PERSONAL RELATIONSHIP WITH HIM

You are not an accident . . . not a copy. You didn't just happen. You are a hand-made original created by the Designer of the universe. ". . . The Lord God formed a man's body from the dust of the ground and breathed into it the breath of life. And man became a living person" (Genesis 2:7).

But you are an *incomplete creation* without our Creator. Pascal, the great physicist, observed: "There is a God-shaped vacuum in the heart of every man which cannot be satisfied by any created thing, but only by God, the Creator. . . ."

Not only did God create you, he *cares* about you! "How precious it is, Lord, to realize that you are thinking about me constantly! I can't even count how many times a day your thoughts turn towards me. And when I waken in the morning, you are still thinking of me!" (Psalms 139:17, 18). So we are uniquely created by God, built for a relationship with him . . . but unable to find him or feel his love!

II. SIN KEEPS YOU FROM EXPERIENCING A RELATIONSHIP WITH GOD

When God created you, he gave you the power of choice. We have used our freedom of choice to reject him and live our own way. This attitude of ignoring or rejecting God is what the Bible calls sin. The Bible says: "We are the ones who strayed away like sheep! We, who left God's paths to follow our own" (Isaiah 53:6).

"Yes, all have sinned; all fall short of God's glorious ideal" (Romans 3:23).

Sin has actually erected a wall between you and God. "The trouble is that your sins have cut you off from God" (Isaiah 59:2).

If you die with the wall between you and God, it will remain there forever. That wall explains why we feel as though there is love we're missing, no way to find out why we were put here, a nagging fear of death. The Person who has the love, the meaning, the life we need is on the other side of the wall!

III. JESUS CHRIST DIED TO MAKE POSSIBLE A PERSONAL RELATIONSHIP BETWEEN YOU AND GOD

You can't take down the wall yourself. No court accepts good as a payment for bad. All the times you have kept God's laws cannot cancel out all the times you have broken them. "He saved us, not because of the righteous things we had done, but because of his mercy" (Titus 3:5).

Only God could take down the wall. "But God showed his great love for us by sending Christ to die for us while we were still sinners" (Romans 5:8). God himself became the Man Jesus Christ. Through his perfect life and his death for our sin, he has broken down the wall between you and God. "God is on one side and all the people on the other side, and Christ Jesus, himself man, is between them to bring them together" (1 Timothy 2:5). Jesus walked out of his grave and is alive today to offer this relationship to you.

IV. YOU MUST RESPOND TO WHAT CHRIST HAS DONE FOR YOU

God will not force his love and forgiveness on you. You must say "yes" to Jesus Christ . . . a yes that involves two actions:

A. Turn *from* your sin.

"You also will perish unless you leave your evil ways and turn to God" (Luke 13:3). You tell God you want a changed life . . . that you are sorry for the sin that has separated you from him, that you're ready to let him run your life.

B. Turn *to* Jesus for forgiveness.

Jesus Christ will come into your life only one way—by *personal invitation*. "To all who received him, he gave the right to become children of God. All they needed to do was to trust him to save them" (John 1:12).

Your relationship begins when you tell Jesus Christ you are ready to make those two turns. The wall comes down forever!

V. YOUR DECISION TO FOLLOW CHRIST WILL BEGIN THE PROCESS OF A LIFELONG RELATIONSHIP

This is not an isolated moment. It begins a new relationship where you are. "Just as you trusted Christ to save you, trust him too, for each day's problems; live in vital union with him . . . see that you go on growing in the Lord" (Colossians 2:6, 7).

Compare your life and body to a physical house. Picture Jesus after you've invited him into your "house." He's just inside the door. He'll go where you invite him in your life, but nowhere else. Ask him to live in all the "rooms" and "closets." He will do much more with them than you can.

God made his move by sending his Son. Now it's your move. He is waiting for your invitation.

That is the message that changes people's lives . . . and their eternal address. For twenty years I have watched that message lead young people to commitment to Jesus Christ . . . and seen that commitment make them into new, complete people!

THE PROGRAM THAT ATTRACTS THEM

I don't have much of an appetite for worms or minnows . . . but fish do. Using the right bait, the right lure is a fishing fundamental. You can have expensive equipment, travel a long way to fish in a good spot . . . but not much will happen if you hang out a bare hook or a slice of pizza (which I love, but fish don't seem to go for).

Jesus described this business of evangelizing people as "fishing for men." That description can help us build a youth program that truly "catches men." To "fish" for young people is to:

- Go where the fish are.
- Look for them, not wait for them to jump into the boat.
- Provide the kind of "bait" that will make them want to come.

I suppose we could just be content to carry on a youth program for a few who *want* to come—and the others who *have* to come (and who act like it!). But what about all those who *need* to come? If you are restless for a larger impact, then you are ready to consider the four ingredients in a "reach out" program. The "pond" is full of lost young people. How attractive is the "hook" we're offering them?

The "reach out" plan begins with:

I. THE STRATEGY
There is homework to be done before action is taken.

A. Identify your kids.

First, you begin with your *actives*. If your program is to grow, the active kids must begin to feel *ownership* of its success or failure. They have sat long enough; it's time to serve. The challenge to them becomes, "Hey, it's up to us. We're no longer coming to watch the leader's show. We are going to be putting this thing on for *others* who don't come right now." Form a Teen Advisory Council (TAC) which will plan and pray for the inactive kids. Give them a Youth Room to paint and decorate so it will be *their* room. The adult leader needs to chair the planning in order to maintain quality control. But the young people become actively involved in creating a new program, a new look, a new climate. Your second step in identifying your kids is to list the *inactives*. That list includes all the young people who have ever come or whose families are associated with the church. They become, in a sense, *the new purpose for your group's existence*. We are making this a place where they will want to come.

That leads to some important questions. Why are they inactive? What could "turn them on"? Which active young person knows each of them best? Could you ask an inactive person to host a meeting at his house?

The first tremors of a "youthquake" in your church will come when your active kids begin to assume responsibility for reaching the inactives!

B. Identify their needs.

A survey is one key to discovering the felt needs of your group. It has to be anonymous. It should list many specific problem and growth areas in kids' lives. Ask your young people to rank those in order of their importance in their lives. Don't just ask, "What are your needs?" They won't be able to think of any.

You might send that survey to all of your inactive kids. You will get valuable input and also show them that the youth program is changing.

Subscribe to publications that are in touch with youth needs. *Campus Life* magazine with the Leader's Guide edition is a good example.

Work with your teenage leadership group to develop meeting themes around issues that mean something to young people (e.g., loneliness, depression, music, sex, self-image, future).

C. Identify your resources.

You have identified your kids, then your target needs. Now you begin to list what resources you have to help meet those needs. What music groups could we use from our area? Who are youth-oriented Christian speakers we could bring in? What Christian movies deal with some of these needs? Who in our church could help us as creative assistants—taking pictures, planning dramas, forming a musical group, cooking for special food events? What are special spots we could use in our area for unusual outreaches? (We have had Candlelight Dinners at the local McDonald's; we have even rented a local steam engine train for a Turn of the Century Train Ride.)

When you have your strategy in place, you are ready for the second ingredient in the "reach out" plan.

II. THE CLIMATE

Your next steps are to create and insure an atmosphere that will make kids want to come . . . and keep coming. A good climate includes:

A. Caring leaders

One active "youth groupie" told me, "Our leader runs good meetings, but he doesn't care much about us." I asked him how he could tell. He said, "Because—he's gone almost as soon as the meeting is over. He doesn't seem to want to just be with us."

A warm climate begins with a leader who makes each young person feel important when he is with him; who remembers names and important details about a person's life;

who arrives early and leaves late so he can just ask interested questions; who even shows up at a school event to see some of "his kids" in action.

B. The right time and place

What's the best time—not for you or the church, but for the kids? A week night? And what's the best place? Probably not the church. You want a setting that feels neutral, where young people will be themselves. Kids' homes? A community building? A gym?

C. Attractive publicity

Have your most creative artist create posters, handouts, and mailings that are bright and imaginative. Bombard your active and inactive list with mail . . . teenagers love to get mail.

D. Variety

Baseball pitchers call it the "change-up." Just when the batter thinks he knows what to expect, the pitcher changes it. Your program should vary the pace—indoors and outdoors; have a sunrise breakfast instead of the usual evening meeting; meet in an unusual meeting place; plan speakers, movies, music, discussions, surveys, concerts. No matter how creative your "new look," it becomes ritual unless you build change-up into your program.

E. More kids

Young people like to walk into a room and see lots of others! If your group is small, look for some other small youth groups in town. Combine with them periodically to give all your groups a bigger, more exciting feel. If there are four groups of ten in your town, why not let your kids enjoy one group of forty every once in a while?

F. Informality

Your youth program should not be mini-church. Try having music playing when you come in, goodies on the table, a casual room arrangement. Kids who feel "at home" are better ground for the gospel.

G. Family feeling

Singing and praying together creates community. Eating, playing, doing together will melt walls. Plan games and activities that will cause people to draw together. The young victims of the "Me Generation" need family.

If the strategy is sound and the climate is right, then you are ready to put the last piece into place.

III. THE PACKAGE

A brief visit to the supermarket will illustrate the importance of *packaging*. There are many similar products on the shelf . . . that's why companies spend so much to develop just the right package. You will probably pass up even the best product if the package doesn't get your attention.

We have in the gospel of Christ *the* product that will answer a young person's deepest needs. Why are so many of them ignoring this great product? Maybe it's because of the *package!*

If you give kids only spiritual reasons to come, then only those with spiritual interest will be there. Our package represents a *reason to come . . . a reason to buy.* Remember the ingredients in an attractive Christian package.

A. Image-building events

You need a big, juicy worm on the hook to get the fish's attention. These "y'all come" celebrations should take place at several points during the year. Of course, they are most important as the school year begins to create excitement for your year's program. Kids like *food.* You should get a crowd if you offer burgers, pizza, a six-foot banana split, build-your-own sundaes, or build-your-own baked potatoes.

Kids like *music.* Build big events around music the young people will like, preferably music with a message.

Kids like to *see themselves.* Take slides at school, at games, in the neighborhood . . . then tell them where they will be starring on the big screen. Have the kids make Super 8 movies, videos, Polaroid slides on a "crazy poses" night. They will be back to see themselves.

Kids like to *get away.* Plan a "breakaway" weekend at an attractive spot . . . one that depends on being at your youth group a minimum number of times.

B. Disarming group activities

When a young person comes to a Christian meeting, he feels unnatural; his guard is up. Use competition and group games to create a *social* reason to come. In Youth For Christ we have used everything from a World's Largest Pillow Fight to a Wild Animal Hunt (using a real turkey, tiger, or goose). In between are many less ambitious activities (Campus Life manuals and youth "ideas" books are full of them) that can break the ice.

C. Creative presentations

When you move into the "message" part of the evening, begin creatively. Use a role play to demonstrate parent-teen conflict; slides to capture depression; a record to open discussion on moral values; a discussion of kids who attempted suicide to get at some of the causes; surveys of what kids fear most to do a talk on fear; a small group experience to demonstrate how hard it is to get into a group when kids lock arms to keep someone out; an object lesson of a very lifelike doll that looks like a person but isn't because she has never been born (rebirth). Always ask yourself: How can I make this truth something they can see, feel, or experience in our meeting?

D. Practical content

Always answer the question, "So what?" What should I *do* if this is true? Why do I need to know this? And always begin your message with a feeling or experience they can relate to.

E. Active purpose

Be sure kids come to a group that has a purpose other than having meetings. Get busy delivering food to hungry families, adopting senior citizen "grandparents," working at a local mission, etc.

F. Feedback opportunities

In our Campus Life Clubs, we usually hand out a REACT card at the end of the meeting. Kids write their name and address and fill out the "my reaction is" section. The card also provides a place to check if they would like to talk to one of us during the week. These cards become a valuable tool in finding out where each young person is spiritually, and in opening up personal conversations about spiritual things.

The strategy . . . the climate . . . the package. Together they form a program that attracts young people. You can't talk to kids who aren't there. But the program can bring kids to a Christian place who never planned to encounter Christ.

However, the program is only a tool. If that tool is offered to the Lord and prayed for aggressively, it can become a powerful means of "catching" young people.

A creative program comes from a restless heart, a heart that is *not content* with the few young people we are reaching. From that restlessness comes a *commitment to excellence* in outreach ministries. And from that commitment can come a roomful of kids without Christ. If the message is clear, then the next step is transformed lives.

THE PERSONAL TOUCH THAT REACHES THEM

If you don't buy the package, you won't buy the product. That's why marketers spend millions to get the right package for their product. Young people, more than any other group in our society, evaluate the package before they buy, especially when it comes to the Christian message. If we have personally experienced the Christ who *is* that message, then we know the product firsthand. If we have created a program that reaches young people where they are, then we will have an audience for the gospel. In a "first impression" sense, your program is the package. But that is true only on a superficial level.

Christians understand, because of Jesus, that *the package is a Person!* When God wanted to reach us, he did not schedule a meeting and ask us to come. He *came among us.* . . . He wrapped the message up in a Person we could see and touch. "The Word became flesh and lived for a while among us" (John 1:14).

The message alone, the program alone cannot change a person's life. That does not happen until the gospel is *personalized* . . . personally appropriated and acted upon. It is human nature to run, to procrastinate. Someone must move in close to demonstrate the message, to get a person to act, to care for him.

Ultimately, evangelism is a *personal* ministry. This "friendship evangelism" acts on three levels: 1) *Contacting* kids; 2) *confronting* them; and 3) *confirming* them.

I. CONTACTING YOUNG PEOPLE
Think of contact paper . . . contact lenses . . . contact sports. "Contact" always means touching. In ministry, it means touching lives, not just teaching lessons . . . loving people, not just leading programs. In youth ministry, contacting is *the establishing and enriching of relationships with teenagers by being with them in their world.* If we are committed to enlarging our impact on lost

young people, then we cannot wait for them to come to our meeting . . . we must go where they are.

The leader establishes a new priority in his schedule, a new entry in his datebook. He sets aside time to visit games, practices, concerts, hangouts, special events, homes. He allows himself to be seen outside his role. It is amazing how much rapport can be built around a frisbee, a football, a trip to the mall, a slice of pizza. Relationships are best built on *their* turf, not yours.

The leader's presence in the youth culture accomplishes four valuable objectives:

1. Contacting demonstrates your personal concern. You *have* to be at your meeting . . . you don't have to be at theirs.
2. Contacting establishes your availability to many young people.
3. Contacting reinforces the confidence of the Christian "remnant." It encourages them to live for Christ in "enemy territory" when they find you there by their side.
4. Contacting extends your influence beyond a meeting.

When a youth leader goes to "teenage turf," he should begin with the kids he already knows. But he should never be content with that. Let the kids you know be the bridge to the ones you don't know. Seek to be introduced to their friends. And don't use your contact to sell your program . . . use it to express interest in him, to make him feel important.

Because there are so many "flavors" of young people to contact, it is imperative that the leader build a *leadership team*. Jesus recruited his "team" from widely diverse elements in his society. Go after volunteers who can be trained for youth ministry. One will mix naturally with athletes; another with music people; still another with the quietly uninvolved. Together your team becomes a highly visible, highly available unit of caring adults in the world of your young people. *That* is reaching out!

II. CONFRONTING YOUNG PEOPLE

Content without confrontation is just religious information. Young people will tend to circle the airport spiritually unless we "bring them in." Presenting the message is not enough. People need to be given a *climate for commitment*. In marriage, that wedding provides a turning point, a place to declare your decision. The youth leader is responsible to help each individual answer that central question, "What will you do with Jesus?" The question is not, "What will you do with the church?" or, "What will you do with me?" Jesus Christ—*only* Jesus Christ—is the issue.

To be ready to confront a young person spiritually, you need to be prepared to:

Get personal

Close the deal

How to get personal:

A. A reaction device

Ask for feedback after your wrapup; provide a REACT card on which they can write it down. Have an "I'd like to talk" box to check. And several times during the year, give kids an opportunity to pray to invite Christ into their lives right at your meeting. Then suggest a way they can tell you on the card that they did that.

B. Spiritual radar

Pray for specific young people before the meeting . . . then go to the meeting *looking* for an opening to talk with them. Time after time a significant conversation has happened after I opened up to the Lord for the name of a specific teenager. I listened to the Lord, then prayed for that person, and an hour later at our meeting the most natural opportunity opened up. Remember, *God* is seeking and preparing people. If your radar is turned on, he will let you know who is ready.

C. Referrals

Encourage your committed young people to refer their friends to you at those "need to talk" times. One young person will often listen to the recommendation of another. "I know this guy who really listened to me and answered a lot of my questions a while back. Maybe we could go talk to him together."

D. Time together

Many spiritual confrontations occur in the relaxed setting of a leader doing something unstructured with a young person.

When a young person does indicate an interest in talking personally, try not to wait more than twenty-four hours. The trail turns cold quickly. Make it a consistent matter of prayer to find a way for each and every young person in your group to be confronted personally with the claims of Christ.

How to close the deal: The leader's responsibility is to help a young person *identify where he is* in the process of coming to Christ . . . and, if necessary, *what is keeping him* from Christ. It helps to ask questions such as, "How do you feel about what you've been hearing about Jesus here?" and, "Where do you think you are in the process of making a commitment to Christ?" Again, the marriage analogy (courtship, engagement, wedding) may help him understand.

After you have had a chance to share the message we outlined earlier, then there are three questions that help "turn the corner" to a commitment. "Do you *want* this relationship with God? What do you think it would take to *start* that relationship? When do you want to take that step?"

If the young person is ready to open the door to Christ now, then help him put it into words. Let him know that there is no magic language for prayer. He can talk to the Lord just as he has talked to you. Ask him to tell you what he would like to tell the Lord right now.

"Well, I'm ready to let him take over. I've run things long enough. I'm sorry for the sins I've committed. And I believe he died for those sins. I know there is nothing I can do to earn him, but I do want to let him into my life. He can have me."

I have often explained to a young person who was at that point that all he needed to do was *tell Jesus what he had told me.* If he can pray out loud, it will mean so much more to him. It often helps if the "attending physician" prays first.

At that moment you are God's instrument, not a spiritual salesman. You are providing a climate in which it would be easy for him to open up to Christ's love and Lordship. If he does, you will be with that young person in the most tender, most important moment of his life. There is no greater thrill on earth!

III. CONFIRMING YOUNG PEOPLE

The personal ministry of evangelizing culminates in confirming that "new baby" in God's family. The issue here is not formal Confirmation, but a personal confirming him in the "what next?" of trusting Christ.

The *event* of rebirth is *the beginning of a lifelong process.* Now that this new relationship with God has begun, how do you develop it?

First, be sure he has a Bible and that he writes in the front the date of his "spiritual birthday." That "birth certificate" can be a real encouragement on the days when the doubts come. Then help him set some goals for the first seven days of knowing Christ.

A. Start a notebook

That is a spiritual diary in which he will record what the Lord says to him through the Bible each day for the next week. Suggest that he read in James or 1 John each day, looking for something he can apply to his life that day. Then have him write it down. A week later, get together with him and see how his "Jesus time" is doing. It is the fundamental factor in the growth of his relationship.

B. Write a letter

To whom? To Jesus! This will help him begin the process of communicating with this Person he has just come to know. That letter can have five key paragraphs beginning with these phrases:

"I love you. . . ."

"Thank you. . . ."

"I'm sorry. . . ."

"Please. . . ."

"I promise. . . ."

C. Go to church

Be with God's people this Sunday. Take notes on the sermon, looking for a personal application.

D. Tell someone

"It is with your mouth that you confess and are saved" (Romans 10:10).

E. Find a buddy

Team up the new Christian with a more mature Christian from his own age group. It will help them both!

What you have really done in these "first seven days" steps is introduce the new believer to his resources in Christ . . . the ones that will be his lifeline for all his days on earth: the Bible, prayer, the church, personal witness, and Christian fellowship.

A commitment to the evangelizing of young people is a commitment to *personal ministry.* The young people you know may never pass this close to Jesus again. Their hearts are still soft . . . the door has not been closed. The program will attract them, the message will prepare them, but it is a *person* who will ultimately reach them. Be ready to deliver them into God's family and to take good care of them as they learn how to grow and walk and talk in Christ.

THE TRAINING THAT REPRODUCES THEM

It must have been in third grade math that I first learned that simple principle: addition is easier, but multiplication equals a lot more, a lot faster.

It's true in reaching people for Christ, too. It's easy to set up a program and see how many kids *you* can introduce to Christ. You're *adding*. If, however, we really want to influence a generation in our town, we will have to be committed to *multiplication:* training our young people to reproduce spiritually.

Paul may have been Super Evangelist of all time. But he knew he had to teach other people to do it. He recorded his "multiplication table" in 2 Timothy 2:2: "And the things you have heard me say in the presence of many witnesses entrust to reliable men who will also be qualified to teach others."

That's the spiritual relay team that carries the torch much farther than any single runner could do alone. No strategy for reaching local young people can ignore the dynamite potential of the Christian kids themselves. They are *not supplemental* to an evangelism strategy . . . they are *fundamental!* There is no more powerful witness in the youth culture than a spiritually alive young person. And yet most reborn Christian kids are fans, not players out on the field. Why isn't the explosion of the gospel being detonated by the kids themselves?

Two reasons: "Lone Ranger leaders" and teenage misconceptions. A Lone Ranger leader has a "do it for the kids" mentality . . . "watch me reach them." The revolution begins with the leader, the day he begins to see himself as a *coach*, not a player. He says in his heart, "I will be a success when the kids succeed in introducing some of their friends to the Lord Jesus."

The other obstacle to multiplication is those teenage misconceptions. Teens may have the wrong idea about what Christian witness is. It is *not:*

1. Changing your friend's religion
2. Getting someone to agree with your beliefs

3. Reserved for perfect people—God doesn't have any of those to work with!
4. An "I win—you lose" argument with someone
5. Doing my Christian duty

The root problem is that our kids think they have a *religion* rather than a *relationship!* It is not a church or a creed or a system we're sharing—it is a Person.

I have no problem telling people about Karen, the very special woman I'm married to. It's natural, spontaneous. I'm not sharing my "beliefs about marriage" . . . I'm talking about a *person* whom I love. In fact, you can't understand me or my life style very well unless I tell you about Karen and her influence in my life.

A follower of Christ is not sharing religious theories, he's sharing *Jesus,* the Person of greatest importance in his life. It is a lot more natural to share a relationship! That is, if you have one. You cannot lead someone where you have not been yourself. We cannot assume that our loyal church kids know Christ personally just because they know *about* him. The worst thing we could do would be to wind up some teenager to witness who has nothing to witness to.

The first step in training reproducers is to be sure the reproducer fully understands the message of the gospel and has acted on it through a conscious, clear-cut, personal commitment to Christ. Once you have some young people who really know him, then you have a team to coach. You say to them, "Let's join hands . . . I will help *you* reach your friends."

What you need now is a *game plan.* You begin to follow this seven-point strategy for multiplication ministry.

I. PRAY FOR GRANDCHILDREN
As Jesus prayed for his disciples just before his arrest, he added, "My prayer is not for them alone. I pray also for those who will believe in me through their message" (John 17:20). He was praying, not only for his spiritual children, but for *their* children. You and I are part of the answer to that prayer. Your training ministry begins on your knees as you lay claim to the friends of the Christian kids you know.

II. HELP YOUR YOUNG PEOPLE UNDERSTAND THEIR TESTIMONY

Do your committed kids know how to express their own experiences with the Lord? In Youth For Christ we call it "the story only you can tell." Give each young person a paper divided into three headings:

> B. C.—My life before my commitment to Christ
> The Turning Point—When, why, and how I opened my life to Christ
> A. D.—The difference he has made

Yes, they need to be trained in the *objective* message of the gospel. But they also need to be able to express how Jesus came to them.

III. ASK THE RIGHT QUESTIONS

Challenge your committed kids with these four questions:

A. In what practical ways could I show my love for this person?
B. What needs to change in my life style? What might be confusing my friend as he watches my life?
C. Where are the hurts and the holes in my friend's life? Those are the "points of entry" through which Christ can get into his thinking.
D. What is it about Jesus that might interest my friend? His unconditional love? Forgiveness? Providing meaning for each twenty-four-hour period in your life? Heaven? Uninterrupted companionship?

IV. FOCUS THEIR INFLUENCE

No witness training or commitment means a thing until it has a person's name attached to it. Challenge your committed kids to prayerfully select a "target teen," one friend for whom they will each pray specifically. It is an exciting spiritual adventure to dedicate your *influence* to Jesus Christ and to watch God use you to bring your friend "home."

V. PROVIDE A VEHICLE YOUR KIDS CAN TRUST

That's where the program comes in. They need to know that their friends will be impressed, no matter what week they come. That commitment to programming excellence must be consistent.

When you challenge Christian kids to use your program as a vehicle for their witness, don't let them down!

VI. PRESENT A PLAN OF ATTACK

Along with the "should" of reaching your friends must be the "how." Here's a plan for a "reach out" young person to keep in mind:

A. Be his friend
B. Win the right to be heard
   Find ways you can express interest in that friend. Ask him to teach you about something he's really interested in; remember special days in his life; be the best listener he knows.
C. Get him to the gospel
   Recommend a Christian movie, a book, try an outreach program—but get your friend exposed to the gospel in a setting where he will feel comfortable.
D. Look for a green light
   The prayer that accompanies this approach says, "Lord, show me when it's time to share the Good News with my friend. I'll be looking for it."

VII. SUGGEST WAYS TO GET STARTED

Here are four examples you can share with your "reach out" team:

A. A book
   Give your friend a Christian book or magazine to read, one carefully selected with his need and interests in mind. Better yet, *lend* it to your friend. When he returns it, ask him, "What did you think about what he said?" Then go from that springboard to explain how you have experienced what he just read about.
B. A meeting
   After your friend has accompanied you to an outreaching meeting, ask him, "How did you feel about what was said?" Again, you go from there into your experience with the Christ he just heard about.
C. An opinion
   Those little words, "What do *you* think?" open a lot of doors. Life provides a lot of opportunities to solicit your friend's views on serious issues: the death of someone close or someone

famous; a movie or magazine article about "the end of the world"; a class discussion on faith or immortality or God; the conversion to Christ of a prominent person. "What do *you* think about it?" The beauty of that question is that it makes it very natural for you to share what *you* think . . . and that's your open door to introduce Jesus Christ.

D. A prayer

Challenge your reproducers to experiment with a dangerous but exciting prayer. It has three parts to it. "Lord, give me a natural, unforced way to start a spiritual conversation with Bill in the next few days. Then help me to recognize that opportunity when it comes. Finally, give me the courage to go through that door when you show it to me." That is a prayer God *loves* to answer!

It is this kind of challenge and training that detonates the dynamite that spreads the gospel far beyond your own influence. Young people will carry Christ to places you could never go!

CONCLUSION

The message that changes them . . . the program that attracts them . . . the personal touch that reaches them . . . the training that reproduces them—those are the powerful ingredients that result in kids being intercepted, surprised by the love of Jesus Christ.

But it all begins with heart trouble. Not the kind that shows up on an EKG . . . this is spiritual heart trouble, the kind of broken heart for lost young people that is incurable! It hits you when you see a group of kids at the mall, hanging out on the corner, pouring out of a local school. Or when you pick up the newspaper and read about another teenage suicide, a young life lost driving while drunk, a teenage abortion. When you have this kind of heart trouble, you just *cannot leave them lost!* You are driven to your knees, where you share your broken heart with the One who wept over his city. And you get up from your knees ready to act . . . to change, to plan, to recruit workers, to train, to go where kids are.

The tools are in this book . . . but the heart comes first. If the lostness of young people has touched you deeply, if the power of the gospel has gripped your soul, then that spiritual youthquake has already begun inside you. And it will spread. Through you, the 2,000-year-old miracle continues.

Ron Hutchcraft is the Area Coordinator for the New York Metropolitan area and lives in Wayne, New Jersey. Working for Campus Life of the Youth For Christ program, Ron has reached thousands of young high schoolers across the East Coast with retreats, programs, summer camps, and a host of other highly successful outreach efforts.

Ron is a popular radio speaker appearing across the nation on weekly broadcasts to youth and youth leaders. He has put together a "How To" program here that shares his insights on reaching today's youth. He is available for seminars and conferences and can be reached by writing The Rev. Ronald Hutchcraft, Youth For Christ/USA, 1459 State Hwy. 23, P.O. Box 68, Wayne, NJ 07470.

A complete listing of materials from Youth For Christ that might assist you in developing your programs can be obtained from Youth For Christ/USA, P.O. Box 419, Wheaton, IL 60187.

CHANGING THE LIVES OF YOUTH IN AMERICA
RICHARD WILKERSON, YOUTH EVANGELIST
WILKERSON CRUSADES FOR YOUTH

CHAPTER

6

WILKERSON Crusades' President, Richard P. Wilkerson, has been counseling and working with troubled youth for the past ten years. The organization has grown rapidly and has been involved in a number of ways in reaching the youth of our country. Concurrently, Rich Wilkerson is also the President of Mainstream, a Christian youth worker's resource network nationwide. Before forming the organizations, Mr. Wilkerson worked in an international drug rehabilitation program in India, France, West Africa, Canada, and several major cities in the United States. He also served on a committee for child abuse in Sacramento County, California, and was a youth pastor for seven years.

These two organizations, under Wilkerson's direction, have sponsored seminars, a vast number of public speaking engagements and crusades, public junior and senior high school assemblies, two books, and annual in-depth youth leadership conferences of over 4,000 youth leaders. Rich Wilkerson's personal counseling and dynamic ability to relate to youth have uniquely qualified him in working with youth and having a dramatic impact on their lives.

Mr. Wilkerson now travels extensively throughout the United States and Canada. During the past three years he has personally held over 700 public school assemblies, in addition to crusade meetings.

Through Rich Wilkerson Crusades, Rich's personal ministry has grown substantially. The ministry's thrust is evangelism to reach the youth of America on a city and area-by-area basis. Rich is scheduled months in advance and plans his crusades through a local church or group of churches in a particular community. The crusades typically begin on a Sunday and continue for three days, ending on Wednesday of the week.

Before the crusade, the local coordinators of the crusade receive a promotional packet which contains lists of preparation and publicity information. The "how to" information gives the local leaders the necessary tools to plan and effectively publicize the coming crusades. The key to success of the meetings is the involvement of the local church people in personally inviting others to hear Rich speak. Suggestions and methods involving local people in crusade preparation are included in the information, as well as directions on how to arrange for public junior and senior high assemblies. The coordinators can follow the guide and, with the help of Christian business leaders and audio cassettes of Rich's school presentation, gain access to the public schools in the crusade area. Rich also gives free school assemblies when he is in an area.

Rich describes his school assembly program not as a method to get the youth out to his crusade meetings (although many times it leads them to come), but as an opportunity to give back to society the positive influence in the world that Christian people have so many times neglected. Our country has been robbed of morals, good attitudes, positive motivating forces, and the overall positive input that Christians should be adding to our society. The school assemblies is one of Rich's ways to give back to a hurting, wounded, and abused world. As it says in Isaiah 61:1: "Because the Lord hath anointed me to preach the good tidings unto the meek, he hath sent me to bind up the broken-hearted, to proclaim liberty to the captives. . . ." These school presentations are not religious, but are among the most entertaining and powerful thirty-five minutes that the students have ever heard. In fact, the response has been so dramatic that the presentation was filmed and has been made available on both video and 16mm film for schools and churches to use. This filming came in response to the many requests our offices receive to have Rich speak in a variety of situations.

We are currently in the process of raising the necessary funds to begin a marketing program to place the film into as many public schools across the country as possible. This current filmed presentation is entitled "Real Love," and it is a very humorous and yet forceful presentation describing the Greek definitions of love. It describes how we must go beyond feelings to a commitment to others in order to develop meaningful, lasting, and solid relationships. The three years of very successful assemblies, coupled with the hundreds of testimonials which follow the presentations, have given us the evidence that we are a welcome organization in the schools and are aiding in a solution to the problems faced by many teenagers.

Once this film project is established, the development of several other presentations, including "Freedom and Responsibility" and "Involvement" will also be filmed and distributed. We expect to have a series of youth films in the future that will make positive impact and contribution to the public school system in the country.

It is Rich's desire to offer another series of youth films designed specifically for teaching Christian youth. This film series could give the local youth worker a unique source of solid, fundamental teaching, with a good portion of humor, designed for a series of three to five meetings in a local church. To the best of our knowledge, there is nothing else designed specifically for youth that would have the power of the series we are planning.

Through Mainstream, Rich's ministry focuses on the youth leaders who are guiding, teaching, and leading the youth in churches across the country. It is Rich's belief that young people will not go any further than the leadership will take them, and consequently he has focused Mainstream on the development of youth leaders.

The first emphasis of Mainstream is to help the young person with his life style. The youth are looking for a model to style their lives after. For many years the Catholic Church has been teaching a holy life in its leadership and the evangelicals are beginning to emphasize it more strongly. Rich stresses the importance of this in youth leadership and spends a good deal of time on it in the annual Mainstream leadership conferences.

The second main emphasis is that the Christian message cannot be compromised. The youth leader must preach and teach the uncompromising standards of the gospel of Christ. Rich's personal messages are clear cut truth on how Christ can set people free. Rich feels youth leaders must have an authoritative message on the key issues of life, "bathed in grace and love."

The Mainstream conferences concentrate on all aspects of leadership, keeping the above two emphases in focus. Each year these conferences are conducted in a different geographic region of the country and are open to youth leaders to attend.

Another area of emphasis from Rich's Mainstream ministry is a youth discipling program called the F.I.R.E. Institute. F.I.R.E. is actually an acrostic that stands for Foundations, Inspiration, Responsibility, and Evangelism. The F.I.R.E. Institute program is published in book form by Mainstream Publishers and is available for study and implementation.

The philosophy of the F.I.R.E. Institute briefly begins with the "F" Foundations. The Bible is the Word of God, it is authoritative, and it speaks to contemporary life in all ways. Rich teaches that if we stick to the fundamentals in the Bible, and use the Word as our source, youth will have a great example to follow. A leader who has an insatiable, growing appetite for the Word, and uses it as the direction for his/her life, will make an impact on the world.

The "I" refers to inspiration from prayer with God. Rich has always emphasized prayer in his own ministry and in the leadership conferences. Rich's ministry and personal life are tied closely to prayer. The emphasis of the leadership conference and F.I.R.E. Institute philosophy is intensely devoted to prayer and getting in step with what God wants us to do.

The "R" refers to our responsibility and authority given to the Lord Jesus. This responsibility is developed into an understanding of what it means to give up the lordship of our lives to Christ. As the Bible states, "It is better to obey than to sacrifice." Rich emphasizes our responsibilities to the church, to society, to our family, and to God.

The "E" refers to evangelism. If the first three are in place—foundations, inspiration, and responsibility—then we will want to spread the good news and evangelize. It is just the natural heart-felt result.

The F.I.R.E. Institute is dynamic and it gives a step-by-step, practical approach to the process of discipling and building the body of Christ.

One of the other areas of ministry which has developed for Rich is the sale of his cassette teaching series. These sets are available not only at the crusade meetings but also at the Mainstream Conferences. Rich deals with everyday subjects on dating, personal relationships, drugs, alcoholism, peer pressure, etc.

This last year Rich also finished a book for the parents of teenagers, entitled, "Hold Me While You Let Me Go." In a warm and entertaining manner, Rich answers some of the toughest and most frustrating questions parents of teenagers face. The book contains practical and sound biblical concepts to assist parents in helping teenagers to become emotionally and spiritually mature adults.

The books and tape series are available to pastors seeking information. The annual leadership conference is also open to youth leaders with participants coming from all over the country. In addition, the first school film presentation is also available in two versions. In one, Rich has added an epilogue challenging young people to commit their lives to Christ. This version is an excellent evangelism tool for churches and youth leaders. More presentations and teaching films will be forthcoming.

Rich stays in touch with supporters via a newsletter publication informing everyone of his itinerary and current happenings in his ministry.

The FOUR PRINCIPLES behind the Wilkerson Crusades are F.I.R.E.

F for FOUNDATIONS
I for INSPIRATION
R for RESPONSIBILITY
E for EVANGELISM

Our concern here is for evangelization, and therefore we would like to tell how the Wilkerson Crusades have enjoyed such outstanding growth in the past several years.

E IS FOR EVANGELISM

"I love humanity, it's people I can't stand!" exclaimed Charlie Brown. This seems to be the unspoken sentiment of many Christians. They know about the Great Commission and may even be consistent givers to the "cause." This, however, does not exempt any of us from our personal responsibility of fulfilling our Lord's final marching orders (Matthew 28:18-20; Acts 1:6-8).

Many sincere Christians who hear Matthew 28:18-20 feel guilty about what they have not done. Others rationalize away their responsibility by declaring, "Well, that doesn't really apply to me because I don't have the gift of an evangelist." Neither of these is acceptable, because the Lord's mandate is just that—a mandate. In other words, it is not optional for anyone who has declared Jesus Lord of his life.

Much of this confusion can be cleared up by following the Master's plan of evangelism: discipleship. Let's take a new look at Matthew 28:18-20:

> All authority has been given to Me in heaven and on earth. Go therefore and make disciples of all nations, baptizing them in the name of the Father and the Son and the Holy Spirit, teaching them to observe all that I commanded you; and lo, I am with you always, even to the end of the age (NASB).

A. THE MASTER'S PLAN OF DISCIPLE MAKING

Every disciple is a potential disciple maker. A converted communist and the former editor of the *London Daily Worker*, Douglas Hyde, in *Dedication and Leadership* states that the use of this principle is important in the communist party. "Every man a potential communist, and every man a potential leader in communism." To illustrate the success of this principle, Hyde tells the story of a most unlikely leader called Jim. Jim "was very short, grotesquely fat, with a flabby white face, a cast in one eye, and, to make matters worse, a most distressing stutter." Jim approached Hyde at the finish of his lecture and said, "C-c-c-comrade, I w-w-w-want you to t-t-t-take me and t-t-turn me into a l-l-leader of m-m-men." Jim, in time and with diligent training, became a national leader within his own industry, and years later his death was given front page coverage in the *Daily Worker*.

What exactly is a disciple maker? Barry St. Clair gives one of the most accurate definitions we have found. A disciple maker is:

> One maturing believer
> Reproducing other maturing believers
> To the degree that they are able to
> Reproduce maturing believers!

Making disciples starts with witnessing and leading someone to a genuine relationship with Christ. Do our responsibilities end there?

Emphatically, *no!* They duplicate what we have taught and lived with them. This, obviously, takes a serious commitment of personal energy, time, and self-giving. The investment, however, can produce tremendous personal and numerical results, as we shall see later.

B. THE MASTER'S PLAN OF DISCIPLING ALL NATIONS:
Some might protest that the process of discipleship is an impractical strategy for evangelizing the world. Approximately 2.9 billion have never heard the gospel preached. Add to that the spiraling rate of population growth. Besides, what about mass evangelism and the use of television? Both of these methods of evangelism, as well as others, are important. They are not substitutes for the original strategy of world evangelization that our Lord offered, however.

Consider the following mind-boggling figures. If one Christian would win one person and then disciple that person, at the end of six months there would be two believers. Then if those two people won two other people, and trained them for six months, there would be four. Continue the process of multiplication as follows:

2 years	= 16 disciples
2½ years	= 32 disciples
3 years	= 64 disciples
4 years	= 256 disciples
5 years	= 1,024 disciples
6 years	= 4,096 disciples
16 years	= 4,294,967,296 disciples

Not only does the process of disciplemaking enable us to reach our world numerically, but professionally as well. Let me explain. Recently, one of the authors was made aware of the following story. A corporate executive for an internationally known company was won to Christ outside a regular church setting. The Christian who led this businessman to the Lord continued to disciple him. It was later learned that the new convert, who had grown up on a farm in Pennsylvania and was now forty-eight years of age, had never read the Bible or had the gospel clearly explained to him. How many more are there just like this "lost" executive?

It is not enough simply to lead others to Christ; it is essential to "disciple them" all the way to the pearly gates. That's why we must teach those whom God has placed within our care.

This, then, is the philosophy behind the F.I.R.E. Institute: It is our desire to give our students a spiritual *foundation* to build upon. Our second goal is to give them *inspiration* to build on that foundation. The inspiration comes in the prayer closet. Third, we strive to develop a sense of responsibility at all levels of relationship in life. Finally, we have a desire for *evangelism*—to see in them a passion for lost souls to meet Jesus.

How is all this working? Thousands of young people have attended and are attending the F.I.R.E. Institutes conducted by Rich Wilkerson and Bob Towell. They have found that the Bible has captured the minds and lives of those they have taught, and they, in turn, have gone out to disciple others. It is a way that works; indeed, it's God's own plan for reaching every soul by the end of this century.

For those seeking further information about Wilkerson's Youth Crusades, or the many books and publications available on youth ministries, write to Wilkerson Crusades, P.O. Box 1092, Tacoma, WA 98401, or call (206) 756-5306.

PART TWO

Outstanding Churches Evangelizing American Youth

THE SOCIOLOGY, PSYCHOLOGY, AND ANTHROPOLOGY FOR ADOLESCENT MINISTRY
A GUIDE FOR THE YOUTH WORKER COLONIAL CHURCH OF EDINA, THE REV. DR. GARY W. DOWNING, EXECUTIVE MINISTER

CHAPTER

7

INTRODUCTION

Jesus commanded his followers to "Go, proclaim, and teach!" everyone, everywhere. The Good News we as followers are privileged to both experience and express has been taken to the farthest reaches of geography and culture in our world. People in high-rise, swank corporate power centers as well as folks in stone age villages have heard the loving message of God's friendship available through Jesus Christ.

But, in the process of going to the whole world, I fear that we have overlooked an important part of that world—many of our teenagers. Now, they have not been totally neglected, but the teenagers who have responded to the gospel have primarily been those who were raised in Christian families and involved in Christian churches. For those not exposed in those settings, or for those who have withdrawn from church or family activities, Jesus often is a stranger.

The next few pages are an attempt to summarize what youth leaders have learned through much research and experience. I will make two key assumptions. First, you are personally committed to Jesus Christ as your Savior and Lord. Second, you are concerned about teenagers. With these as "givens" (in whatever role you find yourself—parent, youth advisor, professional, or pastor), there are three crucial concepts that I believe are essential to a proper understanding of youth outreach and nurture. These concepts are applicable to whatever group of kids you know and will prove to make you more understanding, sensitive, and effective with adolescents.

SOCIOLOGY

Jesus' first command for spreading the gospel was to "Go!" That one word has hundreds of possibilities for you and me. There is a theological foundation implied in that word as well as a practical strategy for youth ministry. Theologically, Jesus is telling his followers to do just what he did to us. God chose ultimately to reveal his love *personally* through the history-changing event we call the incarnation. God offered his love through a Person, not a program. Jesus came into the middle of our world as a real, live human being. His presence was physically felt by people who began to realize that here was no ordinary man. In fact, this man was totally unique—not because he wasn't human, but because he *was* so completely human. In the Gospels we see portraits of a human being who was everything a human being is supposed to be. Furthermore, this same man made it possible for you and me to regain our true humanity which can be found only in a redemptive relationship with our Creator.

Do you understand what I'm talking about? A vast number of teenagers don't! The incarnation of God is an unknown truth to them. God is distant, judgmental, and uncaring for them. They need to understand the truth through the same means that God employed to reach us—personal presence. As God became present to us in Jesus Christ, so we need to become present to teenagers through personal friendships. As God came to us, so we are to go to young people in love.

This "ministry of presence" requires that we begin to answer a simple question, "Where are the young people we seek to reach?" While it seems obvious, most programs really fail to understand the answer to that question. For the greatest portion of a week, young people will not be in a church-related activity. Yet we often assume that our programs can somehow reach and develop the faith of our kids in a vacuum.

We must become amateur "sociologists" in order to discover where kids are, in order to go *to* them, rather than demanding that they come to us. In the past, the many institutions that affect kids' lives were connected with school, home, church, neighborhood organizations, work, police, etc. Now there is a fragmentation and a breakdown in communication between these institutions so that a young person gets pulled many different directions without cohesive linkages. Social relationships for young people become disjointed as each institution experiences internal conflict.

For most young people, their lives are structured by two main "institutions," school and work. A high percentage of teenagers place a priority on work in order to have the things they want. Our school systems also structure the living patterns of our teenagers to an amazing extent. Ask a local teen where he's from and he will likely refer to the school he attends. (He probably won't refer to his church.) That simply means, if we want to be with young people we'll have to get involved as much as possible in the lives they lead, through their jobs and schools. To be effective, we must participate with kids in their activities as spectators at athletic or musical events, as advocates serving as tutors or support people in their school instruction, and as observers in the peer group systems that develop within the social structures of their schools and jobs.

Our presence provides the opportunity to initiate unconditional relationships with young people on their "turf" and in terms they can understand. Our primary witness in this socially oriented ministry is *nonverbal* through our friendship. Our caring to give our lives to teenagers, to become vulnerable to them, can give us insights about the real needs and dreams of young people. We'll also discover how to structure our ministries to fit the social patterns of teenagers (who are inherently nondenominational), rather than imposing our programs awkwardly onto the youth we want to lead. Instead of competing with part-time jobs or school activities, we can try to create an "alternative sociology" that is complementary to the social needs of youth. Young people need and want authentic relationships (even with adults). Our ministries need to reflect that characteristic. Friendships are more important than information to young people. For example, the first question most kids ask about a planned event is "Who's going?" not "What are you going to be communicating?"

In this ministry of presence, the most important thing we have to offer to kids as a Christian adult is our own lives. That takes time, patience, and energy. It's not easy to develop mutual relationships across cultural barriers of age and social structures. But it is the most effective way to communicate the simple truth of God's amazing grace—by how we love and live through caring relationships with young people.

The starting point for this kind of ministry is simple. Make friends with two young people by getting involved in some mutual activities in which they are interested and involved. You'll be amazed at how open most teenagers are to you after they get over the initial skepticism and fear of your unusual approach to them as *real* people.

PSYCHOLOGY

You can read all kinds of books and look at all types of surveys about the psychological needs of youth. But one common thread runs through all of those books and polls: young people need to love and to be loved. Our nonverbal communication through our friendships can lead us to a point of verbally pointing beyond ourselves to the person of Jesus Christ. Even as our relationships speak "incarnationally" to young people, so our words must be communicated in personal terms. God used the medium of people to let us know of his divine love for the world. I suppose he could have used cosmic skywriting, or inner psychic vibrations to tell the world of his desire for our friendship, but he chose to do it personally. Can we do any less?

The "ministry of proclamation" is a reflection of the privilege gained over time through trusting relationships to point to the source of love. We must develop a "platform" for giving verbal witness to Jesus Christ because our lives can only give an incomplete testimony to God's available presence in young people's lives. But we again must ask a simple question, "How do teenagers hear?"

Too often, we can be accused of giving answers to questions

nobody is asking, or addressing truths that may seem unimportant to those we seek to reach. Teenagers hear primarily through their hearts—not their heads. With all of the good information available we might assume that kids know the gospel. After all, many have sat through innumerable church services, confirmation classes, radio broadcasts, or camps and retreats. Yet many teenagers are functional illiterates when it comes to biblical understanding, and religious agnostics in applying the Gospels to their everyday lives.

We need to become amateur "psychologists" as we listen to young people in order to understand their real needs. We must know that teenagers are often caught up with feelings of inferiority, fear, and confusion. They are more concerned about how they will look to their peers than how they appear in the eyes of God. They might be more worried about a potential date than their eternal destiny. That means we must be able to communicate the gospel in highly personal terms, not as propositional truths. Young people hear through their hearts, so we must speak the gospel to them in such a way that it meets their heart needs. We can communicate the way Jesus did with the people around him. He used everyday symbols that were part of life and could immediately be applied to speak to common needs. As the believers moved into different contexts, they began to see the universalities of the simple, profound truths Jesus taught through parables and life-based illustrations.

If we seek to be effective in our verbal "ministry of proclamation," we must take the time and create the sensitivity to listen to the language of their hearts. We will no doubt realize at least four facets of the gospel they need to hear:

First, God created each of us to be special, unique people. Our lives are our greatest gift. "God doesn't make junk!" despite our negative, inferior feelings. God loves each of us unconditionally. Before we were even born, God knew our name and cared for us.

Second, Jesus Christ came personally to communicate God's message of love for every human being. In the Person of Jesus we see evidence that no one, great or small, was insignificant to our Lord. Little children or powerful soldiers, political rulers or widowed pawns of oppressive systems, religious leaders or prostitutes were received by Jesus of Nazareth—and all felt the impact of his love. No matter how badly we've "blown it," or how righteous we might appear, God sees through our masks and defenses and loves us personally.

Third, through Jesus' death and return to life, God did everything necessary to make a restored relationship possible. There is nothing left to prove. There is nothing we can earn. There is no standard we have to meet. Through the dreadful cross and the empty tomb, Jesus removed the barriers of sin, shame, and guilt to God's unconditional offer of love. It's a free gift, given personally to everyone regardless of race, creed, sex, station in life, handicap, or moral history.

Fourth, despite the overwhelming nature of the freely offered gift of love, God never takes away our freedom. We must personally choose to accept or reject God's offer. We never need to feel coerced, manipulated, or pressured. Instead, we can make a decision to affirm God's gift for our lives and become an integral part of the kingdom—with the community of God's chosen people, the family of God and the Body of Christ. We may feel lonely, but we'll never be alone again—for all eternity. As we grow in our capacity to receive God's love along with other believers, we will be able to share that love with others who need us to reach out to them. And so the "ministry of proclamation" reproduces itself personally into the lives of others.

ANTHROPOLOGY

Jesus commanded us to "Go, proclaim, and teach." How we view the teenagers who respond to the gospel and with whom we have relationships directly affects how we go about nurturing them in their faith. Are teenagers kids in adult bodies or are they adults in kid bodies? Are they like empty bags waiting to be filled with "goodies" of information, or are they like potted plants just waiting to flower? As amateur "anthropologists" we must observe the varieties of the phases of development through which adolescents are moving. We must be careful not to generalize, objectify, or dehumanize adolescents. A teenager is not just going through some kind of "disease" that only time will cure. The passage from childhood to adulthood has been elongated, but it need not be ignored. It does not have to be a stormy, rebellious, painful series of conflicts and trauma. Teenagers are real *people* with real needs and aspirations. They are capable of great faith and a transformed life style. They need special attention, not because they are weird or frightful, but because they are special people to be nurtured in special ways.

This special kind of approach to teaching could be called a "ministry of participation." Young people, like most people, learn best by doing. We can work to provide opportunities for them to participate in decisions, relationships, and activities that will shape the rest of their lives. Under the Holy Spirit's guidance, we must seek to be sensitive to the teachable, leadable "moments" that occur with kids (often at odd times and in unexpected places).

The key question we must answer is, "How do teenagers grow?" Our view of the very nature of adolescence strongly influences how we answer that question. Young people should neither be spoon fed nor force fed. Our programs should do more than just entertain them. (Most attempts to try result in boredom anyway, as we compete with TV or multimillion-dollar entertainment centers.) Young people need to be in personal nurturing relationships where they feel support and accountability. At the same time they should be encouraged to take risks to have new experiences, make new friends, and test new truths. Young people need to be challenged. They need to interact with peers as well as reflect on their own sense of identity and religious values. They need "hands on" experience as responsible "members in full standing" to participate in the life and ministry of the church (they are *not* the church of tomorrow only).

At the same time they must be given the freedom to fail. They will encounter conflicting value systems and confusing situations. They will make mistakes as they experiment with new roles and identities. But we must not bind them by legalistic codes or inhibit them with over protective systems of thought. We must allow freedom and diversity in our fellowships. If we do, as young people grow they will contribute new insights and lend new energy to the work of the church.

Young people grow the same way we do. They watch their examples, they model the attitudes, beliefs, and behavior they observe, and they mirror the approaches to life they sense in their environment. They need to see people living in covenant relationships faithful to God, families, and the Body of Christ. They need to experience committed relationships because they will grow best in a context where they feel trust and respect. We can disciple young people by providing the means whereby they can learn to participate in acknowledging the Lordship of Jesus Christ in every aspect of their lives. They can share as deeply spiritual people in the reconciling witness, service, worship, and nurture of the liberating community of Christ. We must give them the special tools they need to grow in "wisdom and stature" and in the love of both God and people. Then we must step back and watch what God's Spirit can do through their lives.

CONCLUSION

We as Christians have been given the mandate to become "friend makers for God," ambassadors of Christ, speaking as though God himself were speaking through us, partners in the great ministry of reconciliation. Through our ministries of "presence, proclamation, and participation" we can have a tremendous impact in the lives of scores of young people in our lifetime. Our willingness to be available, open, sensitive, and obedient to see the needs of teenagers, and attempt to meet them in Jesus' name, will give us many opportunities for celebration. We will see "miracles" happen before our own eyes. We'll watch broken lives get mended, families healed, and communities transformed through the power of God's love. We'll be privileged to excitedly observe new life occur in the young lives we touch, because Jesus' Spirit will use us in a personal way. Will you join us in one of the most rewarding, challenging, and exciting ministries you could have in your lifetime by giving your life to young people?

The Rev. Dr. Gary W. Downing has lectured in both Catholic and Protestant seminaries on adolescent ministries. Probably one of the finest and most inclusive ministries to young people takes place at Colonial Church of Edina, Minnesota.

Dr. Downing is available for consultation and workshops and can be reached by writing direct to Community Congregational Church, 6200 Colonial Way, Edina, MN 55436, or by telephoning 612/925-2711.

HOW TO ORGANIZE AND CONDUCT AN EFFECTIVE YOUTH MINISTRY

THE ASSEMBLIES OF GOD CHURCHES
THE REV. FRANK M. REYNOLDS,
NATIONAL TEEN CHALLENGE
REPRESENTATIVE

THE TEEN CHALLENGE MINISTRIES OF THE ASSEMBLIES OF GOD

HISTORY

"I wonder if they have ever heard the story of Jesus?"

Twenty-five years ago David Wilkerson asked himself that question as he stared at the reporters' sketch of seven young men on trial in New York City for murdering seventeen-year-old crippled Michael Farmer. As the young pastor asked that question, he felt a compulsion to leave Philipsburg, Pennsylvania, and go to strange New York City to find out for himself.

This led him to a crowded courtroom, to being ejected from the courtroom, and to making headlines. He felt defeated.

I read those headlines and wondered, "What kind of a nut is loose in the city now?"

In 1958 large gangs of teenagers, the Mau Maus, the Phantom Lords, the Hell Burners, and other vicious gangs were fighting, rumbling, staking out their rival territories in New York City.

David did not succeed in this first venture in New York City. Had he mistaken the call? In seeking advice from his grandfather, he was told that maybe God never intended that he reach those particular gang members because then he might have considered his task completed.

The next step toward what was to become Teen Challenge took place in mid-summer. The July 6, 1958, issue of the *Pentecostal Evangel* carried an article urging readers to pray for the youth of New York, and it began with this paragraph:

> St. Nicholas Arena in New York will be the scene of a series of youth meetings designed to reach teenage gangs and other teenagers in the area for Christ, July 8 through 12.

The article concluded with this direct appeal for prayer:

> Everyone is urged to pray that this will be the beginning of a great harvest among teenagers in New York and across America.

That prayer has been answered beyond anyone's fondest dream. There were thousands of youths in New York City whom God wanted to reach. And David Wilkerson and thousands of other workers have taken up that vision all over the world. Countless lives have been wrested from Satan's grip in the past twenty-five years.

In 1982 in the U.S. alone, Teen Challenge ministered in 2,390 jail services, 4,780 street meetings, and 1,190 schools, and saw 14,485 persons make personal salvation commitments. These figures do not include the worldwide figures, nor those from the myriad of other centers that have sprung up using Teen Challenge as their model.

The book *The Cross and the Switchblade* and the knowledge of what God is doing at Teen Challenge centers have ignited the enthusiasm of thousands of believers to reach out to others and to believe that God can change lives.

In 1959 Dave was named Director of Teenage Evangelism, Inc., the original name of Teen Challenge in Brooklyn, New York. Area churches helped provide the literature he needed in ministering to gangs wherever he could gather a crowd of listeners.

God provided separate housing for young women, first at another building on Clinton Avenue in Brooklyn, then in Rhinebeck, New York, and now finally at Garrison, New York. The ministry continues also at the Walter Hoving Home, which really is a "home" to over sixty young women.

The Teen Challenge Training Center at Rehrersburg, Pennsylvania, was founded in 1962 as a place of intensive training in the Word of God to develop Christian life styles for the young men reached through Teen Challenge. These young men arrived at the "farm" after a short while in the Brooklyn Center. The ministry of the Training Center has grown, and over 200 are now in residence.

The Teen Challenge Institute of Missions was founded in Rhinebeck, New York, to provide a short-term training program in the Bible and in ministry for those who had met Christ at Teen Challenge and felt called into gospel work. They usually lacked the educational background required for enrollment at other schools, so the Institute of Missions helped train them. The work has continued in Sunbury, Pennsylvania, and is now known as the Teen Challenge Bible Institute.

In 1972 teams of Teen Challenge staff members and graduates were sent to Vietnam under contract with the U.S. Department of Defense. They were effective in assisting military personnel with drug abuse problems.

Camp Champion was acquired in 1974 and became an active outreach center for children from inner-city neighborhoods. Camping programs were established offering opportunity for youngsters to leave the city for a week or so and to hear about God in an atmosphere of love and beauty.

Group homes were also built to serve as residences for young persons in the LIGHT rehabilitation program.

Among the Teen Challenge centers in the U.S. there are ninety-eight ministries and sixty-seven residential programs ministering to nearly 1,500 persons every day. In addition, twenty-eight churches have been planted as a result of these efforts.

Around the world, Teen Challenge International, under the leadership of Howard Foltz, is ministering in thirty-eight countries and has more than 150 outreaches.

We speak of programs, of facilities, of institutions. But Teen Challenge isn't that. We mention them because it is easy to talk of figures and programs. But the heart of this ministry continues to be a personal presentation to *hurting* people of the good news that God is present and powerful on the streets of our cities. The gospel presentation is made to all types of people in extensive street campaigns and church meetings around the country; but particularly to unlovely, unlovable people who desperately need to know God.

In 1973 the U.S. government provided a grant to study the effectiveness of the Teen Challenge drug rehabilitation program. It is perhaps the only time the U.S. government has spent money to document the fact that Jesus Christ changes lives. The results showed that 86 percent of those studied more than seven years following their completion of the residential program were still drug free. No other program can touch this record!

Similar exact figures for all the outreaches this work has had over the years are not available, but multiplied thousands of lives have been presented with the gospel, and we know a large percentage of them have responded.

In the metropolitan New York area Teen Challenge has had outreaches in Greenwich Village, the lower East Side, and Coney Island (while it was an amusement park). There have been outreaches through the Cure Corps department into East Harlem, the South Bronx, and around New York City in clubs called "Seekers" that meet in high schools and colleges.

God has been good. He has bailed Teen Challenge out of much trouble—financial and otherwise. Mom Wilkerson (Dave's mother) says she has prayed us out of more situations than she has prayed us into!

God has proved his faithfulness over and over again. At the end of *The Cross and the Switchblade,* Dave states that the Holy Spirit is in charge of the work. May he always be in charge, leading us as we continue.

BIBLICAL PRINCIPLE
Matthew 28:18-20—"Then Jesus came to them and said, 'All authority in heaven and on earth has been given to me. Therefore go and make disciples of all nations, baptizing them in the name of the Father and of the Son and of the Holy Spirit, and teaching them to obey everything I have commanded you. And surely I will be with you always, to the very end of the age.' "

Luke 14:23—"And the Lord said, 'Go out to the roads and country lanes and *make* them come in, so that my house will be full.' "

2 Peter 3:9—"The Lord is not slow in keeping his promise as some men understand slowness. He is patient with you, *not wanting any one to perish,* but everyone to come to repentance."

Luke 19:10—"For the Son of Man came to *seek* and to *save* what was *lost.*"

METHOD
At the beginning the ministry was primarily street evangelism:

1. Individuals going two by two into areas where street gangs were known to hang out and talking one on one and distributing specially prepared tracts geared to the problems being encountered.

   Those individuals were primarily young people from Bible colleges and church youth groups. They would gather in a central place (church or store front), receive instructions and literature, have prayer, and then go.
2. After "sowing down an area," they would arrange for a place to hold a public rally. This could be a large street corner, parking lot, or playground. A public address system would be set up, and sometimes someone with a trumpet would play music to attract attention. Then someone would preach and testify of God's love through Jesus Christ and his ability to change lives.

ADDED HISTORY
This has continued with variations to this day. The work may not necessarily be that of a Teen Challenge center but may be a church group or several groups working together.

NECESSITIES
1. *People* who care, who care enough to put themselves "on the line," who can relate God's love not only in word, but in deed. Too often we have looked for the highly trained and skilled person, forgetting the force of personal conviction and compassion.
2. *Literature* that relates to the area and culture; therefore, many

times the mass-produced piece is not appropriate. The message does not change, but the method and words used must be relevant to the ethnicity and culture we are trying to reach. It must address the hurts and needs as they exist in the target group or area.

HISTORY
When Teen Challenge first was organized, the philosophy stated that our job was to "evangelize" and get people "saved" and then turn them over to the local church.

PRINCIPLE
Matthew 28:18-20 (previously quoted) notes the two aspects of the Great Commission:

1. Preach and baptize
2. Teach to observe all things whatsoever I have commanded you.

It is not enough to get a person "saved" and leave him to his own devices. Jesus called the twelve, and "they were with him" for approximately three years. They learned from his sayings and his life. In Acts 4:13, "When they saw the courage of Peter and John and realized that they were unschooled, ordinary men, they were astonished and they took note that these men had been *with* Jesus."

METHOD
We try to enlist members of local churches in our street ministry so that there will be someone from the area to follow up new converts.

HISTORY
Reality and ideology sometimes are miles apart. In the inner city and in the areas that Teen Challenge was working, by and large there either was no church or no viable church open to receiving "these questionable characters." The church had largely lost its ability to take "raw heathens" and teach them the ways of the Lord.

PRINCIPLE

Ephesians 4:7, 8, 11-13—"But to each one of us grace has been given as Christ apportioned it. This is why it says 'When he ascended on high, he led captives in his train and *gave gifts* to *men.*' . . . It was he who gave some to be evangelists, and some to be pastors and teachers, to *prepare God's people for works of service,* so that the body of Christ may be built up until we all reach unity in the faith and in the knowledge of the Son of God and become mature, attaining to the whole measure of the fullness of Christ."

There is nothing being done in and through Teen Challenge that should not be the normal life of the local church. God has planted local churches where they are for a purpose. Each church needs to recognize the gifts of its members and provide a way for those members to exercise their gifts. Too often we are occupied in running an institution (church) instead of realizing that it is an

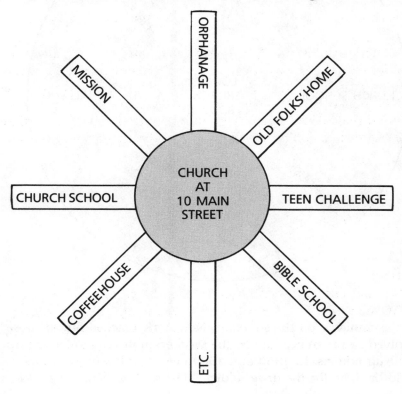

organism that is alive and growing, not brick and mortar and stained glass.

One concept of the church is a building at a special location where people gather for worship. Other agencies are called an arm of the church or parachurch organizations.

Another view is that the church is all of these things. This is the church and its expression in the community and the world, reaching people with all means and methods. The so-called parachurch ministries are in fact arms of the church of Jesus Christ in action.

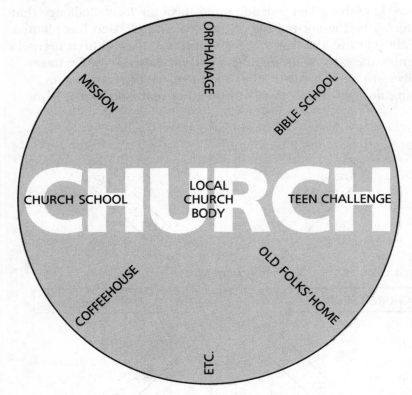

HISTORY

As the ministry on the streets of New York reached out to those involved in the many gangs, the workers noticed another group, the drug addicts. In 1959 and 1960 everyone knew "nothing could be done for the drug addict." The saying, "Once a junkie, always a junkie," was the rule. One day, as Brother Dave was preaching to a group of gang boys, a young man standing on the edge of the crowd heard the message of salvation. The gang boys hated junkies because once anyone started using drugs, he dropped out of the gangs. The young man, Ralph, came up to Dave after the gang had left and asked if he could have that, too. Dave said, "Sure, it's for everyone." Dave explained how God so loved the world that he sent Jesus to die on the cross for our sins, and that by believing on him you can be saved.

Ralph accepted the message, knelt with Dave on the sidewalk, and asked God to "be merciful" to him, "a sinner." They prayed and went their way. The next day Ralph came back to Dave and said, "Preacher, I don't know what you did to me, but it sure is good. I have been twenty-four hours without heroin, and I'm not sick." Normally, someone addicted to heroin would begin withdrawal pains, cramps, chills, vomiting, and all the rest if he did not have drugs every three to five hours. Dave just scratched his head and wondered. The next day Ralph came, saying, "It's still good." He became an "evangelist." He went to all his junkie friends and said, "Hey, fellows, I found the answer." He had been in hospitals and jails trying to find a "cure." He brought his friends to Dave, who explained the plan of salvation to them. Many received Christ as Savior and were instantly delivered without going through withdrawal. It was electric on the streets.

But, in three or four weeks many of them were back on the streets with a needle in their arm. We asked, "Hey, man, God did a miracle for you. What are you doing that for?"

Their answer: "Hey, man, we don't know how to be a Christian."

PRINCIPLE
When a person is "born again," "converted," "receives Christ," he is a babe. New life has come. It says in 2 Peter 3:18, "But grow in the grace and knowledge of our Lord and Saviour Jesus Christ"; and in 1 Corinthians 3:1, "Brothers, I could not address you as spiritual but as worldly—mere infants." In 1 Peter 2:2 it says, "Like newborn babes, crave pure spiritual milk so that by it you may grow up in your salvation." The twofold part of the Great Commission must be fulfilled. In 2 Timothy 2:2 we read, "And

the things thou hast heard of me among many witnesses, the same commit to faithful men, who shall be able to teach others also."

METHOD
We asked these people, "What do you need? How can we help you?" Their response: "If we could only get away from 'our friend' and learn about the Jesus life." From this need was born the training center where we offered an eight-month program of Bible teaching, Christian counseling, and training of "how to live the Christian life." Since 1962 this has been shaped and developed. There are formal structured classes covering the Bible stories, studies, characters, and practical application to the individual life. Included here is an outline of the curriculum material being used. This phase has been referred to as "Christian Growth," "Discipleship," and "Maturing in Christ."

Since most of the people became involved in the drug/alcohol scene at ages eleven, twelve, and thirteen, they had not gone through normal adolescent growth. After conversion, we found that most had to go back mentally and learn those lessons they missed.

The training program takes on a whole-life concept—spiritual, mental, emotional, and physical. So the training involves total life teaching.

Physical health must be restored through proper nutrition, exercise, and general good hygiene.

Educationally, they have been dropouts. Many are illiterate, so it is necessary to teach them a solid, basic education in reading, writing, arithmetic, and religion. Some call it the 4 R's. Filling in these educational lacks builds self-esteem. "I am of worth. I am of value. God loves me."

Vocationally, most have very poor work habits. They are unable to hold a job because of this. One half of each day is spent in productive, necessary work. We try to avoid just "busy work," again to build a sense of worth.

Emotionally, the person involved in substance abuse is stunted. He has been living only by his feelings. You need to teach him responsible action and reaction from a biblical base.

Spiritual life is developed in the classes, which are Bible-based, and through chapel services, prayer meetings, and participating in outreach back to the streets.

There are two essentials that have brought success:

1. The "born-again" (born of the Spirit) experience. This is more than the first flush of accepting Christ. Many times the reality of what this means does not come until the teens get knowledge of the Word.
2. The baptism or infilling of the Holy Spirit, with the physical evidence of "speaking in other tongues." It must be more than just speaking in tongues. We teach them how to live a "spirit-led" life, with its convicting power, comforting power, and directing power.

Both of these essentials are not only classroom and chapel experiences, but occur in daily living in the rooms, on the job, in recreation, so that when a person returns to "normal" life, he knows how to function as a "Christian" person.

HISTORY

The name Teen Challenge means more than reaching teenagers. Originally we were working with the teen gangs. As we began to reach the substance-abuse population, older and older people came to the program. We have not successfully thought of another name. Even the older people with life-controlling problems are still basically responding to life as a youth. Therefore, the principles have worked with the older group.

PROBLEM AREA

In most states there are extensive regulations for the protection of juveniles, which has been interpreted as anyone under eighteen. This has posed problems for the residential programs. Rules and regulations promulgated to protect the interest of "children" quite often prevent a person who could be helped from coming into a Teen Challenge program. Health and human services are not by and large interested in a spiritual program, so heavy requirements in social work and psychology prevent the proper emphasis necessary to change lives.

PRINCIPLE

Matthew 6:33—"But seek first his kingdom and his righteousness, and all these things will be given to you as well." Ephesians 2:1-10—"As for you, you were dead in your transgressions and sins, in which you used to live when you followed the ways of this world and of the ruler of the kingdom of the air, the spirit who is now at work in those who are disobedient. All of us also lived among them at one time, gratifying the cravings of our sinful nature and following its desires and thoughts. Like the rest, we were by nature objects of wrath. But because of his great love for us, God, who is rich in mercy, made us alive with Christ even when we were dead in transgressions—it is by grace you have been saved. And God raised us up with Christ and seated us with him in the heavenly realms in Christ Jesus, in order that in the coming ages he might show the incomparable riches of his grace, expressed in his kindness to us in Christ Jesus. For it is by grace you have been saved, through faith—and this not from yourselves, it is the gift of God—not by works, so that no one can boast. For we are God's workmanship, created in Christ Jesus to do good works, which God prepared in advance for us to do." You must deal with the basic sin-nature before you can change behavior. When a person finds a living relationship to Jesus Christ, then he will begin to seek ways to walk "pleasing to the Lord." There is the motivation to change, and a reason to change.

TEMPTATION

As you minister to hurting humanity, youth as well as older people, you are confronted with so many social problems and injustices, so many physical problems of poverty, hunger, poor housing, inadequate human services. It is easy to become so politically and socially involved that you lose your primary goal of bringing people to Christ.

PRINCIPLE

We must understand that man is paying a penalty that goes back to Adam. Because of sin's penalty, man is earning his bread by the sweat of his face and women are bringing forth children in pain and sorrow.

We must deal with the *sin* problem—the basic nature that

means man is separated from God. A man commits sins because he is a sinner. Therefore, to bring about change you must deal with first things first.

The church should be concerned about injustices and poverty and iniquities, but a well-fed person can go to hell as well as a hungry person. A person in a mansion can go to hell as well as a person living in a cardboard box. The one *sin* that keeps people out of heaven is refusing to accept Jesus Christ as Savior. But because we are born in sin, we commit sins. We need to be careful that we don't use all of our energies fighting sins without dealing with the basic sin nature.

DANGER

There is a danger in producing a manuscript telling "how we do it." It is possible to learn all the methods, use all the materials, do all the things, and then expect God to give the same results. We are tempted to believe that God is obligated to respond in a *certain* way *because* we did certain things.

The Spirit in whose power it is done and the motivation of why it is done are essentials. Only God can look inside of me and know why I do what I do.

For example: the miracles that Jesus did. Is it possible to set down a 1, 2, 3 step of how he did them? You will find as many methods and approaches as you will find miracles. This should be a lesson to us. This does not mean that we cannot learn from each other. There is no virtue in "inventing the wheel" every day.

I must be able to satisfactorily answer "*Why* am I *doing* this?" There is the story of the young bride who cut off the end of the ham before baking it. Her husband asked, "Why did you do that?" "My mother always did it," she answered. "Why?" "I don't know." When Mother came, the incident was related and the question asked, "Mother, why did you cut off the end of the ham?" Mother replied, "My mother always did it." "Why?" "I don't know." So Grandma comes on the scene, the story is told, and the question asked, "Why did you cut off the end of the ham?" Grandma replies, "So it would fit in the pan."

AN ESSENTIAL

Any effort to reach the lost needs earnest, believing prayer. We need to spend as much time *doing it* as we do talking about it, reading about it, and writing books about it.

One lady prayed, "Lord, lead me to souls." No success. She worked in a busy five-and-dime store, and she realized that every day she contacted hundreds of souls. Suddenly she changed her prayer to, "Lord, lead me to hungry souls." Then she began to find many opportunities to share the life in Christ, both on and off the job.

The person and/or program must consider the Holy Spirit's leading and the touch of God on the individual's life. This does not mean some fuzzy-headed approach, but rather becoming sensitive to what is going on around you, what is happening in people's lives—and being open to the fact that God can impress upon you individuals and situations of need without an earthquake and thunder. Read 1 Kings 19:1-18. Elijah had seen God send "fire from heaven." When Jezebel threatened his life, he ran and hid and prayed to die. God spoke to him in the cave. As he stood in the mouth of the cave there was a great wind and a great earthquake, and God was not in either one—but he spoke with "a still small voice" or "a whisper."

Certainly all that has been done through Teen Challenge ministries isn't because of great natural skills and abilities, nor great buildings and programs. When problems arose and still arise, we must ask God for direction to solve the problem. Many times it means trying different things until they fit.

PRINCIPLE

In 1 Corinthians 1:26—2:10 we read: "Brothers, think of what you were when you were called. Not many of you were wise by human standards; not many were influential; not many were of noble birth. But God chose the foolish things of the world to shame the wise; God chose the weak things of the world to shame the strong. He chose the lowly things of this world and the despised things—and the things that are not—to nullify the things that are, so that no one may boast before him. It is because of him that you are in Christ Jesus, who has become for us wisdom from God—that is, our righteousness, holiness and redemption. Therefore, as it is written: 'Let him who boasts boast in the Lord.'

"When I came to you, brothers, I did not come with eloquence or superior wisdom as I proclaimed to you the testimony about

God. For I resolved to know nothing while I was with you except Jesus Christ and him crucified. I came to you in weakness and fear, and with much trembling. My message and my preaching were not with wise and persuasive words, but with a demonstration of the Spirit's power, so that your faith might not rest on men's wisdom, but on God's power.

"We do, however, speak a message of wisdom among the mature, but not the wisdom of this age or of the rulers of this age, who are coming to nothing. No, we speak of God's secret wisdom, a wisdom that has been hidden and that God destined for our glory before time began. None of the rulers of this age understood it, for if they had, they would not have crucified the Lord of glory. However, as it is written: 'No eye has seen, no ear has heard, no mind has conceived what God has prepared for those who love him'—but God has revealed it to us by his Spirit.

"The Spirit searches all things, even the deep things of God."

CONCLUSION

I am amazed at those whom God uses on the street. I am amazed at how God works on the street. Sometimes it's the person who has been delivered from a rough street life, and sometimes it's the "straight" person who accepted Christ at a young age and walked uprightly all his life. The point is, in both instances there is a dedication, a simplicity, an openness to the leading of the Holy Spirit.

DO WE NEED A TEEN CHALLENGE CENTER HERE?

Many people read *The Cross and the Switchblade* and decide they need to start a center right where they are. You may become personally involved with someone abusing drugs and feel a center needs to be started. A property may be made available, thus causing some to be inspired to want to start a center.

God is interested in meeting needs. He will supply the need for a ministry that meets *human needs*.

I. How do we determine the need?
    A. Check with local and state police as to the number of

arrests and types of problems for which youth are being arrested or investigated.

B. Check with the schools to see if a survey has been done, or could be done, to determine the extent and nature of the problems.

C. Do your own survey of youth in the church, in the hamburger joints, and in other hangouts, dance halls, etc. If the survey shows a need, the general rule of thumb is that Teen Challenge Centers should be established in areas of major population, unless there are unusual circumstances.

D. Demonstrate our ability to meet the need by:
   1. Making contact with troubled youth
   2. Leading them to Christ
   3. Referring the ones that need it to an established Teen Challenge Center
   4. Building a track record

II. Can this need be met by the ministry of the local church?
   A. Try to assimilate those reached into the local church.
   B. Get Christian youth involved in discipling them.
   C. Take advantage of any existing facilities or programs.

We have done all this and it seems there is a need. Is there any existing Teen Challenge nearby to which we can send those needing residential care? If not, what then?

BASIC MOTIVATION

Starting or running a Teen Challenge ministry should be motivated by a sincere desire to help people in trouble.

Jesus Christ, in the heart and life of the Teen Challenge worker, is the chief motivator. The best manual, the best buildings, the best program must translate the love of God through people. The approach that worked so well last week or last year or in that other place may not work in this present situation. Our principles and our message do not change, but the approach or package may have to be altered. When Teen Challenge first began in New York, large street meetings were normal—2000 people in one meeting. Then the riots and civil disturbance of the late sixties changed all that. The law would not allow even fifteen people to congregate.

Did this change the command of Jesus? Did this change the love of God? Did this change the call of God? No! So we found another way to tell the story through one-to-one work, literature, store fronts, etc. God is not stopped by rules of men.

Love for people has got to be the motivating force—love that sees through, past, and around the obstacles; love that provides wisdom when there is none; love that drives us to find the answer.

THE TEEN CHALLENGE CENTER
  I. Organizational necessities
    A. Approval must be obtained from:
      1. Sectional presbyter
      2. District leadership
      3. Division of Home Missions
      This is so that proper guidance can be given and good relationships established.
    B. Board of Directors
      This is the governing body and the legal corporate officers. The Board of Directors shall be composed of interested Assemblies of God ministers and laymen, other Christians in harmony with the doctrine and purpose of Teen Challenge of the immediate area, plus the District Superintendent or his representative or a member of the District Presbytery appointed. The National Director and National Teen Challenge Representative of the Division of Home Missions of the General Council of the Assemblies of God shall be ex officio members.
 II. Developing support and interest in Teen Challenge
    A. Church
      In order for Teen Challenge to be a strong influence, it needs strong support by many people. Since the main thrust and motivation is spiritual, it is necessary to develop strong ties with local church bodies. This will build prayer and financial support. It is important to establish a working relationship with churches so that they may realize we are working to build the kingdom of God and the church of Jesus Christ. Teen Challenge is an augmenting force, not a competitive force. The church can be a source of possible staff, both full time and volunteer. A good relationship also means you will find a place to

refer converts and those completing the program who may not need residential care. The churches will be an important part of the financial support as well as the main key to prayer support.

B. Community

The community, city, or metropolitan area to be served must be involved in this ministry. Teen Challenge is ministering to a need and a problem. The solution to that problem can be a big benefit for the community. There are legal agencies that will become involved: health departments, zoning officers, narcotic agencies, juvenile authorities, ad infinitum. We need to build rapport so that our work will not be hindered. We need to show teens how we are going to help solve some of their problems. In larger metropolitan areas, there are block associations that can be a help or a hindrance, depending upon our attitude and cooperation. Our program cannot only help those in trouble, but can become a problem-prevention ministry as well. We deal with those in trouble and provide a ministry to show the newer generation how to avoid trouble. Changed communities come about by changed lives.

C. Individuals

Ultimately, the success of the Teen Challenge program will depend upon your ability to develop the interest of individuals. It is individuals in the churches and communities that will help or hinder. Individuals give money. Individuals pray. Real effort must be given to cultivating good *personal* relationships. The old adage, "It isn't *what* you know but *who*" is still appropriate. Individuals in business, government, and churches will make the program grow. The more individuals you get interested and involved the better.

III. Locating a Property or Building

There are several approaches to providing facilities for the ministry of Teen Challenge. Availability should not be the only criterion. Usability is first. Basic planning should be done to determine the facilities needed.

What phase of the program is being implemented?
What type of ministry is planned?

What rules and regulations will we need to comply with?
What resources do we have (such as money, manpower)?

A. Consideration should be given to renting or leasing property at the outset. Perhaps there is space available in existing community facilities.
  1. Churches with unused or underutilized space
  2. Community centers
  3. Office buildings
  4. Homes that can be adapted
As the work develops, you may find a different area advisable. A lease with option to purchase, with a portion of the rent going toward a down payment, may mean the ability to start with less capital.

B. Some structural considerations.
  1. Plumbing—is it adequate? Are there showers and bathtubs, etc.? Is the location of them accessible?
  2. Electrical—how old is the wiring system? What is the electrical capacity?
  3. Construction—is it fire resistant? Are there good exits? Basic structure should be sound, meet fire codes, have smoke alarms. Does it meet the fire code of the city or municipality?
  4. Internal arrangement—space for office (private and accessible), chapel area. Live-in staff should have some privacy to be most effective. Proximity to neighbors should be considered. Is there space for any physical exercise? This may be on the property; or perhaps there is a "Y" or church or school with facilities that can be used.
  5. Security—dealing with troubled youth leaves a property open to loss or theft. Can the residents easily be supervised or are there too many ways to sneak out? Can the office equipment be protected? Typewriters sell easily on the street.
  6. Maintenance—can the facility be maintained in a clean and attractive way with minimum expense? The original cost may be low, but the daily upkeep could deplete the budget.
  7. Kitchen and dining room—the Health Department will

be inspecting you. It would be good to get some professional advice here. It's still true that "the way to a man's heart is through the stomach." If you can keep the food gripes down, you may find it easier to reach the heart with the gospel.

C. Space needs.
1. Office space—this must be able to:
   a. Handle day-to-day business
   b. Be accessible to public, staff, clients
   c. Provide space enough to accommodate the various ministries
   d. Security (see above)
2. Staff housing
   A conscious decision must be made on how this issue will be handled. In the past, many programs on the community living approach provided room and board and minimum salary. This may be fine for short-term workers, but may be a hindrance to those desiring to make a life-time commitment to the ministry. Long-term workers will want to establish a family and a sense of home.

   It may be necessary to start one way, but long-term planning should consider the options.
   a. Straight salary with each worker finding his own housing
   b. Housing provided as part of salary
   c. Salary plus housing allowance

The choice may be influenced by the facilities available. This building or facility may have to house staff, office, client, and program to get started. The building is not the program, but it may be easier to carry on a ministry with more usable facilities. Do not become so heavily involved in buildings that your ministry to people is hindered. Don't let your buildings become your prisons.

RAISING FUNDS FOR TEEN CHALLENGE MINISTRY

PHILOSOPHY
Fund-raising must be seen as a ministry. Its goal is not funds, but

helping people. People need food, clothing, and shelter, "all these do the gentiles seek." "But seek ye first the kingdom of God and his righteousness, and all these things [food, clothing, shelter] shall be added unto you" (Matthew 6:33). ". . . give, and it shall be given unto you; good measure, pressed down, and shaken together, and running over, shall men give into your bosom. For with the same measure that ye mete withal it shall be measured to you again" (Luke 6:38).

Raising funds is a spiritual ministry. God can lead us to whom we should speak and show us how we should speak.

Prayer is a vital part of this. Expect God to answer prayer through others and through you. When you have prayed, let the Holy Spirit direct your efforts.

I. Mailing Lists
   The bread and butter of this ministry is the free-will monthly contributions received through the mail. Careful attention to acquiring and using the mailing list is necessary.
   A. Methods of building a mailing list
      1. Anyone who does anything for the center gets his name and address on the list
      2. People who you know are interested in solving youth problems
      3. When public meetings are held, have address cards available for those who are interested
      4. People already on your list who have shown an interest in Teen Challenge may enlist other interested people
      5. Some have purchased mailing lists—this is generally the least productive for our type of ministry
      6. Some pastors may be willing to loan you a mailing list
      7. Ask friends of Teen Challenge for their mailing list
   B. Using your mailing list
      1. A monthly newsletter—make *sure* it gives news of what is happening, including special mailings for specific needs or appeals
      2. Have neat and good printing; a good job is not as expensive as a poor one
      3. Do not make it look too expensive—we are a

nonprofit organization; four-color production may not be expensive, but to the average person it will appear to be; try colored ink and/or colored paper

4. Have a specific date your newsletter goes out regularly
5. Do not send panic letters—that usually says you are a bad manager. Emergencies are fire, earthquake, tornado, flood, etc.
6. There are seminars on how to write; study and learn
7. Separate your mailing list for different appeals—by profession, ability, and interest
8. Revise your list at least annually; keep it an active list; use a "cull" letter that elicits response to remain on your mailing list—every letter you mail costs you money
9. Your newsletter should solicit *prayer* and *financial support*

II. Services in Churches

The major source of support will be from Christian people. Most will be active church members. Your opportunity of enlisting their support will come usually through a presentation in a church or to a church-related group.

You will have to make it known that you are available to present a meaningful service concerning a program to help people in trouble. Care should be given that these services inspire. Give and it shall be given. They should be richer for your having been there. Be sure there is an understanding with the pastor concerning the offering, mailing list, length, and purpose of the service.

III. Programs to Civic Clubs, Schools, P.T.A., Special Community Groups

These groups usually consist of motivated people who will accept a challenge. They are working with community problems. Teen Challenge also is working with a community problem, and doing something about it.

In your presentation:

A. Be sure of your facts—about drugs, your program, etc.
B. Present positively our approach without compromise, but do not be "preachy"; Christ is the answer
C. Challenge them to support the effort
D. Clear your presentation with the one in charge

E. Respect their time limitations

F. Be willing to offer appropriate prayer

IV. Drug Abuse Prevention and Education

    A. This could be a part of your presentation under III

    B. It could be a ministry in itself that would encourage support

    C. Many people will give honorariums to a well-thought-out and well-presented program

    D. This can open the door to churches, businesses, and interested people for financial support

V. Group Support

    A. Enlist groups to take on fund-raising projects

    B. Enlist groups to perform voluntarily some of the work of the center

        1. Be sure to train your volunteers

        2. Be specific in what and how they can help; donated effort is money in the bank.

VI. Community Fund, Etc.

Community Fund and/or United Fund may be available in some cities. One word of caution—some community funds make you sign an agreement of no other solicitation, which could hurt unless they assume the total budget.

VII. Goods in Kind

Businessmen and women and individuals may not be able to give money. They need to know specific needs such as: food, office equipment, vehicles, buildings, and building materials; volunteer services such as office workers, building construction and maintenance, counselors, and teachers for the program. Do not be afraid to remind them that tax deductible receipts can be given for the value received. In seeking people to do these services, let us be sure to minister to their need. These can be golden opportunities to share the love of God. Check I.R.S. rulings on in-kind receipts.

VIII. Foundations

There are thousands of philanthropic foundations of varying sizes. To enlist their support, you should do some basic study and research.

    A. Pinpoint specific foundations in your community

    B. Research to see what the purpose of the foundation is; many were set up to fulfill specific purposes

C. Put your effort into those your research indicates have an interest in what you are trying to do
D. Cultivate a relationship to and with key people
E. Determine when and how a proposal should be made
F. The Stewardship Division can be helpful in providing guidelines

IX. Deferred Giving and Memorial Funds
The Stewardship Division should be consulted since this may involve estate planning.
This is long range and should not be counted on for current budget.
Attend Stewardship Seminars.

X. Work Projects
As the ministry develops and there are people involved in the habilitation program there may be the opportunity for light industry or providing some needed service which can generate income. For example: candle making, lawn care service, subcontract in machine shop, picking apples, harvesting crops.
Perhaps there is a needed service that your center can fulfill and at the same time make it part of the life-changing process for those you are helping.

XI. Media Presentations: Radio and television
A. Public service time has been used to acquaint the general public with the need
B. Regular programs paid for by sponsors
   1. This is for those gifted and qualified
   2. Quality is essential

XII. Businesses
Many businesses set aside funds to support local community efforts as a part of their budget.
A. The same care should be given to your approach to the business community as the foundations
B. Cultivate personal relationships
C. Make sure your program business practices are organized, efficient, and businesslike
D. Demonstrate the service and benefit of your program to the community
E. Remember—there are many other community projects

soliciting their support, so be kind, be patient, be understanding and persistent

F. If financial support or material is given, be sure to follow through with proper receipting

G. If support was given to a specific project, i.e., a new roof, let donors know of the progress

H. Many businesses gives their community support through combined funding. You may have to work with and around this

I. There may be community controls on charitable giving

XIII. Banquets, Rallies, Etc.

Large or small public gatherings may be conducted for the announced purposes of gathering support.

A. Plan ahead—the farther the better—who, what, and when

B. Be specific in your goal

C. Target whom you are going to try to reach for what purposes

D. Name personalities may be used; count the cost—success is not automatic because of a big name

E. If you don't know, enlist the help of those who do

F. Check your calendar carefully so that you do not conflict with other activities (church, school, community); that could spell defeat

G. This could open the door to churches, businesses, foundations, mailing lists, etc.

XIV. Films and Slide Presentations

To tell the story of the work of Teen Challenge, several centers have used 16mm films and 8mm films and slide programs (16mm sound film is very expensive if done properly, and this is the only way to do it). While 8mm sound is a new tool and has possibilities, it is limited. The film can be personalized to the local center.

And 35mm slide presentations with taped sound can be very effective. They can be updated more easily than 16 or 8mm movies.

These media have been used in the various types of services suggested above.

XV. Imagination and Inspiration

OUTLINE OF THE TEEN CHALLENGE MINISTRY

The ministry of Teen Challenge is varied and diverse. The services rendered are determined by human need in the city, region, or area served and the purpose of the individual center. The overall purpose of Teen Challenge has been stated. "Evangelize people who have life-controlling problems and initiate the discipleship process to the point where the student can function as a Christian in society applying spiritually motivated biblical principles to relationships in the family, local church, chosen vocation, and the community. Teen Challenge endeavors to help people become mentally sound, emotionally balanced, socially adjusted, physically well, and spiritually alive." Each Teen Challenge Center will have a vital part in achieving this objective.

PHASE I
Coffeehouse, Outreach Center, Satellite. Basic confrontational evangelism. The purpose and method is to conduct evangelism outreach directly to the people; i.e., street meetings, jail and prison services, help-line substance-abuse prevention programs, drop-in counseling, literature distribution, etc.

Purpose:
A. To evangelize the youth in the area
B. To confront them with their need of Christ
C. A place or program that will attract youth in trouble
D. A ministry that goes where the trouble is

PHASE II
Crisis Intervention, Preinduction, and Referral. Persons with life-controlling problems are provided a place to stay long enough to meet the immediate crisis, to receive a clear witness of the gospel, and to evaluate whether they need or desire the long-term discipleship training offered by Teen Challenge.

PHASE III
Teen Challenge Induction Center. This beginning of the discipleship process usually involves ten to twelve weeks of Bible study and character development.

A. Evangelism will be the base of operation
B. Residential care furnished to those reached and needing it
C. Provide induction course and counseling

D. Accept referrals from coffeehouse and satellite or other agencies or individuals

PHASE IV
Teen Challenge Training Center. Long-term residential program eight to twelve months, involving Christian growth and development, academic and vocational improvement.

A. Concentrated discipleship training
B. Counseling with clients
C. Academic and vocational training
D. Six to twelve months' residence
E. Restructuring and resocializing those referred
F. Take referrals from induction centers
G. Regional in scope generally

PHASE V
Reentry. This process is commonly initiated by the induction centers and frequently provides one or more of the following: temporary housing, personal and family counseling, assistance in finding suitable employment and vibrant church fellowship.

A. Clients are those completing first four phases
B. May be in conjunction with an induction center
C. May be through a local church
D. May be at the training center
E. Purpose:
   1. To assist the new Christian in getting established in "normal" church and community life
   2. Assist in restoring or establishing a home
   3. Give guidance in: job placement, further education, family responsibility

OUTLINE OF PHASE I
(COFFEEHOUSE, OUTREACH CENTER, SATELLITE)

I. Purpose
   A. To provide a program that extends the hope of the gospel of Jesus Christ to those with life-controlling problems, by whatever means appropriate for the target population and/or area
   B. Conserve by teaching
      1. Establish classes in local area

      2. Counseling for Christian growth
II. Program
  A. Personal confrontation
    1. One on one on the street
    2. Street meetings, beach meetings, public rallies
    3. Home visitations
      a. Contact people who are reported in newspapers in trouble
      b. Contact relatives and friends of students in residential program
      c. Door-to-door community contact
    4. Jail and prison, juvenile facilities
    5. Help-line telephone ministry
  B. Coffeehouse and/or rap center
  C. Child evangelism program
    1. Clubs
    2. Community centers
    3. Parks
    4. Home that will open
    5. Use your imagination
  D. Street meetings
  E. Beach meetings
  F. Public rallies
  G. Open your mind to the prompting of the Holy Spirit—the command is to preach and teach; the Holy Spirit is our guide and teacher: "not by might but by the Holy Spirit"
III. Organization needed
  A. Board of directors
  B. Advisory board
  C. Full-time Staff
  D. Volunteer Staff
IV. Funding
  A. Local church/churches
  B. United Way
  C. Businesses and corporations
  D. See special section in guidelines on fund-raising
V. Relationship to the church
  A. Relationship of Phase I
    1. Could be a ministry sponsored by the church
    2. Seek a working relationship with the local church

NOTE: Perhaps the word "coffeehouse" could be toned down, to "contact center" or "encounter center."

B. Relationship of Phase II
   1. For the purpose of referral, Phase I should be organizationally and/or functionally with Phase II the Crisis Intervention phase
   2. "Referral" defined:
      a. That type of person who qualified as a prospect for the residential care program
      b. Referrals could be
         (1) Followed up by Teen Challenge and referred to a local church
         (2) Interviewed by Teen Challenge and referred to "live-in"
         (3) Interviewed and referred to others

VI. Followup
   A. To individuals
      1. Introduce to local church in community
      2. Home and/or correspondence Bible study groups
      3. Take through two-week preinduction curriculum
      4. Refer to induction center
   B. Families of converts
      1. Introduce to local church
      2. Home and/or correspondence Bible study individual and/or group
      3. May be nucleus of new church planting

DETAIL OF PHASE I
(COFFEEHOUSE, OUTREACH CENTER, SATELLITE, HOTLINE, HELP-LINE, PREINDUCTION)

I. Purpose: contact evangelism, making contact with people in their area of need
   A. Primarily evangelism: confronting youth with their need of Christ
   B. Providing facilities where youth can meet concerned staff
   C. A ministry on the street to youth hangouts, juveniles, detention facilities, and prisons
   D. Provide a widely publicized telephone counseling service for emergency help

II. Relationships

The amount of formal organization needed will be determined by the extent of the ministry.

A. Local church—this could very well be a ministry run by a local church. If it is a ministry carried on by a local church, the regular church governing body will be sufficient. Well organized, it could provide a place of Christian service for many dedicated Christians. Approval of pastor and church board and working relationships should be established. The church board may want to appoint a committee to handle this phase of the church program with a liaison person or board member carrying this portfolio.

B. This could be a ministry supported by several churches, in city or community, working together. This would require a board of directors that is interested in representatives. An organization with governing board and policy statements would have to be worked out. This board would be the legal entity that would have legal responsibility for policy, procedure, and funding.

C. An advisory council may be helpful in obtaining support and expertise from many people with particular ability in certain areas. These may include people knowledgeable in program, building, or particular community needs. Responsibility for financing and staffing should be defined. (An Advisory Council Guidebook is available.)

D. The staff needed will be determined by the extent of the ministry. One full-time person may be able to enlist many volunteers to work in different types of outreach to the community. It may be necessary to have several full-time staff to plan and carry out the various activities and community outreaches. Lines of authority and job descriptions should be spelled out in order to reach the goals and fulfill the purposes of the organization.

E. The center could be part of the ministry of a local Teen Challenge Induction Phase II, and/or Phase III.

F. An understanding of where converts are referred for followup needs to be clearly understood. Any coffeehouse ministry should seek a working relationship with the local churches, regardless of who is the sponsor.

III. Program and Method

The program and method of approach will be determined by the city or area that is the target.

It may be very simple in its first stages, with one person reaching out to the people. It could be a program of a local church in some areas or a combined effort of several churches, or a separate entity cooperating with many churches and community agencies, with many different approaches.

The complexity of the organization could be determined by the overall population area and number of problems to be dealt with.

The primary motivation is to meet struggling people where they are, with a message and method of dealing with life.

The methods used to fulfill the purpose can and will be as varied as the staff abilities and visions, plus the needs and opportunities of the target areas.

The person-to-person confrontation can come about as a result of any of the suggested types of meetings (see outline). Ultimately the reached person must be able to build a relationship with a compassionate person who can introduce him to Jesus Christ and enlist him in the discipleship process.

Churches and other community agencies will refer people to the center when they see an effective program helping people solve their problems.

Methods should be determined by the need and by what works, rather than doing something just because others do it. Flexibility in approach to an area is needed, as well as the ability to abandon an unproductive method.

Cooperation with other people-helping agencies is essential. There are services provided and paid for that can be utilized to meet some needs. There are those people who will be reached who won't accept the gospel as a solution to their problems. Such people can be referred to other agencies that are available to meet some needs. This will build credibility with the people and the other agencies, showing that Teen Challenge is really interested in helping people.

A. In a building

1. Location of building: where youth traffic is; a building that will motivate the youth to come in
2. What goes on in the building is most important. Services or programs should not be a repeat of a traditional church service or "Christian night club." Suggest staff study *The Coffeehouse Manual* by Don Wilkerson and *The Coffeehouse Itch* by Lyman Coleman before starting.
3. Check any local ordinances, zoning, fire and health restrictions.

B. On the street

Personal witnessing around schools, hangouts, beaches, etc., distributing literature. Should be planned and prayed for: "Lord lead us to hungry souls."

C. Jails, prisons, juvenile detention halls, etc.

In many places this is an open door of ministry. Helps and suggestions for effective ministry in correctional facilities are available through Paul Markstrom, Prison Department, 1445 Boonville Avenue, Springfield, MO 65802. Work in cooperation with those in authority: warden, superintendent, and chaplain. They have the keys to the door that lets you in or keeps you out. "Be ye wise as serpents and harmless as doves." Train, as well as pick your personnel. Plan for followup of those who express a desire to receive Christ with visits, Bible study courses. When they are transferred to another facility, try to contact someone in the new facility for followup ministry.

D. Hotline, help-line

This is a challenge that takes planning. If needed, investigate possibilities of cooperation with an existing service.
1. Proper facility.
2. Recruiting and training for those working on the phone. A community service by a referral center can be effective through a twenty-four-hour telephone help-line. A telephone service must be established and manned by trained people twenty-four hours a day, seven days a week.
3. Assembling information and services available in the

community to meet any emergency. An effective help-line must have a full catalog of other community agencies that provide human services. It should have, on call, professional or backup persons to deal with problems of a special nature.

4. Making arrangements for telelphone. The telephone service should be sufficient so that auxiliary help could be called while the caller is still on the line. It is possible to have equipment where calls may be forwarded to another number, should it be necessary to be away from the main phone. Help-line should not be a part of the business phone system for a center.

5. Seeking widespread publicity for the number so that those who need help can find it easily and quickly. The number must be publicized, especially to areas where needy people can find it. This help-line could be made available to the total community and be a contact for several agencies and needs such as:
   a. Drug and alcohol problems
   b. Suicide
   c. Rape crisis
   d. Child and wife abuse
   e. Family problems, etc.

E. Staff for help-line

It will be necessary to have one person to coordinate the help-line ministry. This person should be able to schedule the manning of the phones, gathering the reference catalog material and general organization of the help-line ministry. He should train and/or arrange for the training of full-time and volunteer help that will be working in the help-line ministry. Workers will need to be trained in:

1. The proper use of the telephone
2. A thorough understanding of the reference catalog
3. Basic telephone counseling techniques

Help-line workers should meet all other staff requirements of spiritual and mental capabilities. They should be mature and stable, with the ability to remain calm in a crisis situation, and able to respond with quick, positive action when it is necessary.

A help-line ministry is a place where many volunteers

can be used effectively if properly trained, scheduled, and committed.

It will increase the effectiveness of a help-line ministry if there are people, volunteer or full-time staff, that could respond to calls for help in a personal call to the home or wherever the caller is. This should be carried out with necessary precautions.

A record system for recording calls, needs, and followup results should be established.

F. Satellite Center, Outreach Center
   1. May incorporate any and all of the previously mentioned ministries
   2. It would be working with and under the supervision of an established center
   3. Primarily referring those in need of help to the main center for residential care

IV. Finances
   A. If run by a local church, the primary source of support would be the sponsoring church.
   B. If run by several churches or the community, support should come from those organizations involved.
   C. Any project should endeavor to be supported by the area being served. If we provide a valid service we should not be bashful in seeking support from the area being helped.

V. Staff
   A. Generally speaking, the more experienced and qualified the staff the less you will need. Someone who is a trainer-coordinator may be able to recruit and train a cadre of volunteers that can carry the load for many outreach projects.

The duties can be broken down so that the responsibility is not a burden but a joy. The task should be large enough to be challenging but small enough to be finished and give a sense of accomplishment.

A beginning operation may well be started by volunteer interested people or part-time workers (i.e., an associate pastor, minister of youth, etc.). As services rendered increase, key full-time staff may be necessary to coordinate and train the volunteer workers.

B. Staff qualifications and training
  1. The director—needs to be trained in ministry of the
     Word and administration of the project. The
     prospective training should be a minimum of thirty
     days in full Phase I and Phase II unit.
     Training
     a. Have a knowledgeable understanding of Teen
        Challenge procedures
     b. Have a knowledge of intake procedures
     c. Spend a few days in Phase III on completion of
        thirty-day stay
     d. Know who is qualified for referral
     e. Know how to win souls for Christ and have won
        souls for Christ—must expose himself to street
        evangelism
     f. Have knowledge of business office procedures
     g. Know how to conduct an interview
     h. Complete reading, tape, and other resource material
     i. Be involved in the ministry of Phase I and Phase II;
        accompany staff on their assignments
     j. Sit in on counseling sessions
     k. Sit in on staff meetings
     l. Sit in on a board meeting—observe financial,
        director's report, observe business meeting
        procedure, understand proper relationship to the
        board
     m. Go with the director on public relations; counsel
        with director on promotion know-how
     n. Fill out in-depth questionnaire for evaluation of
        thirty-day stay
        (1) His response to program
        (2) Fill out questionnaire and interview for personal
            evaluation
     Qualifications
     a. A new program may require that the director wear
        many hats until there is sufficient growth and
        finances to warrant additional personnel.
     b. Spiritually, the director should be saved and filled
        with the Spirit. He should have a concern and
        compassion for the lost. In this type of ministry, he

needs to be able to identify with various cultures and ethnic groups as well as those who are poverty stricken emotionally, physically, and spiritually.

c. He needs to be able to communicate the gospel to those to be reached as well as inspire, train, and lead the staff in this ministry. He needs ability to get along with people and take stress well.

d. He should be able to relate to the religious, social services, and business community. All of these are involved with the people in need. They will provide the people, finances, and services needed to change the life style and situation of troubled people— spiritually, economically, and socially.

e. Maturity—the director should be mature enough to relate to parents and young people with understanding. Maturity is not based on years alone. It includes the ability to make sound judgment (decisions); the ability to know when someone else with more expertise should be brought in; the ability to stay steady when crisis comes.

f. Educationally—it is essential to have a good working knowledge of the Bible and its application to problem solving as well as be theologically sound. Training in the social psychological field will help. This may come from Bible school, correspondence courses, or diligent study. Bible study should be an ongoing part of the director's life—manna every day. Training in counseling method and techniques would be helpful. Some business management courses with the basics of accounting, time management, and office organization are very helpful for efficient and accountable procedures. Two books suggested:
(1) *Time Trap* by Alex MacKenzie
(2) *Managing Your Time* by Ted Engstrom

g. The director must have a servant heart. He leads best who knows how to serve. This does not mean he has to do all of the menial tasks, but he must have the willingness to do them. The director will be an example to the flock (staff).

h. A director may not begin with all of the equipment and polished abilities, but if he is willing to learn and apply himself, if he really has a call of God to help people, he will be open to new ideas as well as opportunities to learn. Love for God and people will help a person overcome his deficiencies.

New directors of centers shall first successfully complete the training program prepared by the National Teen Challenge Committee. No new director will be recognized until he completes the training program and has been recommended by those training him. An evaluation of the abilities of the director candidate shall be given by the established center to the National Director of the Division of Home Missions. Should vacancy occur, the National Teen Challenge Representative shall be consulted by the Board of Directors.

2. Secretary
   a. The secretary of a referral center will be the key to keeping the operation running smoothly. Typing ability, filing ability, and bookkeeping, as well as a pleasant telephone manner are essential. She will need to be knowledgeable of the total program. Staff, including the director, may not always be available. The secretary will be the link. It must be seen as an essential part of the ministry. Records must be kept, correspondence taken care of in an efficient manner.
   b. A secretary must have training in typing, office procedures, and basic accounting; should be a dedicated Christian with an understanding of the referral program.
   c. Technical skills will not be enough. She must see the link between the job of secretary and the ministry to troubled people

3. Street workers
   a. They will be doing largely one-on-one counseling.

Spirit-filled Christians with Bible training and communication skills, they will need to be friendly and easily approached. An appreciation of cultural and ethnic differences helps.

    b. For the public street meeting and rally, they will need the ability to project to the people, be sensitive to the mood of the crowd, and be able to get the message across.

4. Child evangelism

Those involved with child evangelism need the ability to communicate at the level of understanding of those they are working with. Training in basic educational techniques will help in the sharing of the gospel. What is said of other workers concerning spiritual life and understanding the various cultures is also true here. Workers must be sensitive to real needs that may be the clue to helping—this is undoubtedly a learned skill by a loving heart.

5. Home visitation team

    a. Home visitation teams must have the same basic Christian training as well as a gift for basic problem solving. They must be acquainted with the resources that are available to meet many of the physical needs in order to get across the greater need of the gospel: an awareness of community problems, jobs, homes, food-nutrition, broken homes, alcoholism, drug addiction, delinquency, etc.

    b. The purpose of the home visitation team is to help solve basic problems and communicate the hope of Jesus Christ where there is no hope. Volunteers that are trained can be key people, with some basic skills for solving family problems. They should know what is available through the church and other social agencies to meet obvious needs. They will have had much experience of a practical nature, and will need to be trained to know how the community problems can be solved.

6. Jail and prison workers

    a. Not everyone is capable of this, but many are and can be trained. The spiritual essentials are the same for all workers. The prison worker must have a good understanding of the Judicial System, not as a lawyer, but with an awareness of the dos and don'ts of the prison system. Then the basic skills of introducing Jesus Christ and teaching Bible principles for solving personal problems are needed. Judgment has been pronounced by the Judicial System, so the worker must come with a new way of life for those incarcerated. He must also be able to work with the prison authorities cooperatively and be a man of God and friend to the prisoner.

b. Many young people are being held in juvenile facilities. There is a need to minister to these young people. A worker for this field will need the ability to relate to rebellious teenagers or younger children being held under the Juvenile Justice System; these young people often are from shattered homes and troubled neighborhoods. Their trust in the adult world is at a minimum. This condition is often aggravated by the Juvenile Justice System. Workers must be able to reach through these barriers to bring about basic attitudinal changes.

7. Other personnel, even though volunteers, should be Christians with abilities commensurate with their responsibilities.

C. Training

1. Provision should be made to orient and train new personnel for the job expected of them.

2. Ongoing, in-service training should be planned and provided for all staff so that they might progress and keep abreast of new developments, new methods, new materials, and especially new drugs, new laws, changes in community, the youth scene, etc.

3. Thought should be given for those who want to make this type of ministry a lifetime work. The training and experience can fit them to assume leadership in this program or other new or existing programs.

4. Remuneration: Many missionary projects are supported by the salaries the staff does not receive. There are those that want to dedicate a year or two of

their lives to a missionary endeavor and want to work sacrificially. Thank God for them. Those that want to make a career of this work should be paid a salary commensurate with their ability and the responsibility they carry in the program. This should be considered when preparing the budget.

VI. Outreach, Referral

The purpose is reaching the poor, whatever the kind of poverty. The poor include: people and young children in trouble, those battling drugs, alcohol, delinquency, sexual promiscuity. In preparing to meet these obvious needs, we must be conscious that each individual has a circle of friends who can be reached.

Also, he/she came from a "family." His problem may be the result of that family problem. He may be causing a lot of grief to that family, and they are hurting financially, emotionally, and spiritually. The church can and must minister to these people.

So the Outreach and Referral Center needs to have a backup of ministering people tied in with the local church community.

It doesn't take a super-bureaucratic organization, but it takes a network of caring people filled with the Spirit, ready to show and share the love of Jesus in tangible form:

Providing material needs

Providing friendship

Providing wise counsel; i.e., how to be a Christian,
    how to appropriate the promises of God

A belief in the miracle-working power of Jesus Christ.

It may be necessary to do some legwork—surveying what churches are available to really provide a caring community for the hurting people this one contact has uncovered.

VII. Followup in a Referral Center

A. To individuals

1. At an outreach referral center, many people will be contacted. There should be a plan of followup to every contact.

2. The center should make a list and build a relationship with those churches that will put forth the effort to work with those who respond to our ministry. Those

we reach that do not enter a residential program should be enlisted in the community where they live.

3. Christians in the community need to be enlisted to visit and encourage the new converts and disciple them into productive Christian lives. It may be necessary for the Teen Challenge workers to offer a training program for local church workers.

4. Bible correspondence courses may be a way of following up individuals reached through the helpline, in institutions as well as community. The "Discovery of a Lifetime" could be a first course; then courses from the Berean Bible Correspondence School or N.C.I. materials are available through the Division of Home Missions of the Assemblies of God.

5. There may be home Bible study groups that meet in the area that a new contact could be introduced to. It may be necessary to start a small group in an area where there is no Christian group. This could be the basis of a future church in a community without a solid witness.

VIII. What do we do with the people we reach?

The heart of any Teen Challenge outreach is evangelism. The love of Christ is reaching out to people in need. People are hurting physically, emotionally, and spiritually.

As we reach out and sow the seed, we will find these people. They will respond to the love of God expressed through his dedicated workers.

What happens to those we reach, or those that come to us or are referred to us?

A. Find out what the problem is, or the problem as the client sees it.

B. How desperate is the person to do something about it?

C. What is needed to straighten out this troubled life that we have contacted?

D. What destructive ways has the client been living that must be dealt with?

1. Use and abuse of drugs
2. Criminal activity
3. Promiscuous sex
4. Living on the street

     5. Running away
  E. The person has sought help; what is the living environment?
     1. Is there a home?
     2. Is there a caring Christian family?
     3. Is there a caring, loving church that will aggressively help?
  F. Has the person been confronted with tender loving care and the provisions Jesus Christ has made for a new life?
     1. Has the person accepted Christ?
     2. Shown an interest?
     3. Cannot grasp the idea of being saved but wants to try?
  G. Does this person need the protected environment and intensive training of a Christian Growth Center?
  H. Or can this person solve his problems at home in the local church now that he has been shown the way?
  I. If it appears that this person needs to come into a protected Christian environment to bring about a change in his destructive life style, what steps should be taken?
     1. This person should understand the basic principles of the program.
     2. Be willing to try.
     3. Be willing to accept Christ.
     4. Check out any legal complication to committing himself to a one-year program.
       a. Are there court cases pending?
       b. Are there parole or probation restrictions?
       c. Is the person of legal age?
       d. Are there family obligations that need to be taken care of before entrance into the program?
     5. Can the program accept the person at this time?
IX. Families and Friends of Converts
  A. Most every person we contact will have relatives or friends. As we minister to those we reach we should follow the lines to these people.
  B. The family of those individuals that are referred to the residential program should receive attention.
  C. First they need to understand where the referral is going, why he is going there, and what he will be doing.
  D. Second, the family needs to receive the same spiritual life

that the referral will be receiving. This could be the key to successful reentry of the individual. It will also reduce the pressure on the individual while he is in the program.

E. The same stages can be followed with the family as with the individual in followup.

SON CITY: A YOUTH PROGRAM THAT WORKS

THE WILLOW CREEK COMMUNITY CHURCH, SOUTH BARRINGTON, ILLINOIS
DON COUSINS

SON CITY, as the name implies, is a city incorporated in the Son of God, Jesus Christ—a city whose population, foundation, and development are centered on the teachings of Jesus. It is a community of high school students coming to know the Lord as their personal Savior and very best friend.

It all began in one of Chicago's northwest suburban churches. The year was 1972 and a music group called "The Son Company" was formed by the church's youth music director, Dave Holmbo. He decided that if they ever hoped to reach anyone with their gospel music, they'd need to have Jesus Christ come alive in their own lives first.

In August of 1972, with the help of Bill Hybels, some thirty young teens began to experience Jesus Christ through the benefit of music and Bible study. Under the guidance of the Holy Spirit, The Son Company evolved into a ministry of sharing, praying, studying the Bible, and developing friendships with Christ and with each other. The young people began to see their lives changed with real evidence and experience. Jesus had truly come alive in their lives!

Enthusiastic about their friendship with Jesus Christ, these thirty young people began to reach out to their own personal friends, of whom many were actually already church attenders. But they did not experience Christ alive in their lives. The group quickly grew to seventy. These seventy then began to reach out to their unchurched school friends. They told what God was doing in their lives and what he could do for them as well.

By now, they had 150 involved and a Son City Spectacular was held. It was a fun-filled evening of team competition, music, drama, and a message aimed at introducing non-Christian students to Christ. It was an amazing success. It went from one to two nights a week. The Lord blessed the work and it wasn't long before there were about 1,000 members. They were organized into sixteen teams. The two organizers, Dave Holmbo and Bill Hybels, decided it was time to organize a church and implement these same biblical principles on an adult level. They began to meet in a local rented theater, and then they purchased a large plot of land and built an enormous church building, complete with recreational facilities and educational classrooms. Indeed, it has become one of the largest church buildings in the entire Chicagoland area, seating several thousands of people and ministering to one of the largest congregations in the midwest.

From two dedicated young adults and thirty eager high school-aged teens, we have seen one of the most active, one of the largest, and assuredly one of the most dynamic Christian churches come into being in less than ten years' time.

When most churches are thinking that their youth simply are not interested in religious matters any longer, here is proof that the Bible is still the greatest tool in reaching people and building churches. For Bill and Dave, they simply believed what God said and put into practice what they learned from their Bible studies. Here is their plan.

A YOUTH PROGRAM MUST BE BUILT WITHIN THE STRUCTURED CHURCH, AND NOT SEPARATED FROM IT

The ministry of Son City must be viewed as a part of the organized church if it is to succeed. Son City is not a parachurch organization. In fact, Son City ministries are actually bringing high school students back into the church. Son City is simply independent in its focus—reaching and bringing students to Christ. To that end, it does need a certain degree of independence—but not separation.

Here are the goals of Son City. Following are the primary and secondary objectives for this ministry.

I. Build the Kingdom of God
   This aim is to build a community of people who represent God. The process begins when a non-Christian comes into the kingdom and becomes a fellow builder. It continues with fellowship, prayer, sharing, teaching: in all, internalizing Christ so that he sits on the throne of the student's life. Son City is resolved to build a community of high school students who can:
   A. Exhibit God's love
   B. Provide examples of changed lives in Christ
   C. Serve as examples to their non-Christian friends
   D. Demonstrate meaningful relationships
II. Produce Disciples of Christ
   On an individual basis, the goal is to produce a person who is radically committed to Christ, a person whose entire life is controlled by Christ. To be a disciple is to have all life's activities and relationships be Christ-centered.
III. Affect the Total Person
   The aim is to communicate that Christ affects the total person, not just a single part. Son City is directed to that same total person. Its goals are intended to meet the spiritual, emotional, intellectual, and social needs of the youth in its ministry.
IV. Meet the Social Needs
   The purpose is to provide a Christian environment where students can experience:
   A. Acceptance
   B. Belonging
   C. Identification
   D. Supportive friendships
   E. Meaningful relationships

F. Fun in a Christian context

V. Bring the Youth out of the Dark Ages

The goal is to communicate the message of Christ in a manner understood by today's youth. The message is the same truth that has been conveyed for centuries—the methods of conveying it, however, are twentieth century. Since a high school ministry must compete with all the attraction and attention-grabbers present in this world, the message must be communicated in a relevant way. It must talk to a student where he's at, in his language, so he'll understand and react. Christ's message has always been effective, but many times the means of communicating it have been ineffective.

VI. Create a Positive Family Influence

When Christ causes dramatic changes in a student, he will then have a positive influence on his family. As a result, it's expected that the student's eventual marriage and family will be a strong Christ-centered unit.

The desired changes in the student are in the areas of:

A. Speech

B. Behavior

C. Attitudes

D. Morals

VII. Build a Positive Self-image

Son City is resolved to help students know and believe that God cares for them and also believes in them. Students need to understand that Christ's willingness to die for them proves that they have great personal worth.

Son City builds students up, and provides a place where they can use their abilities and talents to sustain:

A. Self-worth

B. Self-confidence

C. Self-love

VIII. Lay a Foundation for the Future

Son City provides the opportunity to bring Christ into a life before major decisions are made. Such decisions involve college, career, and marriage. The aim is to have students make Christ-centered decisions and thereby experience a wholesome and productive future.

IX. Present the God of the Universe As Loving and Personal

The goal is to present God as a personal being who wants to

be the students' forgiver, friend, and guide. God must come alive for them.

X. Reach Students for Christ

Son City wants to expose non-Christian students, as well as churched students, to the difference that Jesus can make in their lives. At the same time, the Christian student will develop a desire for his unsaved friends to experience Christ's love.

XI. Give the Christian Student an Opportunity to Minister to His Friends and Win Them to Christ

The goal is to equip the Christian with the necessary tools to participate in Christ's work within the Son City ministries. This will enable the student to help his friends discover Christ and become his disciple. We call this "Full Cycle Evangelism."

XII. Produce Spirit-filled Leaders

A "Walk in the Spirit" is the totality of our Christianity. Son City builds students who can have a Spirit-filled impact on all their relationships and influence the world in which they live. It is only through Spirit-filled leaders that the Christian community can multiply.

XIII. Produce Students Who Will Have a Positive Effect on the Overall Church

Son City prepares the student eventually to participate in the larger body of Christ, the church. At Son City the student experiences the fulfillment of being a part of the church body on his own level. Remember, this is a youth ministry, and the student is not going to be in high school forever. He needs to be prepared as an active participant in the church as a whole. Son City gives an individual a desire to be a part of the larger church community.

Finally, Son City is dedicated to building the overall kingdom of God and producing disciples of Christ. Son City is building students whose lives count for Jesus Christ. And to those ends, each person is an active participant in the whole ministry and in all its aspects: fellowship, prayer, Bible study, teaching the Word of God, and ministering to non-Christians. Son City's goals are intended to meet the spiritual, emotional, intellectual, and social needs of its youth.

THE FIRST STEP TO AN EFFECTIVE CHRISTIAN YOUTH GROUP: BUILD UP A COMMITTED CORE GROUP

The reason for the success and growth of Son City was the thirty committed and trained leaders in the beginning group. Quality came before growth, training before numbers. The first goal of the two leaders that began this program, which now numbers in the thousands, was to take these thirty students, already members of an existing church youth ministry, and mold them into the core, the body of Christ.

This core is essential to your future. Without this core of trained and committed members, the outreach ministry is doomed to failure. Christ himself demonstrated this by spending three full years with twelve individuals. These twelve men later became the very foundation upon which Jesus built his church.

Here is the suggested process to train and mold your core group.

I. The Characteristics of the Core Members:
   A. Students that are in love with Jesus Christ
   B. Students that are in love with one another
   C. Students that have a desire to reach out to their unsaved friends

   When these three characteristics are present in the lives of a sufficient number of the students, say twenty-five to thirty, an outreach ministry can be launched.

II. How to Develop These Characteristics
   A. Build students who are walking in a mature, love-filled relationship with Christ.
      1. *Getting students into their Bibles.* Students need to know what the Word of God has to say and how it applies to them today. Christ speaks to them through the Bible.
      2. *Seeing who Jesus really is.* Students come to church with all sorts of preconceived notions: "God is a judgmental God," "God is a condemning God," "He is a no-fun God." Getting them to focus on Jesus Christ can rid them of their misconceptions. The aim is to help students accept that Christ truly wants a

relationship with them—not rituals, not rules, but primarily a personal relationship.

3. *Sharing the director's relationship with Christ.* The director has great personal impact in shaping and guiding the students. As a leader, he produces people much like himself. As a model, he must share from his own life and give evidence of his relationship with Christ. It is important for the director to spend time and establish strong friendships with the students. Luke reminds us that if the student works hard, he may learn as much as his teacher (6:40, TLB). The goal is to have students say, "I want Christ as you have Christ."

4. *Learning to value true and meaningful prayer.* In principle, the key to any relationship is the time spent together and the quality of interaction. Students can attest to this from their own friendships. Now they need to recognize that one's relationship with Christ depends on these same two qualities. Meaningful interaction between Christ and the student is nurtured through Bible reading (Christ speaking to the student) and prayer (the student speaking to Christ).

B. Build students who are involved in meaningful, love-filled relationships with one another.

1. *Spending time together having fun.* Sharing good times together builds deeper relationships. Fun times of camping, skiing, bowling, and picnics foster friendships between students. These activities develop camaraderie and break down cliques. The core has to be one unit of people, one body in Christ.

2. *Creating situations for mutual trust.* Trust begins by doing fun things together, leading ultimately to trust on a spiritual level. Athletics enable people to know each other in a nonthreatening, though competitive environment. Students must build solid, trust-filled friendships before proceeding to build Christ-centered relationships.

3. *Accepting responsibility for their ministry.* In this shaping stage, the students must be convinced that this is *their* ministry. They are the body of Christ, with all

its parts, each part with an important role. High school students can handle a great deal of responsibility if they know someone is counting on them and believes in them. This also negates the need for adult youth sponsors.

4. *Participating in meaningful projects.* Working together on worthwhile projects unifies a group. The students may not know each other well at this point, so rallying around a common project will reinforce their self-worth and bring them together. Some projects might be sponsoring a needy family, visiting and caring for the handicapped, deaf, blind, or mentally retarded. This will allow for the students to spend more time together and, thereby, friendships can grow.

5. *Studying the Bible together.* Sharing verses and reading the Bible together will help in molding deep, meaningful relationships—with Christ and with each member of the group. This is nourishment for the body of Christ.

6. *Praying for each other.* Many relational difficulties within the group can be worked out during times of prayer. Prayer also helps to build up and strengthen relationships.

7. *Sharing with friends.* When friendships have been established, structured times of sharing from one's own life are needed. It is vital to growth that friends share their victories, defeats, and what Christ is doing in their lives.

8. *Building deeper relationships through smaller groups.* Smaller interaction groups result in more personal sharing, praying, and trust among individuals and with the director. To build confidence with the students, the director should spend time with these smaller groups, establishing stronger ties for all.

C. Build students who have a desire to reach their unsaved friends.

Without this burden, there can be no Son City. Once the students are in love with God and each other, they feel as though they have discovered a gold mine—one they wish to share with their friends. When people get close to Christ, they become like him, and his burden for the lost spills over into their lives as well. However, one potential problem must be cited. At this stage of development in the students, they might prefer their group just the way it is and not want to change it by including others. If so, here are some directives:

1. *Go straight to the Scriptures.* Scripture provides proof for the students that there is, indeed, a real heaven and a real hell. They must be made aware that real people—just like their own friends, neighbors, teachers, and family—are going to go to one or the other place. It must be emphasized that they, as Christians, can help influence people's eternal destiny.

2. *Help students realize what Jesus thinks about evangelism.* "Jesus called out to them, 'Come, follow me! And I will make you fishermen for the souls of men!' " (Mark 1:17, TLB). " 'The harvest is so great, and the workers are so few,' he told his disciples. 'So pray to the one in charge of the harvesting and ask him to recruit more workers for his harvest fields' " (Matthew 9:37, 38, TLB). James says to be doers, not just hearers of the word (James 1:22).

3. *Share examples of the director's burdens.* The director needs to share his own desires for the unsaved with the students. This must be demonstrated and exemplified through his own outreach programs and efforts.

4. *Explain the emptiness of life without Christ.* Many of these students will have had the benefit of Christian homes and parents and will not realize the emptiness of living life without Christ. They need to get a glimpse of the void that is life without him.

In conclusion, you can see how a commitment will follow, when time is taken to build a sound core of trained students, centered around a committed adult who knows and loves the Lord. The core is, therefore, a body of people who have become committed to Jesus Christ and the building up of his kingdom. Individually, each of them is a disciple of Christ. Corporately, they are the body of Christ. With students who are in love with Jesus Christ and with one another, and have a burden, your Christian youth group will grow.

A MODEL SON CITY EVENING PROGRAM

I. Fellowship and Interaction 7:30 P.M. to 7:45 P.M.
The first fifteen minutes are used as a basic introduction to the evening's program. There are usually five minutes of singing with everyone's participation. The remaining time may be used for announcements, setting of strategy concerning Son City, and preparation for special upcoming events.

II. Teaching 7:45 P.M. to 8:45 P.M.
Forty-five minutes to an hour are devoted to the study of God's Word. Herein lies the key to Son City's effectiveness—expository teaching, i.e., teaching directly from Scripture, God's Word. This is the nourishment, the real meat of the evening.

III. Worship 8:45 P.M. to 9:15 P.M.
After the message, the students are now ready to worship. In fact, it is almost impossible not to worship.
Singing is an important part of this worship time . . . singing together with a spirit of thankfulness and praise. Psalm 98:1 (TLB) says, "Sing a new song to the Lord telling about his mighty deeds! For he has won a mighty victory by his power and holiness." Psalm 100:2 (TLB) adds, "Obey him gladly; come before him, singing with joy."

IV. Prayer 9:15 P.M. to closing
The last portion of an evening with Son City is devoted to prayer. The students thank God for what they are to him and reflect upon what he has said to them through the Scripture message. This may be a small group prayer, team prayer, or individual prayer. The students can be led in directed prayer time and encouraged to whisper their own prayers. Whispering aids concentration because the mind thinks so much faster than words can be formed. At least fifteen minutes is spent in prayer for specific needs.

As one of the most rapidly growing youth movements in the Christian church today, Son City has much to offer the pastor or youth leader looking for a model that speaks to the youth of our time.

You may wish to write for a book entitled, *Tomorrow's Church . . . Today!* It is a full description of Son City and was written by Don Cousins, a graduate of Trinity College in Deerfield, Illinois, and the team leader of the original Son City. You may write to Son City Headquarters, 67 East Algonquin Road, South Barrington, IL 60010.

EVANGELIZATION THROUGH YOUTH RETREATS
COMMUNITY OF CHRIST
THE REDEEMER
DR. JAMES C. KOLAR

"THE Church is an evangelizer, but she begins by being evangelized herself" (*Evangelii Nuntiandi* #15).

Last week I received a telephone call from a rather disgruntled pastor. During the course of our conversation he posed the question which was born of more than a little frustration and exasperation. "What do you do with young people today?" I sensed from the tone of the question that he had some definite things in mind that he wanted to do "to" them, but that his better judgment and pastoral concern prohibited such a course of action.

As I have traveled around various parts of the country during the last ten years I have heard that question, and ones like it, raised again and again. It was raised most often by people who were working with youth in some kind of church context and who wanted to do something for them. The motivation for the question is at least twofold. The first is an awareness that the church, or some people from the church, have a responsibility to do something for young people. Oftentimes that something isn't very clear.

The most pressing occasion for that "something" is to get young people to attend youth groups or youth group activities, or to attend religious education classes or events of one kind or another, especially confirmation preparation. Other times the "something" is to get the young people more involved in parish life by working on a service project or being on the parish council.

The second motivating factor is the awareness or the knowledge that a lot of things don't seem to be working all that well in the lives of many young people. Growing up through adolescence in the best of times was not that easy to do. And today, for many reasons, that process seems to have become more difficult and problematic for many young people. Identity problems, loneliness, rejection, relationships at home, decision making, relating to the opposite sex, school, facing the future, handling the ups and downs of emotions, drugs, and alcohol present some real difficulties for young people. Oftentimes, these areas aren't worked out in a good way, and the results are evident in the lives of young people through the high use of drugs and alcohol, boredom, depression, and general overall anxiety and frustration. It is often these things that motivate people from the churches to want to do something for youth.

The crux of the matter is the "something" that should be done. Regarding this "something," those active in youth ministry have available to them a variety of options that have been offered as the key to opening the door to the "something." For some the key is self-image, helping young people to feel better about them-selves; for others, it's communication skills, learning how to identify their needs, wants, and desires so that they can more effectively communicate them to others; for others, it's relationship building, meeting young people where they're at, and developing warm, positive relationships with them; for others, the key is liberating young people from oppressive structures that adults have placed them in—school, advertising, certain civil laws; for others, it's education that's based on the latest psychological and developmental theories; for still others, it's values clarification, helping young people to recognize and choose their own values and life styles. The problem, then, is not in finding keys to open up the world of "something," but in determining which, if any, is the real key.

In 1972 I was a member of a discussion with the staff of the St. Paul Catholic Youth Center on the topic of what the "something" was that needed to be done with young people, and what the key to that "something" was. The occasion for the discussion was the retreat program for young people at the Center. More particularly, the discussion was focused on how the retreat program could more effectively work with young people. In the year prior to this meeting, we had tried a number of the keys mentioned previously, with varying degrees of success. The retreat program was growing, some of the keys we had used were producing some change and growth, and yet there was a vague sense of something important missing.

It was that vague sense rumbling around in the corners of the discussion that prompted us to continue the discussion when we weren't quite sure where it would lead, or how we could grab hold of that elusive "something" important. One member of the discussion, during a momentary lull, recalled a comment that he had recently heard. "For too long people in the church have been giving good advice rather than good news." At the time it seemed a provocative one-liner, but we were not quite sure how to understand it or how to apply it to the matter at hand. We soon began to find more clarity in both understanding and applying it.

During the next few months of that same year, a number of people involved in the center's retreat program got involved in the charismatic renewal. For one, it was through a conference on healing in a neighboring state; for another, it was a chance visit at a local prayer meeting; for another, it was simply to observe this questionable new "thing." For each of us it was, I believe, a search for that elusive "something" that prompted our inquiries into the charismatic renewal. What we found in the renewal was much more than we expected, and yet it began to clarify for us the nature of the "something" that we were looking for—both for the retreat program and our work with young people generally, and for ourselves.

What we found initially were people who were enlivened with the presence of the Holy Spirit. Their praise and worship of God was joyful and enthusiastic; their stories about how God was active in their lives made it sound as if God was really doing something; their appreciation and use of Scripture to guide, direct, and shape their lives, their trust in the care and love of God, their amazement at the mercy and greatness of the Lord—all these things and more made a great impression upon us.

Those of us on the staff at the Center attended these prayer meetings for a short time, and then began meeting on our own to pray and sing, to worship God, and to share Scripture with one another. Soon, others who were involved on a volunteer basis with one or another of the Center's ministries began to join us.

Looking back on that time now, the "something" more we'd been looking for was the person and work of Jesus Christ. We had begun to see the enormity of what God had done in him and how the way to life was through him. We also had begun to see that the key to this "something" more was conversion. We quite quickly began to see that this "something" and the key to it was the absolutely irreplaceable foundation upon which our lives and the lives of the young people we worked with had to be built. We were, in a word, being evangelized. Since that time we have learned again and again, in some situations that were painful and others that were joyful, that the real power to live the Christian life comes from that one foundation, the foundation of what God has done for us in Jesus.

"The presentation of the Gospel message is not optional . . . for the church. . . . It is unique. It cannot be replaced. It does not permit indifference or accommodations. It is a question of people's salvation" (*Evangelii Nuntiandi* #5).

There is a current saying that has a bit of wisdom and experience behind it. It says, "Anyone who has a conversion experience should be locked up for at least six months." Many of us have stories about being overcome by those who have found the truth. In our zeal to communicate the importance of what we've found, it's more than possible to overwhelm someone else with our discovery. And so it was with us. We redesigned the focus for the whole retreat program and then unleashed it on our volunteer staff (those who work with the young people on retreats), in the fall of 1972.

We tried to do too much with too many too quickly. To move from the focus of feeling better about yourself, to communication skills and values clarification, to conversion and commitment to Jesus Christ in one weekend is a formidable undertaking! Relationships that had been built on one foundation were now being moved and deepened to another; understandings of what the goal of the retreats should be were being changed in substantial and significant ways. There were discussions, testimonies, new songs being written, tears, hurt feelings, and laughter—all at the same time. All in all it was an important beginning—the foundation was being laid.

The focus from that time on was the person and work of Jesus. The Scriptures and the life of the church became the reference points for how we approached the design and content of the retreats. Many of the same topics that had previously been part of the retreat program remained, but the focus was different. For example, presentations on self-image had as their major point of reference what God has done for us, and how the basis for our value is found in our relationship with the Lord. Peer pressure became focused on the question of the truth that we have been given about how we're to live our lives, and how we're to determine the standards to live by.

The overall thrust was to help young people come to a point where they could see more clearly that the greatest need in their lives is to respond to what God has done for them in Jesus. As a result, overcoming obstacles to receiving what God has done for us became a major element in the retreat design. Much of the difficulty young people have in receiving the Lord has to do with basic areas of disorder in their lives. Whether that disorder is in how they perceive themselves, their family, their school, their future—they need to respond more to the Lord's initiative in drawing them to his life than responding to the area of confusion or disorder in their lives.

From quite early on in the redesigned retreat program, we discovered some very significant things. They are in one sense most obvious from the point of view of the teaching of the Scriptures and the church, but they were not obvious to us, nor were they obvious to many of those searching for that elusive "something."

One discovery is the power of God's Word in Scripture. We found that we had tended to replace the Word of God as it's revealed in Scripture with the words of contemporary writing, especially in the area of psychology and human development. We tended, for example, to develop an area and a process around the findings or thoughts of a current theory, throwing in a Scripture verse here and there (if we could find one that had some similarity with the point the secular theorist was making). The real authority behind our approach had been current thinking. Replacing that authority with the authority of the Word of God was a significant change which brought much more effectiveness to our work with young people on retreats.

Catholic young people tend to be uninformed as to what the Scriptures teach about who God is, what our real condition is without knowledge of God, what God has done in Jesus, the purpose that he has for our lives, and how we can give our lives to him. These basic themes of our redemption provide the basis and the power for the Christian life. There is nothing which can replace these saving acts of God, and Scripture as it comes to us through the life of the church authentically presents and interprets these mighty words of God on our behalf.

The Scriptures, then, as they are passed on to us through the life of the church, are the standard by which we are to understand and live out our lives. This is true for young people as well as for those who are not so young. It is hearing and responding to the basic gospel realities that initiates the process of evangelization. It is these basic gospel realities which provide the foundation for or entry way into Christian life. It is no accident that the central elements in Christian life such as liturgy, ecclesiology, and moral teaching are accessible only through the basic gospel message. This may seem a bit abstract, especially with regard to the evangelization of youth, but it does have applicability. Its applicability is something that we learned as we began to redesign our retreat program, and as we began to implement our redesigned models.

Many of the requests that we receive from parishes, schools, and special groups are for retreats with themes on such areas as liturgy, confirmation, Eucharist, reconciliation, or a particular area of personal or social morality, dating, sexuality, drugs and alcohol, family relationships, world hunger, or a specific personal concern such as self-image, peer pressure, friendships, etc. These are certainly significant issues, and ones worthy of considerable discussion and reflection. There are available a large number of resources that make discussion and reflection possible.

The context for these issues or areas—that is to say, the perspective one would take as well as the principles one would use—comes out of the basic realities of the gospel. For example, if a person does not understand the meaning of redemption, of our need for a Savior to overcome the impossible situation we are in, and of how God has given us in Christ the way to a new life, in which we can be what we were truly intended to be—then the church's sacramental life will be essentially unintelligible and opaque. If a person does not understand the unique and irreplaceable role of the person of Jesus in our redemption, and how that is mediated through the Scriptures and the teaching and life of the church, then his following of the teachings of Jesus will be subject to other factors, such as personal preferences, cultural pressure, and the opinions of the latest experts.

The underlying focus of our retreats reflects the significance of the basic gospel, covering topics such as, "Who did Jesus say he was?" "What did he say about our condition?" "What did he say sin was?" "Freedom?" "Truth?" "Life?" "Who is the Holy Spirit?" "What do Jesus' passion, death, and resurrection mean?" The wonderful thing about topics such as these is that they form the backdrop for the whole Christian life, as well as providing the power to live it.

This reflects only one of the fundamental principles of catechetics: namely that *didache* (catechesis) is rooted in the *Kerygma* (the basic gospel message). Some time ago Bishop Flores remarked that many Catholics have been catechized without ever being evangelized. We have certainly found that to be accurate in our work with young people on retreats. I believe it is true to say that the real power of Christian life is in the basic truths of Christianity, and that as we move more and more deeply into those truths we will find not only more clarity, but also more power to live out their meaning in our lives.

One of the things I find most interesting is that when the gospel is presented, it often has an effect on the way young people experience the sacraments of the church, particularly Eucharist and reconciliation. At the end of our weekend retreats, we ask the young people to share one or two things that have had the greatest impact on them, or that made the most difference for them. The part of the weekend that is mentioned most often is the sacrament of reconciliation. For many it's a time of encountering the person of Jesus and of finding in that encounter forgiveness, grace, healing, and life.

The sacrament finds its power and its source in the gospel, and what the gospel teaches about who Jesus is and our proper response to him. It is not a new fact that young people, and older ones as well, are not noted for their frequent reception of the sacrament of reconciliation. The experience of young people on weekend retreats gives clear indication of the sacraments' effectiveness when it's situated within the context of the basic gospel. We have found the same to be true for Eucharist.

None of this is intended to imply that the situation in which the sacraments are celebrated creates the conditions for the grace of the sacrament. It is simply to point out a major factor in the fruitful reception of the sacrament. Nor do I mean to imply that all young people respond in the same way. The simple fact is that they don't. The major point that I want to make, however, is that the central truths of Christian life are found in the Scriptures, and these truths are given so that we might know and have the power to live out the truth.

I want to make two further comments about the focus for our retreat program. The first has to do with some tendencies present in youth ministries today. Many today who are active in youth ministry, either in full-time or a volunteer capacity, are searching for the "something" that will enable them to be more effective in their work with youth. Oftentimes, most often in desperation, the tendency is to grab hold of the latest idea or approach that is being suggested by somebody who has some influence. The latest thing can be helpful if it's integrated into an overall approach of how to help young people deepen their understanding of and commitment to the person of Christ. The difficulty is when someone takes the latest approach and sees in it the whole thing.

More to the point, the danger is to replace the Scriptures and the basic truths of the gospel with the latest approach. I have seen people like ourselves who have replaced the gospel with Transactional Analysis or assertiveness training, or becoming your own person, or nondirective approaches to working with young people, or values clarification. The list can go on, but none of these approaches can replace the gospel. They can be helpful, after they have been measured against the gospel.

The second comment is related to the first. In our desire to work effectively with youth, we run into no little amount of frustration because oftentimes the young people aren't, or don't seem to be, responding in a good way. This frustration can lead to the search for the "latest thing" which accounts for the bag of tricks and gimmicks market in youth ministry. Young people can be difficult to work with. They can be unresponsive, or worse yet, responsive in the wrong ways. I do not want to convey in my reflections on our retreat work the impression that we have found a model that is guaranteed to reach effectively every young person and help deepen relationships with Christ. We share in the frustrations and difficulties that go along with youth evangelism. We do believe that power to change young people comes through the person and work of Christ. Where Christ is preached and his Word taught, his life is released and the invitation is sent forth.

"Young people who are well trained in faith and prayer must become more and more the apostles of youth" (*Evangelii Nuntiandi* #72).

During the mid and late seventies the retreat program continued to grow and develop within our local area. Our volunteer staff grew from forty-five persons in 1972 to 120 in 1979. By 1981 it was 150 young adults. Many of them were young people who had come through the retreat program, and who were involved in the prayer group at the Center. The majority of them were college students who attended school at one of the colleges in or near the Twin City area. Some of them expressed a desire to do something like the early evangelists did as they traveled from place to place telling those who were there about the new life available in Christ Jesus.

Their desire matched a need that was developing. The need was being expressed by a neighboring diocese which wanted us to come down to do some retreats for young people in their area. We had, since the mid-seventies, sent teams out to do "away" retreats, but it was normally for a single group on a weekend. The neighboring diocese wanted us to do a number of retreats in small towns over the course of a few weeks.

So in 1979 we sent a team of eleven young adults with a staff leader from the Center out for a month to do retreats in that diocese. While they were in a town, they would do a retreat, spend time with young people after school, and stay in the homes of one of the local families at night. That worked so well that we did it the next year as well. During 1979 and 1980 we received requests from a number of other dioceses to send teams down. In 1981 we sent a team out for nine months. We did the same in

1982. This last year we sent two teams out for nine months, and three more out for a month, as well as sustaining our local retreat ministry. This coming year, we plan to send three teams of twelve out for nine months to work in twenty-seven dioceses. We also will continue to work in the local area with retreat teams composed of members of our volunteer staff.

Last year the teams, as a whole, worked with over thirty thousand young people. The projection for this year is over forty thousand. The opportunity for young adults to participate actively in the missionary life of the church is a great gift for the church and for them. The opportunities they have to witness to their faith and to share their life in the Lord greatly deepen their own faith. For those who go on the traveling teams, the experience of living with ten to twelve other young adults for nine months is an intense training period in practical Christian living. In that kind of situation, the best and the worst tend to come out, and working that through is a very good process of personal formation.

As members of a traveling team, they work in anywhere from sixty to ninety parishes or schools. They come back with a much broader picture of the shape of Catholic life in this country.

For many, one major discovery is how many of the needs and struggles of young people are similar, even though they come from different parts of the country. For others, a major discovery has been how little impact the church is making in the lives of young people. The media, contemporary cultural biases, and modern ideologies that have filtered down to young people have by and large formed the perspective of their approach to and understanding of life. This, however, has not dampened the enthusiasm of the young adults. It has, rather, intensified their desire to work harder so that the church can have more of an impact on young people. Some of the young adults, after having spent nine months on the road, take two months off and go out with another team for nine more months.

The primary thrust of the work continues to be evangelistic. The talks, music, drama, small groups, relationship building, and liturgies are directed toward that one basic end. There continue to be a variety of ways that that one basic end is approached, but the underlying direction is the same. A primary task is the development of ways to follow up on the work that the retreat teams do. In our local area we have weekly prayer meetings, monthly open house masses, and a week-long leadership training session at our camp in northern Minnesota to offer some followup. This year we are inviting young people who have been on retreats from the five-state area to attend the leadership week at our camp; and we are having a second leadership week in Louisiana for those who have been on retreats offered by our traveling teams in the Southeast.

We also are seriously considering other means of followup, and hope within the next year to have begun use of more printed and video followup resources, as well as to provide more training for leadership within local areas. It seems true to say that the major works of evangelization among young people have been done by nondenominational organizations such as Campus Crusade for Christ, the Navigators, Youth with a Mission, Youth For Christ, etc. These groups are doing an extensive and effective work among young people. Our desire is to do a similar work among Catholic youth.

Our own movement into this area and our growth in it during the last twelve years was not undertaken at our initiative. It was something that we happened into. We recognize the need, especially at this point, to be more deliberate and intentional in our future planning. We also do not want to plan ourselves out of God's leading and initiative. It's a delicate balance, and it's a balance we're praying to keep.

HOW TO LEAD YOUTH TO CHRIST
THE JESUIT HIGH SCHOOL OF
NEW ORLEANS, LOUISIANA
THE REV. JOHANNES HOFINGER, S.J.

CHAPTER

11

FATHER Johannes Hofinger is a man who not only understands young people, but has spent his life teaching them to follow in the footsteps of Jesus Christ. He is a scholar who in recent years has called the church in America, as well as all those who name themselves Catholic, to a new vision for youth. He believes there are two shocking facts that should cause great shame to all Christians in today's world. The first is that two thousand years after the coming of Jesus Christ, the vast majority of men, women, and children still do not know him, or, at least, do not expect anything from him.

The second and even more shameful fact consists in our own poor response to the Christ event. He claims, rightfully so, that the vast majority of those who fill our pews every Sunday are not really committed to Jesus Christ and his gospel message. In fact, he says, "They live as if Jesus had never come into the world."

How can we explain these two facts reasonably? It comes from our own unsatisfactory proclamation of Christ's gospel. In this excellent presentation, Father Hofinger shows how "head

*knowledge" doesn't necessarily lead to "heart knowledge." He says
we must not teach our youth theology which only communicates
solid religious knowledge, but must progressively "evangelize"
them; that means, "help them to accept, with youthful
enthusiasm and conviction, Jesus Christ as their intimate Friend,
Lord, and Redeemer."*

Last fall, Archbishop Pio Laghi, the present Apostolic Delegate,
addressed the participants of a symposium on catechetics
sponsored by the National Catholic Educational Association. In his
discourse he described the religious instruction which is to be
given in family, parish, and school as Evangelizing Catechesis to
which all those who serve in the field of Christian education must
contribute, according to their particular assignment. Especially in
a Christian school, evangelizing catechesis is the task of the whole
school; it cannot be satisfactorily achieved in class by the religion
teacher alone.

What follows is not a summary of the Apostolic Delegate's
discourse, but a reflection on what he very fittingly labels
"evangelizing catechesis" and on some basic principles for
achieving such catechesis in our educational work.

I. What Are Evangelization and Evangelizing Catechesis?
In the catechetical literature of today the term "evangelization"
has a two-fold meaning. Very often it means the first phase of
religious instruction of adult unbelievers, which leads us to a
first acceptance of Christ as Lord and Savior, and by this to a
first commitment of Christian faith. This first and basic
instruction must then be continued and deepened by a second
phase of religious instruction which is called catechesis proper.
It presents the doctrines of faith more in detail and deepens
even more the initial commitment of faith.

When we speak of "evangelizing catechesis," evangelization
is taken in a different meaning, not as the initial phase of the
whole process of religious instruction, but as a particular
aspect and indispensable quality of any authentic religious
instruction. It means religious instruction, as far as it truly
proclaims the good news of salvation "so that faith may be
aroused, may unfold, and may grow." In this sense
"evangelization" was understood by the bishops at the Synod

of Bishops on Evangelization (1974). "Evangelizing catechesis," then, means religious instruction which is not content with some transmission of religious knowledge but aims at leading to ever more conscious, committed, and living faith. By such faith, the human person says a free and truly committed "Yes" to God and his plan of salvation, which is centered on Christ, our Lord and Redeemer.

II. Some Basic Principles of Evangelizing Catechesis

A. *Authentic Catechesis Must Always Be "Evangelizing"; At Any Age Level It Must Be Leading to Living and Ever More Committed Faith.*

From children we cannot, of course, expect mature and committed faith. We can only lead them step by step to genuine religious conviction and commitment. They must out of personal conviction and free personal choice come to accept Christ as their Lord and his gospel as their way of life. Especially in high school when the students for the first time in life become capable of a well-founded personal conviction and commitment, we must not just teach them "theology" which communicates solid religious knowledge, but progressively "evangelize" them; that means, help them to accept with youthful enthusiasm and conviction Christ as their intimate friend, Lord, and Redeemer.

The fact that to many students in upper grades, and even more in high school, Christ, his gospel, and his church mean very little, is an irrefutable proof that we have not succeeded in evangelizing them. What can and must we do to win them for Christ and to a thoroughly religious outlook on life?

B. *Evangelizing Catechesis Assumes an Evangelized Christian Educator of Conscious, Committed, and Living Faith.*

In order to make a school or a parish program an effective means of evangelizing education, obviously, above all, the leaders, principals, directors, and coordinators of religion must excel by their conscious, committed, and living faith, and must be able and willing to share their conviction and vigor of faith with their co-workers. In the selection of the teachers, in elementary and high schools alike (also of those teachers who do not teach religion), committed and living faith is an indispensable requirement; it cannot be validly compensated by special professional excellence or educational skill.

The teachers need to be encouraged and helped for further progress in their life of faith. Responsible principals, DREs, and CREs will be eager to find suitable ways of bringing the teachers together in common prayer and sharing of faith, and to provide special opportunities of religious renewal and deepening, such as retreats and days of recollection.

C. *Evangelizing Catechesis Requires a Favorable Atmosphere at Home and in School.*

At home and in the whole life of a Christian school, our Christian values must be acknowledged and lived. A Christian outlook on life must be operative in the making of decisions and the setting of priorities. The atmosphere in which they live and grow up forms young people more than verbal teaching. A truly Christian atmosphere must not only characterize all classrooms of the school, but also all extracurricular activities, especially also entertainments and sports. For creating a genuine Christian atmosphere, practice of prayer is indispensable. But all will depend on the way prayer is sincerely valued, how prayer services, especially Eucharistic celebrations, are carefully prepared and performed in a Spirit-filled manner, and participated in by the faculty—not just out of duty, but with the fervor of committed Christian faith.

In order to evangelize the students effectively, the Christian atmosphere of the school must be paralleled by the Christian atmosphere and life style of the family. In the vast majority of cases we work in vain with students who come from a badly secularized atmosphere in their homes. The evangelizing task of a Christian school does not end with students; it extends to their families. The school will caringly but strongly insist on the active collaboration of the family in the whole process of religious education. It will in any way possible support the educators at home in their task of authentic Christian education. A close, friendly contact with the parents of the students offers many excellent opportunities of evangelizing their homes.

D. *There Is an Important Difference in the Process of*

Evangelizing Catechesis with Regard to the Age of Those to Be Evangelized.

In the evangelization of children, we must start with the fact that they are not yet capable of a full commitment before they reach high school age. So we have to present to them the details of our Christian faith gradually, before we can expect a religious commitment in the strict meaning. We lead them step by step to such a commitment, and in presenting to them the content of Christian religion we will try hard to present everything in the light of God's redeeming love. But we have to get into details, such as the teaching on the various sacraments and commandments, before the students can make mature commitments. We have, of course, to avoid overburdening them with unnecessary details.

In the evangelization of adults, on the contrary, we present first the very center of our Christian religion, often called the "kerygma"; that means the central message of God's loving plan with man, that God calls us to life with him through his Son Jesus Christ, our brother and Redeemer, crucified and risen. Through this proclamation of God's saving love, we lead unbelieving adults to a first deep commitment of faith in Christ our Lord and Savior, and only then we acquaint the adult convert, according to his needs, with the details of our Christian religion and try to deepen ever more the first commitment of the convert.

E. *Evangelizing Catechesis Is of Particular Importance for Adolescents and Young Adults. It Must Help Them to Overcome in Time the Religious and Moral Crisis Which Is Characteristic for This Age and to Arrive Early in Life at a Lasting Commitment to Christ, Founded on Personal Conviction and Choice.*

A religious and moral crisis during adolescence and/or young adulthood is perfectly normal and must be accounted as such. But the present situation of a badly secularized environment, which proclaims an unchristian outlook on life, most unduly aggravates this unavoidable crisis. Catechesis of this age group evangelizes by presenting in a convincing and winning way the solid reasons for our conviction of faith and the true values of an authentic Christian life. It must equally avoid an excessively rational and excessively emotional approach to religion and give to deep, sound religious experience its due important place.

It is at this blessed period of life that the Christian for the first time can arrive at true commitment to Christ and his gospel. Catechesis of this age evangelizes in the very measure as it makes Christ real in the life of the young Christian and leads him to an acceptance of Christ as the Lord of his life, based on personal conviction and choice.

Adolescents and young adults are, even more than the other age groups, exposed to the pressures of a secularized environment. Evangelizing catechesis must convince them of the irreconcilable opposition between the gospel of the world and the gospel of Christ, and lead them to an unwavering decision for Christ and his gospel.

F. *The Method of Genuine Catechesis Must Be "Evangelizing"; That Means, It Must "Reach the Heart" and Not Just Address the Brain; It Must Facilitate a Personal Encounter with God in Faith and Prayer.*

There is no particular method of evangelizing catechesis. Any good method and technique which fits a particular situation can be used. But it always must lead the students to a personal contact with God through committed faith and a prayer of love. Good evangelizing catechesis not only starts and ends with well chosen prayer, moreover it is given in a prayerful atmosphere and during the class of religion leads often to genuine religious experience. Audiovisuals will be an excellent aid in this respect. But they must be chosen carefully and used in the right measure. It is not enough that they make the religion class "interesting"; they must convey the respective religious message in such a way that they touch and form the hearts of the students.

Because evangelizing catechesis proclaims the Good News of God's overwhelming love, a deep, all-pervading and liberating joy is one of its indispensable characteristics. Sad and stern catechists may be good teachers, yet they are surely poor evangelizers.

G. *The Content of Evangelizing Catechesis Is the Gospel and*

*Challenge of God's Redeeming Love As Manifested to Us
Through and in Jesus Christ.*
What we proclaim is above all a "gospel"; that means,
"Good News." Its content can be summarized with the
statement of Christ: "Yes, God so loved the world that he
gave his only Son, that whoever believes in him may not
die but may have eternal life" (John 3:16). And St. Paul
adds: "Is it possible that he who did not spare his own Son
but handed him over for the sake of us all will not grant us
all things besides" (Romans 8:32). Whoever sincerely
accepts this message of love comes necessarily to a well-
founded optimistic outlook on life, since "we know that
God makes all things work together for the good of those
who have been called according to his decree" (Romans
8:28).

The love of God challenges us to an answer of grateful
love, a love which is proved by keeping God's
commandments, not out of fear but out of love: "He who
obeys the commandments he has from me is the one who
loves me" (John 14:21). To this our love now, in the time of
our test on earth, God will finally answer by his final gift
of love: "Eye has not seen, ear has not heard, nor has it so
much as dawned on man what God has prepared for those
who love him" (1 Corinthians 2:9).

Evangelizing catechesis distinguishes itself by its
concentration on the center of the Christian message, the
gospel of God's saving love. All the particular doctrines
receive their right and proper place from their connection
with the center.

H. *The Principal Agent of Evangelizing Catechesis Is the Holy
Spirit.*
Pope Paul VI in his magnificent Apostolic Exhortation on
Evangelization makes this point very clear: "It is the Holy
Spirit who, today just as at the beginning of the Church,
acts in every evangelizer who allows himself to be
possessed and led by Him. The Holy Spirit places on his
lips the words he could not find by himself; and at the
same time the Holy Spirit predisposes the soul of the hearer
to be open and receptive to the Good News and to the
Kingdom being proclaimed" (n. 75).

Authentic trust and openness to the action of the Holy Spirit will never permit the responsible religion teacher to neglect a careful preparation for the class of religion or consider himself or herself exempt from following the syllabus which determines the topics to be covered and the order of teaching them. But a Spirit-filled religion teacher is deeply aware that the technical preparation is not all that is required for conducting a good class of religion. Only a life of prayer can make the religion teacher truly open to the action of the Holy Spirit during his or her class.

LEADING A CHILD TO CHRIST
THE HIGHLAND PARK PRESBYTERIAN CHURCH OF DALLAS
THE REV. ROGER O. GREEN, YOUTH MINISTER

"LET THE CHILDREN COME"

Nothing but the best is good enough for our children. This is an old adage and needs to be remembered by the church and society. Many centuries ago Plato tried to encourage his friends to keep perspective. He said, "You men of Athens, how is it that you vie for places of authority and yet you have no time for children to whom you shall leave it all?"

I am thankful to God for the men and women who work with me in our church—men and women who do not "have time" but who *make* time to "feed the lambs" of the flock of God. At Highland Park Presbyterian Church we have 100 two-year-olds, 100 three-year-olds, 100 four-year-olds, and so on, right up to sixth grade. That amounts to at least a thousand children to whom we are seeking to minister in some way. We keep reminding ourselves that it is not only important to instruct the children in their faith (and we do), but it is also vitally important for them to share experiences of the faith with adults so that "the community of faith" can transmit the faith committed to its care.

In other words, there is both a corporate and an individual responsibility to be borne.

Recently, a Canadian churchman walked up to me after a morning worship service and said, "Are you the Roger Green that ministered to my children in Canada twenty-five years ago?" I acknowledged that I was the same. He told me that he was now senior chaplain of the Canadian Military Forces and that he had brought his son down to go to school at Southern Methodist University. His question came quickly: "Have you written any materials on how to organize a youth program?" So, with this in mind, I have set forth some of the principles most relevant to equipping God's saints for the work of ministering to children between age two and sixth grade.

EVANGELIZING CHILDREN

At the beginning of their book, *How Children Learn* (David C. Cook), Glenn Heck and Marshall Shelley say, "Jesus Christ did not intend for His church to be run by experts, by specialists, by professional consultants. He knew that his church would be made up of reasonably informed lay people who would do their best to carry on a loving and effective ministry."

I believe that. I believe that we need to discover new models for making the church what God wants her to be: a place to celebrate good news and to build bridges to the lost, sharing that good news with others. You can have a part in that; and children are included in the mandate, for Jesus said, "Let the children come and do not hinder them." Two or three important questions need to be raised. One might be, "What is children's evangelism in New Testament terms?" Another, "How is it done?" and/or "Who is qualified to do this?"

I. PRINCIPLES OF EVANGELISM OF CHILDREN—
WHAT ARE THEY?
There is no joy like it. A boy sat opposite me and said, "When I came to those sixth-grade Bible studies last year, that was the first time I thought seriously about my need of Christ and I committed my life to him." God's Spirit is at work; God is calling children to himself. The church is his primary instrument to effect this. The fact that we have institutionalized the church isn't God's fault;

neither does it change his mandate of what the church is for. We need to rediscover New Testament models. I believe that the church is the place for children's evangelism and that this is not only a biblical perspective, but that sociologically it is imperative to put the child and child evangelism back where it belongs—in the local congregation. Children need to belong to a community of faith and love, especially in this day of changing family mores and peer pressure.

In the gospel narrative when the children knew who Jesus was they trusted him (Matthew 18:3); when they came to know him they loved him (Matthew 19:13-15); and when they really encountered him they were spontaneous in their worship (Matthew 21:15, 16). Children of our day are no different.

Another principle that needs to be considered is what John R. W. Stott said in regard to evangelism (and he said it, I believe, in regard to children's evangelism): "There needs to be a lot more education in all of our evangelism, and a lot more evangelism in all of our education." That should be said again and again. We, in the churches, have approached the learning process riding on our own particular "rail." We need to ride on two rails. What we do evangelistically needs to pass the education test, realizing that the goal of all of our education is to lead children to know Christ and walk with him. We do need to teach doctrine to children.

The third thing we need to wrestle with is the question that John Inchley raises in his book, *Kids and the Kingdom:* Why is it that we in the church have failed to differentiate between children from godly homes and children from ungodly homes? Whether we want to or not, God does. He is the God of the covenant.

What that means evangelistically is beyond the scope of what we can discuss today, but it does raise the question of what is the appropriate response of the children of God. Oversimplified, it means that children from godly homes should be called to make a commitment to Christ (that is, to continue of their own choice and desire in a path modeled by parents), while children from ungodly homes need to be converted to Christ (that is, to experience a complete turn-around in their attitude to God, Christ, and the life style he asks of them).

We, as evangelicals, have been fuzzy in our thinking. *All children* need to make a decision for Christ of their own free volition. We need to encourage that, and when we start to think our way through this we will feel freer to preach in order to lead all children to a decision for Christ.

Inchley also raises the question of the age of accountability and challenges us to come up with the chapter and verse which authorized us to make profound statements about our children's relationship to their Heavenly Father.

He infers that all children are morally accountable to God and their parents, whatever their age. From each child-developmental stage, God expects a response of trust, love, and commitment.

So let us regroup. We are laying down three basic suppositions. First, God purposed that the local church should be the base for the evangelism of children, and it is best accomplished in the context of family and church. Second, teaching evangelism is biblical evangelism. We need more doctrine in our evangelistic program. Third, we need to understand what a true response of faith is within the context of child development stages.

II. MODELS OF EVANGELISM—HOW IS IT DONE?

I want to share with you some models that have been effective in our congregation. Although ours is a large church, I have for over twenty-five years seen these ideas work effectively in churches where the membership was less than 100 as well as in churches where membership was over 5,000.

1. The first idea is *Children's Evangelistic Week.* You can call it a "Children's Week" or a "Bible Adventure Week," or just "Celebrate Children." It runs for five nights after school, usually one-half hour after the grade school has been dismissed. The program must begin at a fast-moving tempo with happy children's songs and quizzes geared for a Christian and non-Christian audience. There is nothing worse than immediately excluding all non-believers by a Bible quiz; include secular as well as biblical quiz questions.

One key to making this into an effective week is to have some sort of "serial" material; for example, five film strips on the life of David or Paul; a five-day puppet serial on *Pilgrim's Progress,* or five Jungle Doctor "Monkey Tales" for puppetry. Puppetry can play an important part. One word of caution here: *Do not* design your program for seven-year-olds because you will never attract a fifth or sixth grader. Aim over the heads of first and second graders but include a song or two for them. A serial story will help provide continuity and, well done, it will hold the interest of the older children.

If you want to include Bible verses, *teach them creatively.* I prefer to make "the verse" the theme of each day. Then there is the heart of the program, one doctrine taught each day through a *well-told Bible story.* The themes I have found to be important are:

1. Meet Christ and all is changed (e.g., Zacchaeus)
2. Sin separates us from God and one another (e.g., Jonah)
3. Christ died for our sins (e.g., The Brazen Serpent)
4. Decide for Christ (e.g., Ruth)
5. Grow in Christ (e.g., Timothy)

Learning how to tell stories effectively or finding someone who can is the key to success.

Songs set the mood and change the pace. One other question is important: What time of year? The first weeks of fall are preferable. The beginning of the calendar year is a good alternative. Children's weeks should complement Daily Vacation Bible School, and if you have to limit D.V.B.S. to one week so as to include a children's week, do it. It has worked for us in outreach to the lost and it will work for you. It also means that the children you reached through D.V.B.S. are now being reached within the school year and can be channeled into a regular followup program (preferably mid-week) or the Sunday school.

III. DAY CAMPS.
The second model has to do with summer outreach. You need to ask yourself, "What are the needs of our church?" "What is the purpose of Daily Vacation Bible School for this year?" "Are there any other alternatives?" One such alternative is to have a "day camp" program. If you are not geared up to reach for the standard that name may imply, call it "Summer Splash" or "Street and Sidewalks Missions," or come up with your own name. At H.P.P.C. we hire three college students as "Summer Interns" to implement this program. We have found this to have a double value: namely, a service to the children and also an equipping of the student for future lay ministry for God in the church.

A very effective and attractive model was established by Jim

Welsh when he was associated with Fox Chapel Presbyterian Church in Pittsburgh. The model was duplicated by St. Stephen's Episcopal Church in Sewickly, Pennsylvania, where the Rev. Dr. John Guest is the rector. These models use "the track" at a private school for their athletic program, and probably the school pools for their swimming events.

A less structured approach can be made by smaller churches, and indeed we have opted not to include such a competitive approach in our summer outreach. However, what you need to know is the impact that such an event has on the whole community. They know that you care, that Christ cares about them.

IV. LEISURE-TIME EVANGELISM.

Leisure-time evangelism is the opportunity of the next decade. We have been working at this on the beaches (Children's Sand and Surf Missions) for twenty-four years. We have excellent results. About 50 percent of the children who come are unchurched. When you move these ideas back home into the context of the local church, maybe using a park, you will probably find that you are only reaching about one-third unchurched; but that, by God's grace, is what we must try to do.

The plan for such a program needs to be kept simple. The key parts that we have found useful in C.S.S.M. are 1) the focal program, fast-moving, fun, involving puppets and prizes, Bible stories, and singing; 2) swimming (a lot of one-on-one friendships can be built around swimming); 3) a Bible reading time—we have found it invaluable to use Scripture Union's children's Bible study packets (designed for use at camps) and to use some time to teach the children the skill of Bible reading; 4) games, not all competitive. Learn to minister to children in a holistic way and expect that they will seek you out when they are ready to commit their lives to Christ.

What is the difference between the C.S.S.M. model and the day camp model (Model III)? A day camp model runs for ten weeks—the leisure-time model probably for two. The more creative difference would be if the church sent a team of its college young people (including a few senior highs) to a beach or resort area in the state to run a two-week program of evangelism and discipleship aimed at the children of tourists between the ages of five and twelve years. Children's Ministries sponsors thirty such programs in conjunction with local churches (most of them along the Eastern Seaboard, but one or two now in California, the Great Lakes area, and Texas). The program has two main parts: The morning program, which is a simple, low-pressure presentation of the gospel, employing puppets, songs, skits, memory verses, and an illustrated Bible story, focusing primarily on evangelism; and the evening program, which is split between Bible Diggers (small group Bible studies) and recreation, focusing on discipleship.

V. KING'S KIDS.

The cast consists of twelve children, ages seven to eleven, who clap, bubble, snap, and crackle like no group of kids you have ever seen before. The program takes place in a castle, the King's castle, to be exact, but you will often see kids venture out on exciting little trips around the country. They go where kids go.

"The instant appeal of a first class story, worth telling, forms the basis for all of our programs," says Rod Brown. A great story has a magic all its own and characterizes the main teaching point of each individual program. The stories used are a delight to six-year-olds as well as to those ten times that tender age. The programs already are widely acclaimed in the Washington, D.C., area.

VI. "EXCELEBRATE."

Excelebrate is an eight-lesson course for preteens that meets once a week on Sundays from 4:30—6:40 P.M. In the sessions, everyone has a lot of fun and exciting things happen as they share together.

Some of the purposes of the course are: to build the self-esteem of preteens, to help children learn that they are very important to God and to us, to learn how to have more confidence in the things they do, to learn how to make friends and how to deal with anger and problems.

Excelebrate is a very exciting and dynamic course. It's designed to help a child develop his communication skills and build a healthy self-image. Self-esteem is the greatest gift we can give to any child, influencing the rest of his/her life. A child usually acts consistent with his self-image. If he sees himself as capable and able to communicate, he will act that way. If he feels inferior his whole attitude and performance level will be affected. Failure weakens self-esteem.

So this course is designed to create an atmosphere and program in which the child experiences success. It is the impact (the introjection) of success experiences that changes a person's self-image. It is not changed by cognitive input. We need to polish the child's self-image; we want the child to have a healthy self-esteem.

One parent observed that "my child has grown as much in this course as she will in the rest of her lifetime." I see such a course not only meeting a need but being an outreach into the community for evangelism and building bridges to new families in the community.

VII. COORDINATED CHILD AND ADULT EVANGELISM.

There are two further exciting models for evangelism that I remember from my early ministry. The first is a valuable way to get a church moving for God, and it involves a strategy that was used effectively by Dr. William Fitch, who was then pastor of Knox Presbyterian Church in Toronto. Before he conducted a preaching mission for adults (a revival), or evangelistic week, he would propose that there first be a Children's Bible Adventure Week. The children were the first to build bridges to the unchurched families in the community. Parents noticed that their children were singing different kinds of songs around the house after they had been at the programs.

However, this was not an isolated week, for it was followed up with a visitation program that used the invitation, "What this church has done for your child we think it can do for you. Why don't you come and hear the good Doctor?" And they came.

In many ways the effectiveness of this kind of approach depends upon the quality, effectiveness, and imagination put into the Children's Week. It involves more work than an adult crusade, but I want to assure you that it is one way to see that there are fish to fish for in an evangelistic effort. Let's learn to coordinate our outreach. This model is far more effective than the simultaneous crusade, i.e., for adults and children.

VIII. CITY-WIDE EVANGELISM OF CHILDREN.

The other model is a more ambitious model of claiming a city's children for Christ. It was attempted back in the sixties in the city of Toronto under the leadership of the late Lionel Hunt. This man had a compelling love for children that drove him to expect great things from God. We divided the city map up into blocks of one mile square, and it was our vision to see a Children's Evangelistic Week held in walking distance of every child's home in that city within the space of a year.

We marshaled all of the resources of the church that we could find. If any denomination had children's evangelists, we asked them to come to develop their own program within some guidelines. The outreach was endorsed by the boards of evangelism of the Presbyterian, Lutheran, Convention Baptist, Evangelical Baptists, and by the Bishop's Evangelism Committee of the Anglican Diocese of Toronto. I remember conducting some ten or twelve mission weeks in three or four different denominations in Toronto that year; but the full results will never be known till glory because of the untimely (in our eyes) death of Lionel Hunt. We must not forget his vision. There were probably sixty or seventy special weeks coordinated through his office. We need to develop this kind of trust among the people of God.

OUR PURPOSE . . .

Children's Ministries is a nationally recognized, interdenominational program which organizes and operates a specialized ministry to children, young people, and their families.

The mission of Children's Ministries is to bring the Word of God to children and young people through evangelism so that they might be led to a personal faith in Jesus Christ. Ultimately, we strive to foster in each child a desire to be a part of the local body of Christ in their own communities.

Through Children's Ministries, young people across America are encouraged and instructed in the development of Christian character, fellowship, witness, and a sense of vocation.

The activities and programs of Children's Ministries combine a strong biblical application of basic Christian truths with a practical application to the problems of everyday life.

As a complement to all Christian churches, we provide young people with quality teaching, leadership, and spiritual guidance.

Because children are the church of today, and the leaders of the world tomorrow, it is critically important that we reach them with the "good news" of Jesus Christ.

For pastors and youth leaders interested in the full details of Children's Ministries, you may write direct to the president, the Rev. Roger O. Green, 250 N. Highland Avenue, Pittsburgh, PA 15206; or telephone (412) 363-0425.

PART THREE

Outstanding Organizations Evangelizing American Youth

THE OBEDIENT CHRISTIAN IN ACTION
THE NAVIGATORS
RICHARD SMITH GREENE

The Navigators primary aim: To multiply laborers in every nation thus helping fulfill Christ's Great Commission by evangelizing converts, establishing disciples, and equipping laborers

CHAPTER

13

THE NAVIGATORS

1. We have 2,288 Navstaff—including 848 wives—committed to this aim, including thirty-two nationalities:

   Americans Australians Brazilians British
   Canadians Chinese Colombians Costa Ricans
   Danes Dutch Egyptians Filipinos Finns French
   Germans Ghanaians Indonesians Jamaicans
   Japanese Kenyans Koreans Lebanese Malaysians
   Mexicans New Zealanders Nigerians Norwegians
   Singaporeans Spaniards Swedes Syrians Ugandans

2. 390, or 17 percent of these staff are foreign missionaries . . . including 140 wives.
3. 774 of these staff are Representatives and Contact Staff.

TO MULTIPLY LABORERS
1. God used The Navigators to raise up about 3,000 new laborers during 1982-83.

2. Specifically, 1,009 of our laborers qualified as Disciplemakers for the first time: That is, they led at least one person to Christ and were the major influence in raising up at least one new Basic Disciple; 40 percent of these new Disciplemakers were Women . . . and 48 percent were non-Americans.

IN EVERY NATION
1. The Navigators minister in 691 locations:

Community 224   32 percent
Military 115   17 percent
Student 352   51 percent

2. We have a sustained ministry commitment in at least forty-seven countries, using thirty-eight languages:

Argentina   Australia   Austria   Brazil   Canada
Colombia   Costa Rica   Egypt   Finland   France
Ghana   Great Britain   Hong Kong   Indonesia
Japan   Jordan   Kenya   Lebanon   Malaysia   Mexico
Netherlands   New Zealand   Nigeria   Norway
Philippines   Singapore   South Korea   Spain
Sri Lanka   Sweden   Switzerland   Taiwan   Uganda
USA   Venezuela   West Germany

3. Seventeen of these countries have sent at least one Staff Missionary:

Australia   Brazil   Canada   Denmark   Great Britain
Japan   Lebanon   Malaysia   Netherlands
New Zealand   Norway   Philippines   Singapore
South Korea   Sweden   USA   West Germany

"Unless the Lord builds the house, its builders labor in vain."

NAVIGATING FOR CHRIST

Who are The Navigators? Are they a close-knit unit of retired Air Force pilots from World War II? Are they a special branch of the U.S. Navy with a confidential mission? How about an instrumentation firm, or even professional ship salesmen?

These are good and logical guesses. But each is incorrect.

The Navigators are an international, evangelical Christian organization. Their mission is rooted in the final mandate delivered by Jesus Christ after his resurrection and before his ascension to heaven. He commanded, "Therefore go and make disciples of all nations, baptizing them in the name of the Father and of the Son and of the Holy Spirit, and teaching them to obey everything I have commanded you . . ." (Matthew 28:19, 20, NIV).

For the past fifty years, the purpose of The Navigators has been to help fulfill Christ's Great Commission. Our objective is not only to win people to Jesus Christ, but to continue working with them until they are able to reach and train others.

During his personal ministry, Jesus expressed a major concern, saying, ". . . the harvest is great, but the laborers are few . . ." (Matthew 9:37). This need is as true today as it was the day Jesus spoke those words.

For example, the U.S. Center for World Missions in California reports that there are approximately three billion non-Christians in the world today. Most of these have yet to hear the gospel of unconditional forgiveness and eternal life through faith alone in Jesus Christ.

In response to Jesus' call for spiritual laborers, The Navigators help people develop a personal relationship with God and train them to serve Christ over their lifetime . . . no matter what the context. Almost 2,400 Navigator staff men and women of thirty-one different nationalities are ministering in fifty countries and all fifty states. They communicate the love of God in thirty-eight languages. In the United States, Navigators minister with singles, couples, and families on 144 college campuses, 114 military bases, and in 96 communities.

Making a permanent difference in the lives of people is an essential ingredient in any Navigator ministry. We believe the most effective way to help individuals to work and witness for Christ is to enable them to walk with Christ. Concentration is more on people than on programs, and on individuals rather than large groups. We therefore focus on the personal growth of believers, emphasizing the disciplined cultivation of fundamental habits of effective Christian living.

Navigator staff members conduct their ministries on a one-to-one basis and in small groups. They spend many months with new believers, teaching them how to study the Bible, how to have a consistent devotional life, how to memorize Scripture, how to pray, how to share their faith, and how to become more involved in a local church and its outreach. This personalized training helps Christians center their lives around Christ, apply the Bible, and reach out in love to meet the needs of others. Not only are principles and skills taught, but convictions and vision are instilled.

How can this training best be illustrated? For years, The Navigators have used the wheel.

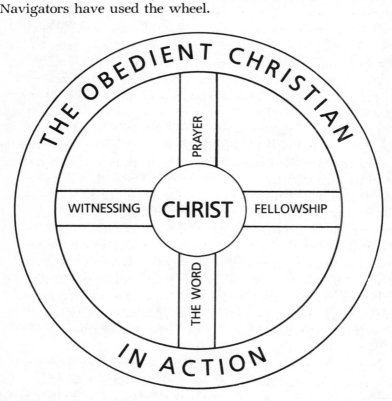

The wheel illustration, devised by Navigator founder Dawson Trotman and later refined, visually depicts the key components of a vital Christian life . . . and the areas in which The Navigators help individuals mature.

Just as the driving force in a wheel comes from the hub, so the power to live the Christian life comes from Jesus Christ the Center (2 Corinthians 5:17; Galatians 2:20). Christ lives in us in the Person of the Holy Spirit. We must choose individually to give Christ the place of true lordship in our lives and surrender totally all areas to his authority.

The rim represents the Christian responding to Christ's lordship through wholehearted, day-by-day obedience to him (John 14:21; Romans 12:1, 2). When we are actively obedient to God's Word, people will see the evidences of our Christianity. But some of these acts of obedience will be internal, such as attitudes, motives, values, and daily thoughts. We become like Christ.

The spokes show the means by which Christ's power becomes operative in our lives. We maintain personal contact with God through wholehearted, day-by-day obedience to him (John 14:21; to us through the Bible, we learn his principles for life and ministry (2 Timothy 3:16, 17; Joshua 1:8). A personal intake of God's Word on a regular basis is key to a healthy and growing Christian life.

Through prayer we have direct communication with our heavenly Father (John 14:13; Philippians 4:6, 7). Prayer should be the natural overflow of time spent in the Scriptures. When God speaks to us through the Bible, we need to respond to him in prayer. He also wants us to share our hearts and needs with him as well as pray for the needs of others. As we pray, we demonstrate our dependence upon and trust in him.

The horizontal spokes concern our relationship to people— believers through Christian fellowship and unbelievers through witnessing. Fellowship centered around the Lord Jesus Christ, with others in his church, provides the mutual encouragement, admonition, and stimulation we all need (Matthew 18:20; Hebrews 10:24, 25). Christians cannot afford to operate independently from other Christians.

The first three spokes help prepare us to pass on to others what we have received from the Lord. We are commanded to share this experience with others and to proclaim the gospel to those around us (Romans 1:16; Matthew 4:19). This involves friends, neighbors, relatives, colleagues, and yes, foreigners on other continents. We need to explain that Christ is God, that he died on the cross for our sins, and that we need to personally accept him into our hearts as Savior and Lord.

When we are living a balanced Christian life and are developing in each of these areas, then the wheel rolls freely. People will not see the individual spokes of the wheel, but they will notice the hub—Christ.

Since the ministry of The Navigators is an outreach to people, it can be explained in personal stories. How the organization began is an example.

In 1933, Dawson Trotman began teaching a young sailor in Southern California, Les Spencer, the principles of Christian growth. A shipmate of Spencer's soon asked him about the secret of his changed life. Spencer brought the new man to Trotman and said, "Teach him what you taught me." Trotman's answer, "You teach him," was the beginning of The Navigators.

Spencer did teach the second sailor, and the two in turn reached others. Soon, 125 men on their ship, the USS *West Virginia,* were growing in Christ and actively sharing their faith. They were practicing the truth of spiritual multiplication conveyed in 2 Timothy 2:2: "And the things you have heard me say in the presence of many witnesses entrust to reliable men who will also be qualified to reach others" (NIV).

By the end of World War II, men on a thousand ships and military bases had surrendered their lives to Christ and were learning the principles of Christian discipleship. After the war, this ministry spread to college campuses and numerous communities throughout the United States and around the world. In 1948, the first overseas Navigator missionary was sent to China. Others soon followed to Europe, Asia, Australia, the Middle East, Africa, and Latin America.

Exhibiting unselfishness, Trotman refused to keep his multitalented Navigator staff to himself. He adopted early a policy to "lend out" his staff to many organizations. Trotman was not interested in building Navigators but in multiplying laborers. Thus, he wanted to help guarantee the success of other evangelism and discipling ministries.

Trotman drowned in 1956 after saving the life of a young woman conferee at a Navigator meeting in New York. Lorne Sanny, friend, confidant, and co-laborer with Trotman for fifteen years, took over. Under Sanny's presidency and leadership, the Navigator ministry grew rapidly.

God continues to bless! Oklahoma State University is a

beautiful example. In late 1982, Navigator staff held evangelistic meetings in fifteen fraternity and sorority houses on campus. About 2,000 heard the gospel presented by Oklahoma businessmen. Over 200 indicated that they had prayed to receive Christ personally while attending these formal dinner meetings. Navigator-trained students and staff from local churches and other Christian groups are following up these collegians.

Navigator staff at Oklahoma State have also taught several dozen students how to share their faith individually with others. One-on-one or in groups of two, they intelligently and respectfully present the gospel message to their friends or to other students they meet at meals or elsewhere on campus. Securing permission from university officials, students also explain about Christ's death and resurrection at dorm meetings and then help students make commitments to him. They also enjoy, in private conversations, challenging their professors to give their lives to Christ. During the 1983-84 academic year, almost three dozen students and two professors received Christ.

Another strong area of outreach for The Navigators is the military ministry. Targets not only include all American Armed Forces personnel in this country, but also in Europe and East Asia. Out of an attitude of personal concern, The Navigators are committed to influencing enlisted servicemen and officers for Christ.

Military ministries are not carried out in secret behind a chaplain's back. Instead, Navigator staff request permission to be on base and coordinate their activities with the chaplains, especially through the official chapel program. One chaplain in San Diego, California, says, "I am thankful that The Navigators have helped me to be more fruitful in discipling others."

A very significant area of ministry where church laymen are being equipped to know Christ and make him known is in the community outreach. Navigator leadership have a growing burden to help bolster the ministry of local churches. One way to serve local congregations is by designing practical discipleship materials for the laity.

The Navigator 2:7 Series is a two-year discipleship training course designed for use by the church with laymen and women. It helps each believer to enjoy daily the richness of Christ's fellowship and to walk obediently, even when professional pressures, family commitments, and community activities compete for his or her time. The program's scriptural base is Colossians 2:7, which says, ". . . rooted and built up in him, strengthened in the faith as you were taught, and overflowing with thankfulness" (NIV).

Rather than offering a spiritual quick-fix program, this discipleship training course helps Christians focus on growing in between Sundays and not just one day each week. This 2:7 Series equips Christians with proven skills in the practical how-to areas of the Christian life. It also helps instill biblical convictions that can stand the test of time in today's secular society.

The 2:7 Series is being used in over four hundred cities in the United States and Canada and is also being used in fifteen other countries. It has been translated into four languages and is being translated into ten others. Several hundred churches are now incorporating the 2:7 Series into their curricular programs. Churches involved cross mainline Protestant denominations and also include numerous Catholic parishes. Participants include high school students, collegians, young adults, business professionals, homemakers, and couples. Individual lives, marriages, and churches are being changed. Men and women are maturing in their own faith and are leading others to faith in Christ.

An additional feature of The Navigators' work is Eagle Lake, a nationally respected camping program. Eagle Lake provides a colorful environment for adventure, fun, and spiritual direction for young people ages eleven to twenty-one. It is known for its excellent camping programs, professionally qualified staff, and ideal location high in the Rockies near Navigator headquarters in Colorado Springs.

Eagle Lake programming goes beyond the immediate joys of its wilderness experience. It plays a meaningful role in helping fulfill the mission of The Navigators. After a group of campers hear the gospel presented by trained staff counselors, several campers commit their lives to Christ. And all the campers are taught how to develop and deepen their personal walk with the Lord.

Measuring the effects of the overall Navigator ministry in the half-century since 1933 is difficult. What's exciting, though, is that The Navigators' global commitment to help fulfill Christ's Great Commission has not abated but still burns brightly. The vision begins with a heart for the individual. But the vision must extend to the whole world. That's who The Navigators are determined to help reach.

Richard Smith Green is communications director for The Navigators, a position he has held since January 1983. Before moving to Colorado Springs with his wife Lynda, Richard was a staff reporter and religion editor of the Chattanooga *News-Free Press*. Richard is a graduate of the University of Tennessee, where he became a Christian through The Navigators' ministry on campus.

TEARS, OPPORTUNITY, AND JOY
CHURCH YOUTH DEVELOPMENT INC.
J. DENNIS MILLER, PRESIDENT

TEARS

"John, wake up—time to get ready for church."

"I'm not going this morning, Mom," John yelled back.

"Yes, you are, dear. Now get up and get dressed. You know we go to church every Sunday."

"Aw, Mom."

"Come on, dear, we don't have much time."

"Well, I'm not going, and that's final." John pulled a pillow over his head. He didn't feel good about what he was telling his parents, but he was so tired. After all, he'd been out until two in the morning. "The stuff I get at church is so boring," John thought. "They don't know what's going on with kids anyway."

John's father entered the room. "All right, son, on your feet now or you're grounded this week and no car Friday night."

John slipped out of bed. He thought to himself, "Well, I may be standing up on the outside, but I'm still asleep on the inside." He begrudgingly got into his clothes.

"Hurry, dear, breakfast has been ready for twenty minutes."
John struggled down the stairs. He sat down and took each bite
as slowly as he could. John's father said, "John, I know you're
just trying to aggravate us. Now hurry up and eat or we'll just
have to leave before you're done."

John pushed his plate away. "I'm not real hungry anyway, Dad.
Let's get it over with, OK?"

John's mother looked at John's father and shook her head. "I
just don't understand why John feels this way about church." The
door closed.

Does this story sound familiar? I'm sure it replays in home
after home, Sunday after Sunday. Most of the time we opt for
simple solutions. Well, John was just tired this morning. Or, John
just doesn't appreciate a good thing. But the truth is that John
was giving a signal that cannot be ignored. Obviously, he felt that
church was not relating to his needs. John's parents felt that if he
went he might at least get something out of it. But in John's
heart, he was growing colder and colder to the things of God.

John's religious education has focused him on who he needs to
be and on who he isn't. The result has been a series of guilt trips.
He associates church and Christianity with unpleasant memories.

He has now discovered he feels very negative toward church
because what he hears there is unpleasant. Therefore, he tries to
resist going and becomes rebellious to his parents as a result.

Most of the kids at school who seem happy are in the party
crowd. He looks up to one teacher in particular because he seems
so secure and understanding. His teacher doesn't believe Christ is
God and scoffs at religion as a whole. He believes man made
religion up out of his imagination.

John begins to wonder if what his teacher says is true because
he doesn't see any Christians as attractive as his teacher.
Therefore, he concludes that, even if Jesus is God, it doesn't make
any difference to him.

After trying to discuss his doubts with several unsympathetic
adults, John decides to accept his conclusion as what he believes.
He knows this differs from what he has been taught in the past,
but he wants to be committed to a life style that really works.

So, until something convinces him otherwise, he will choose to
believe that it makes no difference if he believes or doesn't believe
Jesus is God.

Thousands of students are deciding to put their spiritual lives on the back burner in just this manner. Unfortunately, when decisions are being made in this way, information alone has little effect on motivating students to reconsider spiritual truths. In fact, a heavy emphasis on content may serve to convince them that Christianity is only something to be understood and believed, but not necessarily lived.

QUESTIONABLE INFLUENCES

The student of today is being enticed by questionable influences from many different sources. These influences have helped to create a generation of pleasure worshipers seeking their gratification from materialism, sex, drugs, and alcohol.

Secular companies selling everything from makeup to pornographic magazines are focusing up to 70 percent of their advertising budgets on the teenage market. NBC News reports their success by noting that the American teenager accounted for over 35 billion dollars in sales during 1977. This figure represents 20 percent of the total sales made in America.

ALCOHOL AND DRUGS

The beer and liquor industry aims most of its advertising themes directly at the teenager market, and has successfully lobbied in twenty-seven states to lower the drinking age to eighteen or nineteen. Many commercials present a very distorted image of love and sex, and encourage the young person to expect pleasure and success as a right, regardless of their achievements or productivity.

The fact is that the teenagers of America have been deceived by this vast appeal to their senses. The decline of the home and the astronomical divorce problem have left them without the counsel they desperately need to cope with these influences. The results have been tragic.

Teenage alcohol and drug problems have risen at an alarming rate. The national President of the P.T.A. stated in 1978 that, "86 to 94 percent of school children have had experience with alcohol by the time they reach high school." National Clearing House for Alcohol Information indicates that 70 percent of all school children drink; and 50 percent of the teenagers ages sixteen to eighteen drink. The medical foundation reports that 95 percent of college students now consume some alcohol, and that drinking patterns are set in high school. It is very evident that the youth culture has accepted the glamorous image represented by the commercials on TV, radio, and magazines. NBC News opened their television special, "Reading, Writing and Reefer," by stating, "Suddenly, in just the past few years, hundreds of thousands of American youngsters have become daily marijuana smokers. They are smoking marijuana with a frequency, and in ways that are potentially disastrous. Dr. Nicholas Pace, assistant professor of clinical medicine at New York University Medical School, estimates that marijuana intoxication is responsible for about 8,000 highway deaths—or one out of every six fatalities. What's more, 150,000 disabling traffic injuries are due to the drug's use.

SUICIDE

Materialism is at an all-time high among youth, as is evidenced by the figures on sales mentioned earlier. Students today possess more material things than any previous generation; nevertheless, at least 30,000 students will commit suicide this year—and the actual number of suicides, experts believe, is at least double that. Even more startling is the statement by Dr. Calvin J. Frederick of the National Institute of Mental Health: "I believe that among young people, suicide attempts outnumber actual suicides 50 to 1." A recent article in *USA Today* listed suicide as the number two cause of student death. The article by Anita Manning stated that the six most common causes for suicide are: 1. The extreme pressure to perform well in school; 2. the competition for jobs and colleges; 3. the fear of nuclear annihilation creating a sense of hopelessness; 4. the divorce rate; 5. parents who are overworked or preoccupied with their own problems; 6. frequent family moves.

CRIME

Crime has also become the undercurrent of today's youth culture. During 1977, youths seventeen and under accounted for a tenth of all murders, a third of all robberies, a fifth of all rapes, more than half of all burglaries and motor vehicle thefts, and 43 percent of arrests for larceny and thefts. From 1967 to 1979 there was a 98 percent increase in arrests for violent crimes among those seventeen and younger. Since 1960, arrests of juveniles for violent crimes have shot up 283 percent, more than twice the increase among adults. In the first months of 1984, the Baltimore School System reported seventy-nine cases involving weapons on the campus.

DIVORCE
The horrible blight of divorce has turned 17 percent of American children to latchkey kids. The family is disintegrating at an alarming rate.

Child abuse and incest are becoming so prevalent that it is difficult to keep statistics current. The Justice Department's Bureau of Justice Statistics estimated 4,108,000 instances of violence from 1973 to 1981 in which the offender was either the spouse, ex-spouse, parent, child, brother, sister, or other relative of the victim.

MEDIA
Many of the most popular movies of our day depict brutal violence and/or sexual exploitation of people. For example, an article from *USA Today* reads, "A carefree teenage boy is combing the kitchen for a corkscrew, but can't find one. That is, until the elusive utensil, wielded by an unseen assailant, flashes out from nowhere and impales his hand against the countertop—a bloody greeting that's promptly followed by an axe between the eyes. Not a very pretty sight, but legions of teens are paying to see it— and scream. The scene is a typical one from the movie, 'Friday the 13th—The Final Chapter,' the fourth in Paramount's violent 'slice-and dice' horror series. The film scored the biggest box-office opening of any movie so far this year, grossing $11.2 million when it opened two weekends ago, then tailing off to a still-hot $5.7 million last weekend. Its audiences are composed primarily of teenagers."

SEX
The current Pop charts for the week of April, 1984, featured these song titles: "1. I Want a New Drug, 2. Give Me Tonight, 3. They Only Come Out at Night, 4. All Night Passion, 5. Hold Me Now." It is obvious that teenagers are being fed a constant diet of sexual themes.

Overemphasis on the role of sex has bloomed into a venereal

disease epidemic. "Youth Letter" estimates that one in four high school students will have contracted some form of venereal disease by graduation.

As if this bleak picture weren't enough, students are demonstrating an increasing inability to identify, evaluate, and use spiritual truth to form their values. For example, if a pastor made this announcement from a pulpit—"I feel it is God's will that we share Christ with one person this month"—an adult would likely accept his statement as a valid discernment from God and decide either to submit to it or ignore it.

The student, however, would more likely respond by saying, "I don't feel anything like that. Besides, what would my girl friend think?" He evaluates truths and challenges by how he feels about them at the time. "If it feels good, do it" reflects his subjectivism.

He determines what he believes by comparing information with his opinion, and then he acts upon what makes him feel good. This obviously places him at a great disadvantage when he considers biblical absolutes and content-oriented Christian teaching.

HELP?!

But who can students turn to for help and answers to these complex and dangerous issues? Teenagers desperately need youth workers and volunteer adults who care and know that a personal relationship with God is the first and most important step in finding the answers.

Where can those qualified individuals be found? We would hope to find them in the 135,000-plus churches throughout our land. It is a sad fact that in the face of tremendous teenage problems, the appeal of the local church to youth is relatively weak. While secular interest groups pour billions of dollars into influencing teenagers, the church spent less than 2 percent of its budget on the same age group. In spite of a host of individuals pushing dope, selling material things and influences, the church has a great lack of clergy working with youth. Only 2.8 percent of the total clergy work with youth. The effectiveness of the secular world in capturing the minds and hearts of students is proven. One executive with a large denominational mission organization reported that 92 percent of the students who graduated from their youth groups failed to continue a life of commitment to God or to the church within eighteen months of graduation.

"Further evidence that religion, although important, does not have primacy in the lives of teens is seen in the results of a recent Gallup Youth Survey. A national sample of teenagers was asked how important they feel eight personal qualities are for a person their age to learn. About half (52 percent) said, 'religious faith' is 'very important,' below the proportions naming the other seven traits on the list.

"The perceived importance of these personal qualities generally increases with age. Older teens (sixteen to eighteen years old) give higher or equal ratings to all the qualities measured except religious faith, the importance of which substantially decreases with age.

"Also, Protestant youngsters tend to outvote their Catholic counterparts on the relative importance of personal qualities. The difference in opinion is largest for those qualities that make up the Protestant work ethic: hard work, obedience and religious faith, with proportionately more Protestants than Catholics citing these values as very important."

Local churches must begin to sharpen their ministry philosophy and skills in order to reach out to the thousands of non-Christian students in their communites. Our role is that of a consultant. We are committed to helping youth workers think through and find applicable solutions to meet the astronomical problems the church faces in youth ministry.

OPPORTUNITIES

FINDING ANSWERS
Perhaps an overview of church youth development will underscore our commitment to develop men and women who love and disciple students. We are men and women who are training church leaders to rescue the spiritually dead and develop the spiritually alive inside and outside of the youth culture.

We train youth pastors, pastors, and volunteer youth leaders to custom-design effective pre-evangelism, evangelism, and growth opportunities; philosophies of discipleship, modeling, teaching methods, challenging and leadership development. We research and author training tools and text books for those desiring to make a significant impact through the changed lives of others.

In the Scriptures, Christ and the apostles have inspired us by spending their earthly lives multiplying themselves through others (2 Timothy 2:2). There are so few effective leaders focused on the youth culture. Not many are focused on life change as a standard for successful student or adult ministry (James 2:14-17).

Millions of students and adults have yet to be personally encouraged by trained Christians to begin a love relationship with God through Jesus Christ that continues to increase with age. This will happen most effectively when someone *leads* the charge.

1983, A YEAR OF JOY, TRAGEDY, AND HOPE
We ended the year 1983 with mixed emotions.

First, there was joy at the remarkable way in which God worked his sovereign will in our ministry; many new opportunities were opened to us; more than a thousand students found Christ a fulfilling life partner; and hundreds of others heard his claims clearly.

But there was also a string of staggering shocks. Unspeakable horror stories of suicide, child abuse, incest, rape, alcohol, and drug casualties came to us by telephone from many youth workers.

The depression, hurt, and loneliness of youth pastors as they face monumental barriers and problems from without and within remind us anew of the enormity of our task. We are reminded that only 2.8 percent of American churches even have a youth pastor. Hundreds of thousands of students remain virtually untouched by any church that focuses on the Bible as a means to solve life's problems.

While we have been doing an excellent job, much more is demanded of us. The specter of thousands of students taking their lives each year drives us to press on, working from early to late in the day at loving, encouraging, and training youth pastors, pastors, and volunteer youth workers. Who else is there to motivate the Body of Christ to share the gospel with 20-plus million needy students?

Youth ministry reform must come. I sincerely believe that this is one of those appointed times in history when God majestically intervenes, confounding feeble efforts at youth ministry and promoting major movements of well-thought-through evangelism and discipleship. The key is the commitment of the local church. The church must understand the great needs of students and adults in the eighties and respond with a sacrificial willingness to pray, give, and become personally involved. In short, it is up to you and me, because we comprise the church.

Youth leaders express several needs in common as they consider effective ministry to students.

THREE GENERAL NEEDS OF YOUTH WORKERS

NEED ONE
A greater emphasis on training youth workers.
At present, only a handful of seminaries offer a major in Youth Ministries and the courses are mostly theoretical in nature. If there are no laborers, who can reap the harvest?

NEED TWO
People who have a long-range calling to youth work.
The average stay of a full-time youth worker at a local church is only eighteen months, while the average stay for a pastor is four years.

NEED THREE
Specialists who help the youth worker do his job.
A myriad of specialists exist to help pastors; however, practically none exist for the youth worker.

SIX SPECIFIC NEEDS OF YOUTH WORKERS

NEED ONE
Better defined working relationships.
Most youth workers have a very nebulous reporting relationship with their co-workers. Some do not report to anyone, while some report to several individuals. Often the pastor is not aware of the youth worker's ministry until a problem arises. What communication there is between them is often only admonishment from the pastor.

NEED TWO

A better-defined personal vision.

The average youth worker has very little assurance of God's desires for his life. The youth ministry is often a stepping stone to the pastorate or a temporary assignment. Young people need to be led by people who are called by God to lead them.

NEED THREE

Ability to relate a large-group emphasis to small-group discipleship.

Often the youth worker sees a contest between ministering to the whole group, and discipling a few. Pressure to gather large numbers of students forces many to do very little if any personal discipleship of students. This often results in students who turn away from the church and the Lord after graduation.

NEED FOUR

A good idea of what a student should be like when discipled.

When the youth worker has little idea what qualities and qualifications a discipled student should learn and apply, he rarely understands the purpose of the activities he does. His students don't either. Thus, they grow very little through them.

NEED FIVE

A clear understanding of the current youth culture.

Many leaders work with students as though they were the same as when *they* attended high school. This creates a communication gap between the church and the secular student which hinders the gospel.

NEED SIX

Ability to relate activities to fulfillment of objectives.

Activities for activities' sake is a dangerous trap many fall into. The program itself becomes the goal and no direction and purpose are established. This puts the youth worker at the mercy of the ever-changing whims of the students.

FOUNDATIONAL PRINCIPLES

These are only a few of many key needs youth workers face . . . but they can be met! I have seen much success at helping youth workers identify these problems and think through solutions to them. The solutions will vary with the uniqueness of each church, but there are several principles which remain the same. By God's grace, he has given me insight into many of these foundational principles.

Understanding and using several principles prepares a youth worker to begin answering these problems.

PRINCIPLE I
The youth worker relates everything he does to developing a discipled student.

This assumes that the youth worker knows what a discipled student is like. Most do not, so a worksheet is given to help them develop a profile of such a student. The rest of the training is designed to help the youth worker see how what he does, and what the youth group does, help him develop what Doug Hartman calls in his book, *A Guide Book for Discipleship*, a *relational thinking style.*

PRINCIPLE II
A student has been adequately prepared by the youth group when he can think for himself and make his own decision.

This principle has helped to reorient the youth worker's thinking on how to develop students. If the student has these abilities, he will almost always assume the responsibilities for his own spiritual growth and development when he leaves the protective wing of his parents and his church. This is vital if we are to stop the horrible attrition now taking place among high school graduates.

PRINCIPLE III
The youth worker's responsibility is to create an environment where the Holy Spirit develops students at his own rate.

Only the Holy Spirit can produce growth in the lives of students. God in his own unique way has entered into a partnership with his church to win and build his body. Our part is to provide him with an excellent environment for that growth. The student grows as the Holy Spirit uses the activities, relationships, and programs we make available. Now what is needed is a way to picture that environment and put it into operation. That is the focus of training in this area.

PRINCIPLE IV
The youth worker must have a clear personal vision to lead his ministry with confidence.

The word "vision" actually originates from the Hebrew word *chazah*, and means "to perceive, to contemplate, to meditate on." A clear, well-thought-through written record of the events and Scripture verses God used to make his desires known are vital in the youth worker's calling. A dream of future things becomes his motivation. Confidence and motivation are the key results of having a well-defined personal vision.

Our training includes assisting the youth pastor in:
1. Creating objectives and goals for the spiritual development of students.
   a. Identify spiritual qualities to be developed
   b. Determine the use of each activity to develop these qualities
   c. Determine the criteria to measure growth rate of the student
2. Developing a vision of God's desires for your life ministry.
   Procedure:
   a. Prayer together
   b. Coming to an agreement concerning the Lord's desires for interim period
3. Assessing the needs of the students.
   Procedure:
   a. To lead your staff in an overview of the youth culture
   b. To develop a survey for use with active and inactive youth
   c. Tabulating and interpreting this formation
4. Troubleshooting immediate problems.
   Procedure: Discussion
5. Creative modeling of spiritual needs and truths to students.
   Procedure:
   a. Brainstorm on creative ways to accent spiritual needs
   b. Brainstorm on creative ways to illustrate spiritual truths
6. Creative outreach to secular students in the community.

This past year has been a visible fulfillment of 2 Timothy 2:2: "And the things you have heard me say in the presence of many witnesses entrust to reliable men who will also be qualified to reach others." Although there is much more to report than we can include, here are four ministries we have trained. I'm sure you will be thrilled as you hear of God's handiwork in the lives of students through these men.

RICHARD McFARLAND OF BETHANY BIBLE CHURCH,
PHOENIX, ARIZONA
This has been God's year to use our youth staff on high school campuses and to see hundreds of kids come to Christ. As a result of their new faith, many of their families are now also taking part in Sunday school and worship services. One situation illustrates this well.

Jeff came to one of our outreach programs without any previous knowledge of Christ. Our campus leaders had been really praying that God would draw him to Christ. That night, Jeff came to Christ, accepting him as his Savior.

At 2:00 A.M. that morning, he called his mother to tell her what had happened. She rejected the call and said that he was stupid. Both parents severely rejected and criticized him for the next two weeks. This made him feel he was stupid. They told him that he was too sensitive and emotional. His dad said that he didn't want any more hugging and to just leave the Jesus stuff out of the home.

The kids in the group surrounded him with love and affirmation. They began to pray with him every time they saw him.

Four weeks later, Jeff was in his room getting ready for church when, out of the blue, his father entered his room and put his arms around Jeff and began to cry. He said, "What you have, I need." He promised that the whole family would attend church for two weeks. Two weeks later, he and his wife not only attended church but came to the youth group and complimented the kids and thanked them for helping in their boy's life change. They said that it showed them that God was real too. They are now committed to Christ just as Jeff is.

Jeff has a tremendous desire to help students find Christ. In February he challenged several hundred students to discover the life-changing power of Christ, mostly in large outreach groups and some one on one. Jeff represents only one of many changed lives through our ministry this year.

STEVE WILLIAMS OF THE FIRST CHURCH OF GOD, SACRAMENTO, CALIFORNIA

One of the most positive experiences we have had in our youth ministry in recent months has been the restructuring of our weekly meetings to a student-led, adult-directed approach. This has done more to foster group unity and personal ownership than anything we have attempted in a long time. In working to develop personal leadership and responsibility, we are also seeing an exciting breakthrough in student/staff relationships. As our youth and staff regularly share, study, and support one another, it is a joy to see them discover their ministry with students. I am indebted to Dennis Miller for these training skills and how they are being used by God to bring about a fruitful and effective ministry to our youth.

JIM PAGAN OF BYNE MEMORIAL BAPTIST, ALBANY, GEORGIA

On December 11, 1983, Dennis Miller completed his training with me at Byne. As I reflect on the year, I can see the emergence of a revitalized outreach ministry with the students. Our outreach level events have tripled in attendance, with close to 100 young people accepting Christ this school year. Our attention now is on developing relationships with our babies.

Our kids are increasingly seeing the need for spiritual growth. Just recently we challenged the young people to greater personal involvement in God's Word. Over 100 responded to this growth challenge.

GLENN SMITH OF CHRISTIAN FELLOWSHIP CHURCH, EVANSVILLE, INDIANA

This year started great. Five cheerleaders at one high school accepted Christ, along with three varsity wrestlers. We began our outreach activity to secular students, and during the course of the spring, fifty-four students accepted Christ.

This summer we began a new ministry in Evansville, Indiana,

and we are just beginning to penetrate the secular student community here.

DON DUNSCOMB OF GRANT MEMORIAL BAPTIST CHURCH, WINNIPEG, MANITOBA, CANADA

One girl in our group struggled all through her high school years with drugs. She knew she couldn't make a genuine commitment to Christ because of it. One day she came to talk, and it became obvious that she wanted to be free of drugs. I asked her what sacrifices she would be willing to make in order to be free from the drug situation. She said that she would be willing to make some sacrifices, but that she didn't know what kind to make.

I suggested to her that she go to all of the people that would be offering her drugs and tell them she didn't want to take them any more. She was willing to do that, and so she told her friends not to offer her drugs any more. She has been free from drugs for quite a while now and has begun a relationship with Christ.

Learning the skill of challenging has been very helpful in my ministry. I often ask, "What are you willing to sacrifice in order to allow Christ to change your life?"

CONFERENCES

In addition to these reports, God allowed me to speak at several strategic conferences. They include The National Conference on High School Discipleship, 1,000 delegates; The National Network, 80 of the most successful youth workers in America; National Evangelism Leadership Conference, 350 youth workers; Christmas Breakaway, 225 students and youth workers; several church conferences, over 600 students and adults. To the praise of God, the responses have been marvelous. Several lives were changed as a result of these speaking times. Praise the Lord.

WRITING PROJECTS

Several writing projects highlighted the year: Three chapters in *Working with Youth, a Handbook for the Eighties,* Victor Books; an article entitled "Destined to Succeed," in *Extra Ordinary Christian Students of America;* an article entitled "Christian Students, They're Leaving the Flock" in the September issue of *Moody Monthly.*

A manuscript on *Philosophy of Youth Ministry* has been

completed and is in the process of publication by a major Christian publisher. Over seventy responses have been received from many sincere individuals who desperately desire more effectively to minister to students. We are pleased to be able to share in this way.

YOUTH MINISTRY COLLEGE COURSE

A course has been written and taught for Northwestern College in Roseville, Minnesota. The reviews have been excellent and plans are being made to offer the course work to other Christian seminaries, colleges, and Bible schools. A taped series of the classes has been produced for resale.

For information regarding the materials and services of Church Youth Development, please respond to P.O. Box 24354, Edina, MN 55424. If we can be of service to you, please write or call (612) 944-9647.

A CHALLENGE FOR THE FUTURE

I must leave with you the sobering reminder that the task ahead is a staggering one—impossible but for God.

Our charge for the future is very much like one given 200 years ago by John Wesley, to a young, recently converted member of parliament, William Wilberforce. It was written six days before he died, the last document, in fact, that Wesley wrote: "Unless God has raised you up for this very thing you will be worn out by the opposition of men and devils. But if God be for you, who can be against you?"

Wilberforce faced a seemingly impossible task in challenging the slave trade. Public opinion was overwhelmingly against him; powerfully vested economic interests opposed and slandered him at every turn.

Wilberforce and his associates, who became known as the Clapham Sect, continued their battle for twenty years. Though they designed a masterful campaign, they never lost sight of Who was in charge; they devoted three hours every day to prayer. When victory came at last, in 1807, it came not through the endeavors of mere men but by the sovereign accomplishment of Almighty God. And their work not only led to abolition of the slave trade, but it kindled a mighty spiritual awakening which lasted half a century.

We dare to dream that ours is just such a time. And we dare to pray that God might grant us the courage and faith of those like Wilberforce who have preceded us.

I am eternally grateful to God that he has called us—you and me—to a cause such as this.

Dennis Miller is the founder and president of the fast-growing Church Youth Development Inc., a youth ministry founded in 1978. He is a much published worker in the field of youth and has seen his programs grow as much as 300 percent in the few years they have been in operation.

His primary emphasis is on the high school ministry, and he is available to give workshops and seminars in this field. His background includes city-wide programs and staff training. He can be reached at Church Youth Development Inc., J. Dennis Miller, President, P.O. Box 24354, Edina, MN 55424.

SERVING STUDENTS OR SELF?
AMERICAN STUDENT MINISTRIES
TIM ALTMAN

C H A P T E R

15

        ACCORDING to Dawson McAllister, nationally known youth communicator, over a million teenagers run away from home each year. In a video seminar held in Denver, "How to Get Along with Your Parents," McAllister said, "Throughout the many years I have spoken to students around the country, I have discovered that most do not have a healthy relationship with their parents. I believe it may be the single greatest problem plaguing the American student."

This problem and the answers from God's Word are the focus of this four-part video seminar created by American Student Ministries. This presentation, featuring Dawson McAllister, was done in conjunction with the Youth Ministries Department of Western Bible College. It explores student/parent relationships as they are today and provides biblical truth about how they should be.

Tim Altman, Director of American Student Ministries, said, "This video presentation utilizes a dynamic personal approach combined with a step-by-step workbook. It is designed, first, to help students identify the problem areas in their relationships, and, second, to display and explore the solutions God has provided in the Bible."

The question of student/parent conflict goes beyond just getting along within the home. McAllister says, "The whole parent relationship issue boils down to what a student's relationship with God is all about. I don't know of an area that causes as many students to stumble in their walk with God as does the student/parent relationship."

"How to Get Along with Your Parents" is the first video seminar produced and distributed by American Student Ministries. Altman supports this new approach to student ministry by saying, "Television is the primary source of information for American students. It has had a powerful influence in teaching them how to live. Because is has been a constant companion, it may well be more authoritative to these students than their parents. The situation is sad, but not hopeless. 'How to Get Along with Your Parents' uses this same authoritative technology, programmed with correct information. It will entice students to listen willingly and be open to making positive changes in their lives."

Altman also said, "Dawson McAllister is one of the nation's most dynamic youth speakers. His communication gifts are rare and powerful. His clarity and personal charisma are very appealing to today's beleaguered and confused youth."

American Student Ministries suggests many uses for this video seminar, including student/parent encounters and personal counseling. But the real story concerning usage of this product is its flexibility. It can be valuable in endless scenarios. The user can move the program forward and backward with ease to find a special section or a specifically stated principle. Because it is video rather than film, it can be used in total darkness or a fully lighted room. Perhaps its greatest strength is its biblically based teaching. In McAllister's words, "The Bible is just chock-full of truths about how to get along with your parents."

American Student Ministries, located in a suburb of Denver, Colorado, is also involved in coordinating a conference ministry to both students and youth workers, featuring Dawson McAllister.

DAWSON McALLISTER:
"PROBLEMS WITH THE AMERICAN STUDENT"

The American student is in trouble! Four years ago I delivered a talk to 600 Christian youth workers called, "What's Gone Wrong with the American Student." This sobering message pointed out that although Christian churches have youth ministries, they have not significantly altered the trend of spiritual ignorance and moral decay in the youth world.

We as youth workers have been serving God and we have seen God work miracles in some kids' lives; yet for the most part, American youth continue to slide further away from Christ. God is sovereign; God is going to build his church. But America is seemingly on a path of self-destruction.

Now, four years later, there seems to be little to cause us to alter our previous viewpoint on the dying youth culture.

Homes are not any healthier than they were four years ago. Drugs, alcohol, and the misuse of sex are still doing their menacing destruction to the young. Me-ism, self-centeredness, and rebellion are now part of the American tradition. Even the Christian students on the average are less likely to love Christ than the godless world they live in.

It has become painfully obvious that there needs to be a change in the way we as youth workers attempt to transform the youth world for Christ.

But what should our response be to the continued spiritual decline of the American young? The only true plan that will work to turn around today's world must come out of the Bible. After all, God has had to deal with generations of godlessness before. It would be enlightening for us to look into Scripture to find out how, for example, the Apostle Paul would counsel us on what to do to make a significant impact for Christ in the twentieth century.

One thing is for sure, the Apostle Paul would, in giving us a plan to change our youth world, first talk directly to us about our own attitudes. I believe the first thing he would say to us is that our egos must be in the right place before God. Let's face it, so often our egos stand in the way of lives being changed for eternity. But look what Paul says about this in Galatians 6:14

(NASB): "But may it never be that I should boast, except in the cross of our Lord Jesus Christ through which the world has been crucified to me and I to the world."

Now what does it mean "to glorify" or "to boast"? Literally it means to give praise, honor, or worship. It seems obvious that we were created to boast or praise about something or someone. The Bible teaches that we will either boast about Christ or praise ourselves. It is our own rebellious, prideful egos that demand that we praise ourselves. But Paul says, "May it never be."

Now if there was ever a person who had good reason to boast about himself it was the Apostle Paul. In Philippians 3:4-6, you see he had seemingly every reason to boast about himself, but he refused to do so.

Most of us as youth workers also seem to have reasons to boast. Some of us are really good with kids one on one, while others are gifted communicators, or administrators, or counselors. There is a lot of power in working with teenagers. Students are hurting so much that when we appear on their scene with answers that work, we get a following.

It's easy to get an ego-feed in youth ministry, yet God does not want us boasting about our gifts and power, but about Christ and the Cross.

In the early seventies I heard a youth speaker, Josh McDowell, for the very first time. I said to myself, "I sure would like to be like Josh." Several years later, with my traveling and speaking ministry already launched, I met Josh again at Arrowhead Springs, the headquarters of Campus Crusade for Christ. I happened to be speaking that night and asked Josh if he would come and critique my message.

What a thrill it was that night when I looked out over the audience and saw Josh McDowell in the crowd. After the meeting Josh and I went out for coffee. Looking for some affirmation and for an ego boost, I said to Josh, "You heard me speak, what do you think? Do you think I have the shots?"

I shall never forget his reply. He said, "Dawson, of course you have the shots, that's why you're up there." He continued, "Let me ask you a question, would you be willing to be an usher in a Billy Graham Crusade?"

You see, many of us with such strong egos wouldn't humble ourselves to be an usher in a crusade. In fact, often youth workers are not glorying in the Cross. We are glorying in ourselves and using the Cross for our own advancements. And so we get on the treadmill. We brag about how many are in our youth group, and we church hop, competing with the youth minister down the street, and always looking for advancement up the career ladder.

But Paul is clear on all of this frustrating activity. He said, "May it never be. The Bible says that we should 'glory in the Cross.' " The Cross is ugly, cruel, and degrading—the very opposite of pride and puffing ourselves up. The world looks for the ego-feed, anything to puff itself up and make itself look better. But that is not God's way.

Teenagers are looking for someone different from the world, someone who is so caught up in a cause that he is not constantly trying to feed his ego. When they find someone like that they will follow that person.

When the kids in our youth group look at us, what do they see? Do they see us glorying in the Cross or do they see us being all caught up in power, charm, gifts, sureness, etc.? What do they see? Do they see in our life style a living model that says, "God forbid, save I glory and boast in the Cross of Jesus Christ." Without this truth being lived out in us, we will never see a lost world changed.

—*Dawson McAllister*

Dawson McAllister, one of the nation's top communicators, has spoken to more than a million high school students during the past twelve years. He has also written seven books to further help students grow in their personal relationship with God and their peers.

In 1973 Dawson began a nonprofit organization called Shepherd Productions. Shepherd Productions developed a nation-wide conference schedule consisting of student relationships conferences and "Walk to the Cross" conferences. These meetings offer students and youth leaders an opportunity to mix with their peers in the exciting atmosphere of teaching, music, and worship.

These conferences make use of the different manuals that Dawson has written for high school students. His books include:

Discussion Manual for Student Relationships, vol. 1, 2, & 3
Discussion Manual for Student Discipleship, vol. 1 & 2

A Walk with Christ to the Cross: A Discussion Manual
A Walk with Christ Through the Resurrection: A Discussion
Manual

In addition to the above-mentioned conferences, Dawson
McAllister speaks for numerous organizations and churches,
including Youth For Christ, Campus Crusade for Christ, Youth
Specialties, denominational conferences, camps, and high school
and college groups.

Dawson's formal education includes undergraduate study at
Bethel College in St. Paul, Minnesota, and graduate work at Talbot
Theological Seminary in La Mirada, California. His expertise in
working with youth comes from being a youth pastor, running a
coffee house for "street people," being a probation officer, an elder
in a local church, and spending consistent time with students on
the high school campus. He has also hosted a high school
television show which ran for fourteen weeks and aired in
twenty-two cities coast to coast.

Dawson and Ruth Hill Fulton married in 1977. They live near
Baily, Colorado, about fifty miles west of Denver in the beautiful
Rockies, with their newly adopted infant son, Franklin Fulton.
Dawson's special interests include his great love for horses and
riding in the national forest.

For more information on "How to Get Along with Your Parents," or any aspect of this
ministry, contact American Student Ministries, P.O. Box 465, Morrison, CO 80465, or call
(303) 761-8696.

INVOLVING YOUTH IN MISSIONS
TEEN MISSIONS INTERNATIONAL
ROBERT M. BLAND, DIRECTOR

INVOLVING YOUTH

"Come back when you finish college," many teenagers are told, "and then you can get involved in the work of the Lord." There is a need to gear missions to youth and youth to missions. For this reason, Teen Missions International, Inc., was formed in 1970. If we fail to reach young people at that age level they will fail to develop the missionary vision and compassion necessary to get the training for service in the future.

When the idea of a missionary organization for young people was formed, it was felt that a team needed to do more than simply visit a mission station. The teenagers needed to accomplish something while they were there, so that they would feel a part of the work after returning home. Consequently work projects were planned. The program has expanded to include evangelism projects as well. Our purpose on a Teen Missions team is not to go to a foreign place for sightseeing, but to spiritually build teenagers and expose them to every facet of missions—in hopes that they will "catch" a missionary vision, begin mission work immediately in their churches when they return home, and prepare, as God leads them, for future missionary service.

Today, teen missions alumni are serving around the world as full-time missionaries under the auspices of mission boards such as World Evangelization Crusade, International Crusades, Operation Mobilization, Wycliffe Bible Translators, and many others. Many are currently in Bible schools preparing for the areas that God has called them to. Many still too young for college or career have become active in their local congregations and church outreaches.

One girl who has served on three Teen Missions teams before and immediately after graduation from high school has this to say: "After the first team I went on I knew that I would never be the same. When I returned home that year from Honduras, my parents realized as well the amazing transformation that the Lord had put me through. My attitudes, my words, my actions, my thoughts, and my goals completely changed—not to mention my grades in school! In the seven years since that first team experience, God has not ceased to work in me. As Philippians 1:6 states, 'Being confident of this very thing, that he which hath begun a good work in you will continue to perform it until the day of Christ Jesus.' That verse has become true in my life."

TEEN MISSIONS OFFERS TEENAGERS AND ADULTS SERVICE OPPORTUNITIES

Work and evangelistic teams are sent out around the world each summer. Since the mission's founding, over 12,000 teenagers have served the Lord as team members in fifty-eight countries including Nepal, Papua New Guinea, El Salvador, Norway, Korea, China, and Egypt.

With each team, six adult leaders are sent to supervise, take care of, and discipline the teenagers. All leaders are carefully screened and have attended a Teen Missions Team Leader Seminar. This is a thorough one-week program required before taking a team on the mission field. During Team Leader Seminar the potential leaders are taught how to deal with teenagers, as well as the policies and practices of Teen Missions. David and Diane Rodriguez said of their seminar, "You have no idea what a wonderful blessing we received from the seminar. It was truly a very encouraging and challenging time. We just thank the Lord for giving us such an opportunity. The discipline of having devotions and Bible study have set a precedent in our lives. We have always tried to get into the Word each day, but now we needn't just try because it has become a habit."

It is very important that each team we send does not become a burden to the host mission. We seek not to hinder the missionary by using all of his or her time, but to be of help. Many missions have had a bad experience involving a couple of kids visiting for a summer to "help." Practically every mission organization has had its hands burned by having a few kids visit for the summer to work with the mission. Often the teens lacked motivation and didn't really want to work, or perhaps they came only to sightsee and didn't have the proper concern for the mission. Many times the missionary is forced to become a baby-sitter for the visiting teenagers and loses effectiveness in his or her own work for lack of time.

Appearance and the testimony of some teenagers has been a problem for mission organizations. Often missionaries end up "footing the bill" for visiting teens. Since missionaries generally live on a limited income, having to provide food for a couple of extra people can really cut into the budget. This places the missionary in an embarrassing situation, especially if the teens are from a home church that is supporting the missionary. To overcome the hindrance and conceptions that many mission boards have, Teen Missions endeavors to properly train the teens. They are trained to be a help and not an embarrassment to the mission with which they are working. Implementing the training on the field, of course, is greatly dependent upon the leadership of the team. A missionary in Colombia wrote: "I confess we were somewhat fearful of what the outcome might be with thirty teenagers descending upon us. From the news media one wonders, 'Can any good thing come out of the teens of the U.S.?' We want you to know that we were more than happy with your Colombia team."

BOOT CAMP
One might ask, "How can you train so many teenagers to be well behaved—much less put up buildings and evangelize? I can't even get Johnny to do the dishes!" At the Lord's Boot Camp Johnny

and Sally do their own dishes, as well as many other things they never dreamed of doing. The Lord's Boot Camp is a two-week tent-type training camp designed to acquaint guys, girls, and adult leaders with conditions and customs of the mission field. Teens get up at the early hour of 5:30 A.M. and work hard all day. Classes include laying blocks, mixing mortar, tying steel, personal evangelism, Bible memory, music (teams have many opportunities on the field to do open-air meetings and presentations in churches), letter writing, and even learning to do laundry by hand. A timed obstacle course with a maze of tires, rope swings over a moat, the twenty-five-foot-cargo net Jacob's Ladder, and a twelve-foot wall, among other things, is used to unify each team and teach them how to work together. Boot Camp is not all hard labor because the training emphasizes the spiritual man as well as the physical. Daily personal devotions, team prayer times, and evening rallies are a large part of the training. Boot Camp climaxes with a commissioning of teens and leaders, as teams depart for their particular field of service.

Boot Camps are now being operated in several different countries including Scotland, India, South Africa, Colombia, and the Philippine Islands. In these and other countries national team members do work and evangelism projects in their own countries, with the exception of European teens who meet in Scotland for Boot Camp and serve on teams throughout Europe. Doors are closing in many countries, but through the Teen Missions Overseas program we can train an average of 120 missionaries per Boot Camp to minister to their own people when we no longer are able to go.

One need not feel guilty about disciplining someone else's children. We cannot take a team to a foreign country or within the U.S. where there are dangers without organization and discipline. One teen's irresponsible act could hinder the work of a mission board for many years. Teen Missions' policies are not just a set of rules to have rules, but are policies that have grown out of many years of experience on over 469 teams in fifty-eight countries. The most common mode of discipline used is "Special Blessings Training." It is an effective extra-work detail accompanied by a short devotional which is given by the detail supervisor. Should a severe discipline problem be encountered, the teenager is sent home at his or her parents' expense. The ministry of a team will not be hindered by one rebellious teen. One mother shares, "Wendy had been a typical rebellious teenager for some years and always told us, 'You won't get me on the mission field.' She went on a Teen Missions team simply because she saw how other teens in our church had changed after their summers with TMI. In September she arrived home having committed her life to the Lord for full-time service! Now she is working to earn enough money for Bible school. She plans to train as a teacher so that she can teach on the mission field. We are grateful to God and to Teen Missions."

Prior to involvement with Teen Missions, teenagers are not screened in any way, but accepted on a first come, first serve basis. However, there is a "self-screening" process that each teenager goes through. If they come we believe that the Lord has brought them here. A teen must face the challenge of trusting in God to supply his support, and of giving up his or her summer to work for the Lord. Teenagers go through two very tough weeks of training with very strict rules as far as dating, dress, and discipline. If a teen isn't willing to meet those challenges, he won't come. We get all kinds. Anyone, age thirteen and up, is eligible to serve on a Teen Missions team. Teens simply need to be willing to work and abide by Christian standards. A handicapped teen may still serve on a team as long as he or she is willing to work at the things he is able to do and it isn't against the doctor's orders. One totally blind young man commented, "Because of this summer I have made a sincere commitment to the Lord to go into full-time Christian service, no matter what the cost. I don't know what the future holds, but I am willing." Teen Missions is trying to screen kids *into* missions, not out! There is no racial, ethnic, or denominational discrimination.

BRINGING PEOPLE TOGETHER
We seek to be truly an interdenominational ministry. We believe that the teaching of a specific doctrine is the responsibility of the local church, and have agreed to disagree over the controversial doctrines that divide the church, and to work together as Christians for the sake of the gospel. We do not want to become like porcupines who cannot work together for sticking one another.

"Isn't a team expensive? How can a teenager save that much

money?" In 1984 the team cost ranged from $1,190 to just over $3,000. A valuable lesson for each teen, and a humbling experience for some, is that of raising missionary support. Upon receipt of a registration form, registration fee, and photograph, Teen Missions prints and mails a Teen Team Packet. The packet includes printed letters with the teen's picture on them explaining their work or evangelism project. Teens are to mail letters to friends, relatives, church people, youth groups, etc. The letter states that the teen has been accepted by Teen Missions for a team and asks friends to enable Teen Missions to cover his or her missionary expenses by contributing fifteen dollars per month for only three or four months. (It takes twenty to forty sponsors to cover expenses.) Also included in the packet are prayer cards printed with the teen's picture, name, and home address. Trusting the Lord and seeing him provide can be a great spiritual blessing and faith-building experience for young people. Former team member Debbie Dover commented, "One of the most outstanding lessons I learned is that God can provide any need, no matter how great or small that need may seem."

Included in the cost of the team are food, lodging, and travel (in the U.S. some transportation is provided from or to designated areas), airfare and ground travel in foreign countries, Boot Camp training, and printing of support packets and prayer cards. Also, on work teams, $100 per person goes to the mission board with which Teen Missions is working for purchasing building materials. A percentage of the cost of team involvement is used to send third world teenagers on Teen Missions teams in their own country. Therefore, each financial supporter is not just sending one teen, but two.

No staff personnel are salaried, but instead raise their own support much like the team members do. Teen Missions is a faith ministry supported completely by those who wish to donate to the organization. Each staff member tithes 10 percent of his or her income to meet the operating expenses of the ministry.

Prayer is a major factor in the ministry of Teen Missions. The person in prayer is truly on the front lines in today's spiritual warfare. Believing this, Teen Missions practices prayer. Every hour of our work day, staff members pray for the teams, team members, other staff members, and special requests in the prayer closet. Staff members are asked to spend at least one hour each week in the prayer closet.

Teen Missions requires that each team member have a network of sixteen prayer partners. If the number of prayer partners was multiplied by the total number of team members, the figure would amount to a lot of prayer on behalf of the summer teams!

The ministry of Teen Missions is not successful because we love young people and give all of our time to spiritually strengthening them. It is not successful because we have tremendous missionary vision. Teen Missions is only successful because Christ is our focus. Only he can do the work of redemption in lives. We seek to simply be his work glove.

For complete information on Teen Missions, their Training Camp program in Florida, and other printed material, write The Rev. Robert M. Bland, Director, Teen Missions Int., P.O. Box 1056, Merritt Island, FL 32952; or telephone direct to (305) 453-0350.

WORKING ON A UNIVERSITY CAMPUS FOR CHRIST
CAMPUS CRUSADE FOR CHRIST
ANDY WINEMAN

YOU may be wondering how a young college graduate who was headed toward the business field got into full-time Christian work, and is now working on the university campus for Christ. Actually, as I was growing up I was like most kids. I enjoyed going to church and Sunday school, although I went mainly out of an inward sense of obligation. It never really had any effect on my day-to-day life, until I entered high school.

Even though I had many friends and probably looked like I knew where I was going, in reality I was lost. My life was characterized by confusion. I liked to get involved in things, but then was unsure about how to respond to situations that came up. I had no basis in my life from which to determine what was right and wrong. This became very evident in several areas of my life. Until high school there was not much difference between what I had been taught was right and what everyone else was doing. Confusion entered in when those two became different and I was forced to decide what to do. It was more appealing to go along with the crowd than it was to do what I had been brought up to believe was right. I compromised some of my values because I did not have anything firm on which to base them. In addition, in athletics I was so competitive and concerned with winning that I did not care about what I said or did to people. For example, I played on the soccer team all four years in high school. During the homecoming game of my junior year I was thrown out of the game for swearing at a player and yelling at the referee.

In the fall of 1978, Steve, a young seminary student, began working with the youth group at my church. It was through him that I began to understand that I could know God in a personal way. I learned that if I asked Jesus Christ into my life, he would do two things. The most important was that I could know for sure that through Christ I would spend eternity with God in heaven. I also learned that he came to make my life full and meaningful. He was the solid foundation I needed as the basis of my life. I knew that these things were true and that Jesus was who he claimed to be; so on a weekend retreat I asked Christ to come into my life as Savior and Lord.

Since that time I have been growing in that relationship with him. I graduated that year and then went on to school at Ohio University. This was a fresh start. I did not know anyone there and I had a new basis from which to make decisions. In the fall of that year I got involved in a student organization called Campus Crusade for Christ. Over the next four years, through the people I met and the training I received, I was able to grow in my relationship with God and have an impact at Ohio University for Christ. As I approached graduation with a degree in Organizational Communication, I realized that I wanted to invest my life in something that would last for eternity. I also had a strong desire to continue to help college students understand how to know Christ personally and be involved in the discipleship process. I joined the full-time staff of Campus Crusade for Christ International. Campus Crusade is an interdenominational organization with a staff of over sixteen thousand working in 150 countries around the world. I am involved more specifically with the campus ministry, and am currently at the University of Minnesota.

Our vision for working with university students is centered around the Great Commission given by Jesus Christ, to make disciples of all nations. College students are so strategic in this because they are the leaders of tomorrow. This is also a unique time in most people's lives. They are beginning to think for themselves and are open minded and willing to consider different viewpoints. As Christians we need to take advantage of this by making Jesus Christ and the truth of his claims known. As this happens we will see every facet of our nation and eventually the world affected for the kingdom of God. The students that graduate will go on to be the doctors, lawyers, senators, representatives, businessmen, and missionaries of tomorrow. Christ's command involves going into the world and preaching the gospel. Our university campuses are a very strategic place from which to influence the rest of the world. In summary, our motivation is centered around the Great Commission, a desire to be obedient to Christ, and a love for others who need to hear his message.

My vision for working with college students does not stop on the college campus; if it did I would be very short sighted. I say that because I believe it is an important area in helping to reach the world for Christ. A great majority of our leaders for this country as well as many international leaders are there right now. In addition, their campus is their Jerusalem (Acts 1:8). Our greatest ministry is where people can spend time with us and see us as we live day to day. It is very important not to bypass our Jerusalems on the way to reaching the world. If you combine these factors with the numbers of people attending our nation's colleges and universities it is plain to see what an important area this is to concentrate on.

My experience on the university campus as a student, and now as I work full time in the ministry on campus, has taught me quite a bit. I have seen a wide variety of student interest (and noninterest). I have seen certain things that God has used and that have worked very well in reaching students. I have also seen things that have not been very effective.

One of the most encouraging things I have noticed on campus today is a variety of different evangelical Christian student organizations. Some are national and international in scope, while others are local. The encouraging part is that all are reaching out to the nation's college students with the gospel of Jesus Christ.

Each group has distinctives. In Campus Crusade our distinctives center around evangelism, living by the power of the Holy Spirit, and training believers to grow in and share their faith. In the area of evangelism we have found that a straightforward, but sensitive approach is something that God has used to draw many to himself. The word evangelism means many things to many people. To one person it may bring up scenes of someone on the street corner preaching to those who walk by. To others it may mean sharing the most important discovery they have ever made, with their closest lifelong friend. We all have different thoughts about how it should be done, but in the most basic of terms it is taking the gospel message to people.

Ever since the beginning of Campus Crusade for Christ in 1951, we have stressed the importance of taking the unique claims of Jesus Christ to college students. We act on the promises and commands of the Bible. For example, in John 4:35, Jesus tells us that the fields are white for harvest. And in Matthew 28:18-20 he commands us to go and make disciples of all the nations, and promises that he will be with us always.

We reach out to the whole campus, but an important part of our strategy is to target the leaders. These may be people in formal leadership positions, fraternity and sorority officers, members of the student government, or those in other student organizations and clubs. There are also those informal leaders who have an influence in their living area and the classroom. As these leaders are changed by Christ, their natural spheres of influence will be affected also.

Another important distinctive of Campus Crusade is the importance of walking in the power of the Holy Spirit. It has been estimated by some that up to 90 percent of the Christians in the world today do not know how to be filled (directed and empowered) by the Holy Spirit. Next to leading a person to know Christ personally, there is no greater thing we can do for a Christian than to teach him how to trust God's Spirit to be in control of his life moment by moment.

The third area of emphasis is on training believers to grow in their faith and to communicate that faith to others. This is done mainly through small group Bible studies consisting of five to ten students. These stress the basics of our faith in Christ as well as providing an environment for the students to mature in that relationship. This training takes on many forms, but the emphasis is always on learning how to share that faith. The critical event, according to Mark McClosky, area director for Campus Crusade in Minnesota, is to have one trained Christian taking one untrained Christian to talk with one interested non-Christian.

We incorporate these distinctives into a win, build, and send strategy on the campus. This is the basic structure that characterizes our movement. As we share our faith on campus we are trusting the Lord to draw many people to himself. Many are won to Christ during their college years. The second aspect is building these believers in their walk with Christ. Whenever someone becomes a Christian we carefully follow that person up with information to help establish him in the basics of the Christian life. As the student graduates and enters the business, professional, or mission field he is being sent into the world for a lifetime of ministry.

Often when I think about strategy, I wonder if it will work. I think the most important thing is to trust the Lord. The Psalmist writes, "Commit your way to the Lord, trust also in him, and he will do it" (Psalm 37:5). As I look back on many experiences at Ohio University, one in particular shows how this strategy works. We had the opportunity to speak in a fraternity house on the topic of being a man from a biblical viewpoint. At the end we asked for the students' honest comments about what was said. I went back and talked with those who wanted more information. I talked with Dave, and later on that night he asked Christ into his life. I personally went through followup with him to help him understand more about his relationship with Christ. As a result of the things that Christ was doing in his life, he had an impact on the rest of the men in his fraternity and dormitory. Dave continued to influence people as they saw the changes in his life and as he explained how important Christ was to him.

In summary, our strategy on each campus is fairly simple. We work at developing a winning, building, and sending movement that is centered around evangelism and discipleship. As we work on college campuses our goal is to help reach the campus in obedience to the Great Commission. I believe that the college campus is one of the most strategic places to have an impact for Christ.

A thermometer that could measure the "spiritual temperature" on a campus would be very useful. It would be helpful to know exactly what students are thinking about God as well as what nationwide trends are. We do not have that thermometer, but I think it is possible to determine what the spiritual climate is on campus today.

In recent years the campus environment has gone through many changes. The 1960s were characterized by tension and student unrest. The 1970s leaned more toward disinterest and lack of involvement by students. I think so far in the 1980s we are seeing student interest in many areas, both positive and negative, rising again. For example there is a view of morality that is quickly leaving traditional values behind. The phrase, "If it feels good, do it" is often characteristic of what people are thinking. Another alarming sign is the number of cults attracting people to become involved with them.

On the other hand, I believe students are more interested in Christianity than they have been for many years. I think we are seeing the beginnings of a great revival across our nation. Many are open to and searching for truth, although sometimes it feels like a race to get to students. So many stop short of finding that truth and settle for a lie.

I have been asked several times, "Are college students really interested in hearing about God?" assuming they are not. I have found as I work day in and day out with students that there is a strong interest in that very subject. Often the real problems are misconceptions that people have about Christianity. For the most part the students who show little interest have not rejected Christianity, but a misconception of it. The most important thing is to lift up Jesus Christ, and as he said, he will draw all men to himself. We have a great opportunity as well as responsibility to use this open climate to make Christ known to every college student.

One of the greatest thrills as well as challenges in this work is seeing how God provides what you need to accomplish it. He draws people to himself and to involvement in our movement. It is amazing to see God working in another person's life and how he helps that one mature in his relationship with him. Also, as we do creative things to expose many people to the gospel, the Lord brings to the surface those who want to hear more as well as those who are already Christians. Another area that continually strengthens my faith is seeing the Lord provide the materials and finances we need. In addition to the day-to-day operating expenses, special evangelistic outreaches can run into the thousands of dollars. Every time God provides the resources we need.

For example, we just finished our biggest evangelistic outreach of the year. Josh McDowell, a traveling speaker with Campus Crusade, spoke on seven of the smaller campuses in the area. As we trusted God for everything from the finances to the people who would come to hear Josh speak, we saw all of our prayers answered. Several thousand people heard the gospel, and of those, hundreds trusted Christ as their Savior. The bottom line is that as we have trusted God, he has always provided all that we have needed. I have been learning that whenever God calls us to do something he will *always* provide the necessary resources to accomplish it.

My goal has been to give you a broad picture of what is going on in the university environment and how we are penetrating it with the gospel. I hope to have shared some practical information for relating with and ministering to college students. I have tried to communicate my vision for college students, our strategy for working with them, and the spiritual climate on campus today, as well as how faithful God is in providing what we need. I count it a great privilege to be serving the Lord on staff with Campus Crusade for Christ on the college campus. I hope that you too have caught some of my excitement about the significance of working with college students today.

Andrew D. Wineman graduated from Ohio University in 1983 with a B.S. in Communication. While there he majored in Organizational Communication. Upon graduation Andrew joined the full-time staff of Campus Crusade for Christ International. He currently works with Campus Crusade at the University of Minnesota.

BUILDING THE CHURCH IS THE KEY TO FCA'S EVANGELISM

FELLOWSHIP OF CHRISTIAN ATHLETES
JACK ROBERTS, VICE PRESIDENT

GOD usually, or at least frequently, works his greatest miracles in what the world would consider to be the least likely people and places. So it has been with the Fellowship of Christian Athletes, conceived by an unknown graduate assistant coach at Oklahoma State University in 1947.

With the help of baseball immortal, Branch Rickey, and esteemed churchman, Dr. Louis H. Evans, Sr., the idea became an organized movement in 1954. Now, thirty years later, FCA's challenge and adventure continue.

The purpose of FCA is "to present to athletes and coaches, and all whom they influence, the challenge and adventure of receiving Jesus Christ as Savior and Lord, serving him in their relationships and in the fellowship of the church."

One of the very basics of FCA is that it is a *presenting* ministry. "Presenting" is more the focus of FCA's work than "discipling." While FCA staff is involved in equipping volunteers to conduct the ministry when and where paid staff can't be present, and that involves discipling, the main charge of FCA is to present the gospel while promoting the family and the church as the primary places for Christian growth.

A second basic of FCA is that it is an *athletic* ministry. Athletes and coaches are the focus of staff time and organizational resources; athletes and coaches are the focus of the summer conferences and camps and the year-round local Huddle program. Athletics is the platform, and coaches and athletes are the role models for influencing young people and society.

The original vision of FCA was that if coaches and athletes could endorse commercial products, they could also endorse a life style and a person on whom it is based; and that vision has become a reality over the past three decades. The notion of "harnessed hero worship" is likely to remain a part of the ministry of FCA in its fourth decade. While the media uncover more of the bad traits of many sports figures, the media continue to make other sports heroes more available to public worship than ever before. Thus FCA will attempt to promote the positive role models at least as vigorously as the negative models that parade across the public landscape.

Another basic of FCA is that its primary method of evangelism is through *fellowship*. It is the Fellowship of Christian Athletes, "Christians" surrounded by "fellowship" and "athletics." If either fellowship or athletics is missing, it is not the true FCA ministry.

Another basic of FCA is that it is a *volunteer* ministry. FCA has fewer than 200 paid employees nationwide who do things *with* volunteers rather than *for* them. Thus we have the effect of a large movement but the budget of a small one.

But above all, what makes FCA unique among parachurch evangelism is that FCA does not separate its work from that of the church. Support of the church is part of the stated purpose of FCA. FCA's staff are expected to be active members of local churches. And the evangelism in which FCA is involved is not complete until the new believer is united to a local fellowship of believers: the church. FCA does not have a statement of faith but presents the gospel to coaches and athletes and then urges them to link up with the local church of Jesus Christ and affirm its statement of faith.

The success of FCA as a movement of Christ's evangelism is linked to and measured by the success of Christ's church. Parachurch groups cannot fulfill the Great Commission; only the local church can do so. So FCA activities are usually scheduled to avoid church conflicts and geared instead to direct young people back into a high level of involvement in the local church.

If we do anything else in FCA other than build the local church, we've lost effectiveness and lost sight of our goal in evangelizing young people.

FCA in its fourth decade will challenge young people and coaches to receive Jesus Christ as Savior and Lord and embark on the adventure of serving him in their relationships, especially at school and in the home—but above all in the church.

THIS IS FCA

The FCA approach might well be termed "evangelism through fellowship"—centering on the person of Jesus Christ, the Bible, and the institution of the church. Through FCA ordinary people help each other become better people and better examples of what the Lord can do with a yielded life.

FCA is national in operation and composed of men and women from the athletic/faith community who desire to advance the ministry of Christ in all areas of life. The FCA "ownership" voluntarily contributes time, talent, and money toward the movement's objectives. As the members have teamed up, the following structures have emerged:

Huddle—junior high and high school; **Fellowship**—college; **Chapter**—adults in the local community.

FCA policies are established by a Board of Trustees and implemented by a central and regional National Staff. This not-for-profit organization is supported by tax-deductible gifts from individuals, foundations, businesses, churches, etc.

FCA PURPOSE

To present to athletes and coaches, and all whom they influence, the challenge and adventure of receiving Jesus Christ as Savior and Lord, serving him in their relationships and in the fellowship of the church.

FCA MEMBERSHIP PLEDGE

As a member of the Fellowship of Christian Athletes I shall endeavor to know more about Jesus Christ and his way of life, to be active in his church, to strive to be Christian in my personal life, and to share my convictions with others.

FCA AND THE CHURCH

The Fellowship of Christian Athletes is a church-oriented movement. Its working tie with the church was inherent in its conception, and its compatibility with the church is attested to by its history. Where FCA programs exist the local church is usually stronger, and vice versa.

The FCA is interdenominational, embracing Catholics and Protestants. Its focus has always been upon the person of Jesus Christ and not upon traditions or denominational labels.

Recognizing the potential danger of creating splinter groups when its Huddle/Fellowship/Chapter program was launched in 1966, FCA stresses that the only working relationship local FCA groups should have is with the institutional church. Each FCA member is urged to faithfully attend and serve the church of his or her choice. Some Huddles and Fellowships occasionally worship at various churches as a total group, and FCA events are planned so as not to interfere with one's church participation on Sunday.

In the first twenty-five years of FCA's history an estimated 125 athletes and coaches entered seminary after being influenced by some phase of the FCA program. The seminarians span the gamut from cross-country runners to wrestlers to men in the prime of coaching careers.

Persons interested in the complete program book on how to design and conduct a Fellowship for Christian Athletes in either their school or church may write direct to the National Headquarters office at 8701 Leeds Road, Kansas City, MO 64129; or telephone (816) 921-0909. FCA has regional offices in Colorado, Indiana, Texas, Georgia, Oklahoma, Pennsylvania, and Missouri.

PART FOUR

Outstanding Agencies Where Help Can Be Found

DISCOVERING JOBS FOR AMERICA'S CHRISTIAN YOUTH
INTERCRISTO
DICK STAUB, EXECUTIVE DIRECTOR

INTERCRISTO—A PLACE FOR EVERYONE

With the upsurge of young committed Christians across the nation, where do they go to put their newfound faith into action? Many come with college degrees and considerable work experience; others are just committed to Jesus Christ and seek a place to serve him.

Where will these people find a place to work? Many simply are not called to the ministry as pastors, but they do wish to serve Jesus Christ and the church.

From Seattle, Washington, comes an answer: INTERCRISTO. Under the dedicated direction of Dick Staub, the Executive Director, this organization has established a computerized matching service into which more than one thousand Christian service organizations feed various job descriptions, and into which Dick feeds the names of thousands of persons seeking work.

The listings are international, and at the present time there are more than 30,000 open jobs to which any young Christian can apply. Listen to these three accounts of happy persons who found a place to work for Jesus Christ:

PAM MEEKINS:

"I'm so grateful for Intercristo!" exclaims Pam Meekins, twenty-three, a recent graduate of Messiah College in Pennsylvania. "I was just dying to do some kind of Christian work on a short-term basis. My roommate told me about Intercristo after seeing an ad in a Christian magazine, so I called the toll-free number." Pam, who is now teaching elementary school music, spent her Christmas vacation in Matamoros, Mexico, with Operation Mobilization's Christmas Crusade, an opportunity she discovered through Intercristo.

"I worked on a team of twenty college-age people," reports Pam. "For ten days we worked with churches in the town, supporting a city-wide evangelistic outreach. We distributed literature and went out into neighborhoods and marketplaces inviting people to attend films and concerts in the various churches. Just feeling like you were forsaking the comforts of home to do the Lord's work was so satisfying!"

JOEL SUTTON:

Facing graduation from Wheaton College last spring, Joel Sutton, twenty-two, had a degree in Christian Education but did not have a permanent job lined up. He heard about Intercristo through friends and went through the job-matching service before commencement.

After spending the summer working as a camp supervisor, Joel was driving home to Denver from Boston. The camp had just closed for the season and Joel had no idea what he would be doing in the ensuing months. Halfway to Denver he called home and learned that Aloma Park Methodist Church in Winter Park, Florida, had discovered him through Intercristo, and were interested in him as a candidate for their Youth Minister position.

Upon his arrival in Denver, Aloma Park Methodist flew him to Florida, interviewed him, and offered him the job. He accepted. "It was an enormous faith builder," says Joel.

TED RORK:

After years in real estate and automobile sales, Ted Rork felt restless. Despite his successful record as a salesman, several months of job searching bore no fruit.

In a conversation after church on Sunday, an acquaintance mentioned a friend who had found work through Intercristo.

" 'You mean Intercristo really works?' I asked. Funny thing is, I'd carried around an Intercristo ad in my wallet for the past two years, thinking I might use it someday."

Ted decided to contact Intercristo. "I was still skeptical, though; I didn't see how God could use an old car salesman."

Within weeks Ted was hired as a radio advertising salesman with WIVE-AM in Ashland, Virginia, and his skepticism vanished. "I highly recommend Intercristo," he said.

A PROGRAM CALLED INTERMATCH

Thousands of Christians wonder if God could use their vocational skills in a Christian organization. Every year Christians from all walks of life ask the same question, "Where can God use me?"

This new service called Intercristo offers good news. Right now there are thousands of Christian organizations searching for individuals to fill key positions in virtually every vocational field. Intercristo knows this as each day they receive hundreds of calls from organizations throughout the world, seeking a person for a particular job. At this very moment they have some 23,000 job listings to be filled.

They have a program called Intermatch. It is Inter-Cristo's unique service that personally matches applicants with a Christian work opportunity that fits the applicants' education and experience.

Each applicant is able to find the full particulars about the work through this computer match, information such as: Which organization is seeking someone with the applicant's vocational background? What are the specifics about the job? Where is it? How much does it pay? . . . and much more.

WHAT KIND OF JOBS ARE AVAILABLE?
The reason for Intercristo is not to fill in the gaps in our present economy—that makes jobs hard to find. The reason is to find

Christian people to fill Christian jobs. Now, just what kinds of jobs does Intercristo have? During one month in the past year, a listing of the top ten most sought-after people were to fill this list:

1. Arid Soils Specialist—Somalia
2. General Medical Doctors—Third World
3. R.N.s—U.S. and Third World
4. Houseparents—U.S.
5. Director of Communications—Latin America and Asia
6. Financial Development Director—U.S.
7. Church Planters—Overseas
8. Executive Secretaries—U.S.
9. College Professors—U.S.
10. Summertime Camp Staff—U.S.

Nor should one get the idea that the applicants come from among the unemployed or the unemployable. At the same time the top ten jobs listed above were open, here is the listing of the top ten people that were seeking a Christian position through Intercristo:

1. Corporate Manager; M.B.A., ten years' experience
2. Human Resources Supervisor; six years' experience
3. Journalists, Writers
4. Lawyer; nine years' experience, Yale Graduate
5. X-Ray Technician
6. Corporate Marketing Director;
   twenty years in major U.S. corporation
7. Business Administrators
8. Carpenters
9. Church Staff: Pastors, Christian Ed. and Youth
10. EDP: Programmers, Analysts and Managers

A CHRISTIAN PEACE CORPS
Our nation experienced a real concern among college-age students to help others in need. As a direct result, the Peace Corps was founded, and jobs for thousands of young people willing to dedicate themselves to social causes became a reality. In like manner, young Christian students desire to apply themselves and their talents to the cause of Jesus Christ—not so much in the role

of clergy, but simply to use their God-given talents in God's work. One staff member states, "We have an obligation, as Christians, to make evident our Christian values in the marketplace, to put our best foot forward . . . to behave as Christ would behave were he in our shoes."

WHAT ABOUT EVANGELISM?
While the real purpose of Intercristo is to find Christian jobs for Christian young people, it lists thousands of positions each year in the field of evangelism. Some are in this country, but most of them are overseas.

HOW TO GET INVOLVED
Intercristo invites churches to become "agents" for them, to list on their bulletin boards positions that Intercristo has open, or to offer information on how young people can get in touch with them.

A Vocational Information Packet is available for writing to: Intercristo, 19303 Fremont Avenue, North, Seattle, WA 98133; or you may telephone direct by calling (206) 546-7330. Or call toll-free: 1-800-426-1343.

RESOURCES FOR BUILDING
AN EFFECTIVE YOUTH MINISTRY
IN YOUR CHURCH
GROUP *MAGAZINE*

CHAPTER

20

"MY youth group has a problem with cliques."

"I wish I knew how to spark some enthusiasm in my kids."

"Attendance has been dropping off in my youth group, and I'm not sure why."

These comments are typical of the needs of many youth groups.

Group magazine arose out of an awareness of such needs. The founders of *Group,* who were working as youth directors in local churches, recognized these needs. They went in search of a publication that would provide some answers. Finding no such publication, they decided to launch out and create their own magazine.

So, in October of 1974, a twenty-four-page tabloid newspaper-type magazine was born. Five hundred subscribers received the first issue of *Group* magazine. The staff, working in their spare time, operated on a shoestring budget. From those humble beginnings emerged a magazine that now serves over 50,000 subscribers.

Group is read by youth and youth leaders all over the world. The leadership is universally shared by all Christian denominations. Since its birth, *Group* has been interdenominational and independent—connected with no other organization.

Group's offices are located in Loveland, Colorado. It is here that the magazine takes shape every month. Writing, editing, research, typesetting, art, layout, and advertising all come together to form the final product: *Group* magazine.

"*Group* magazine is a resource for both leaders and young people," says Managing Editor Gary Richardson. "In fact, it's got something for everyone in the whole youth group. For leaders it's got ideas, tips, and actual sessions. For young people it's a source of encouragement; and most of all, it's fun."

Art Director Laurel Watson says: "The most important thing about my job is to enhance the writer's message with a visually stimulating one and to combine the two into one unified and very readable product. Personally, my goal is to produce a youth ministry resource that is both flashy and fun, yet thought-provoking; it should be a resource for messages that are easy to grasp. It should be creative, colorful, professionally presented—I just want it to be a real pleasure to open the mailbox and see it there each month."

Other divisions have developed under the *Group* banner also. For example, there's the book department. Editor Lee Sparks explains: "Group Books began as a direct result of *Group* magazine. Several years ago, some people asked for collections of the magazine's "Try This One" selections in book form. So we put out *The Best of Try This One*. As it turned out, it did very well—it sold several thousand copies, and encouraged us to put out two more Try This Ones: *More Try This One* and *Try This One . . . Too*. Some of the books we've put out include *The Hard Times Catalog for Youth Ministry* by Dennis and Marilyn Benson, and *The Group Retreat Book*. Some others are *The Basic Encyclopedia for Youth Ministry* by Dennis Benson and Bill Wolfe, and *The Youth Group Travel Directory*. And now we're going into more varied aspects of youth ministry. Our goal has been and will continue to be to produce authoritative, practical, and theologically sound youth leadership resources."

The events department at *Group* is directed by John Shaw. Here *Group* offers a wide range of camps and conferences that challenge young people and their leaders. "*Group* events include the Christian Youth Jamboree and the National Christian Youth Congress," explains John Shaw. "These events focus on workshops, speakers, and concerts. The purpose, of course, is to provide quality resources for youth groups. We expect from 3,000 to 4,000 young people and youth ministers to be involved in these events this summer (1983).

"*Group* work camps are a very different type of event which includes 200 to 300 young people working for a period of one week to repair and weatherize homes in poverty and disaster areas. This kind of event is very special because it brings together young people from many different parts of the country. In the work camps, evening sessions help the young people focus on understanding the culture in which they're working and also develop a feeling of common commitment in their Christian service.

"The third kind of event we have is the Colorado Ski Spree, which grew out of a concern to provide Christian programming for youth groups traveling to Colorado to ski. We are finding that *Group* events are growing very quickly, and within this growth we constantly strive to provide the most meaningful and highest quality Christian experience possible."

The events department fits in well with the rest of the organization. Together, the editorial, book, and event staffs complement one another in special ways. They serve as a springboard for new ideas and group support. You'll find the editorial staff helping the events staff at *Group*-sponsored programs. This kind of personal involvement helps the editorial staff stay on the cutting edge with *Group's* readers. In turn, the *Group* events personify the magazine and the books—giving readers a chance to actually experience *Group's* philosophies and purposes face to face.

Group's goal is to support youth ministry in the local church.

Group is *not* a parachurch organization. Rather, it is a servant to the church; it provides resources to enhance already-existing programs.

Group offers a clearinghouse for ideas. Through research, the best resources are gathered from different denominations across the country. Those resources are then attractively packaged and made available to church youth groups everywhere.

Group's ministry focuses on Christian growth. Its primary thrust is not evangelistic; *Group* aims to help *Christian* young people grow in their faith. While appreciating the work of those involved in youth evangelism, *Group* staffers find their gifts in the equally important area of promoting spiritual growth among Christian young people.

Group promotes respect and responsibility among young people themselves. *Group's* approach encourages full involvement of young people in determining the direction of the youth group. The use of a powerful adult dominating the spotlight is discouraged.

Helping young people develop decision-making capabilities is a strong objective of *Group* magazine, books, and events. *Group* staffers believe that learning Christian decision making assures more Christian maturity than does forceful spoon-feeding of dos and don'ts.

Young people are entrusted with a lot of respect and responsibility at *Group's* work camps—where they learn decision making and Christian maturity. One work camper said: "I've really found out the joy of giving. Time, I think, is the most precious gift, and whenever you can give that to the Lord, especially when you're doing something that you know he wants you to do, the feeling of satisfaction is unbeatable."

Another key element in *Group's* philosophy is fun. Learning can be fun, and when learning is fun it is most often retained by the learner. *Group* magazine, for example, is a colorful publication. The events are often spectacular in nature. But all of this flash has a purpose. Beneath the glitter and fun, you'll find real issues being confronted.

It's the frosting on the cake that captures the attention. Another youth at an event explained: "When we first came out here I was thinking it was going to be a lot of fun, and I didn't really care about God being in the picture. But as the nights went on and the week progressed, and with the programs at night, I really thought that he was here, too."

Once the attention is gained, the environment is right for receiving the message. The serious message is not diminished by the fun . . . it is simply enhanced. Young people are eager to learn when learning is fun. "Since I've started using *Group* magazine," explains one youth leader, "I've noticed a new energy level in our group. It's neat to see the teenagers having a lot of fun, and I'm content because I know that they're learning something."

That's a brief look at the ministries of *Group* . . . helping young people, youth groups, and adult leaders to grow . . . closer to God, to one another, and to those around them—to grow into the kind of loving servants that Christ wants them to be.

To obtain a catalog of the large number of youth ministry resources *Group* has available, simple write to Group, Box 202, Mt. Morris, IL 61054.

LEADING BOYS TO CHRIST
CHRISTIAN SERVICE BRIGADE
PAUL H. HEIDEBRECHT, VICE PRESIDENT

CHAPTER

21

MILLIONS of boys in the United States are unreached for the Lord Jesus Christ. Most of them lack the benefit of a positive male influence who can help them reach a mature manhood. Boys everywhere are looking for men they can trust; a man they can model themselves after—a coach, a leader, a friend, a father.

Think of the boys in your own church, home, and community and ask yourself this question: "How would you help them become effective Christian men?"

That is the goal of Christian Service Brigade, a program of outreach for churches of all denominations who want to make an impact on the boys of their community. The boys are divided into three major groups called (1) *Tree Climbers* for boys in grades one and two, or between the ages of six and seven; *Stockade* for boys in grades three through six, or ages eight to eleven; and finally, *Battalion* for boys in grades seven through twelve, or ages twelve to eighteen.

With a carefully planned, year-round program, with uniforms, camps, and goals to be reached, the average American boy will find both fun and adventure in belonging to Christian Service Brigade—but with the added dimension of a Christian atmosphere. CSB can only be conducted in a church congregation and works closely with that parish.

THE PHILOSOPHY BEHIND LEADING BOYS TO CHRIST

Being the human instrument which the Holy Spirit uses to lead a boy or young man to Christ is one of the privileges of being a friend of boys. Likewise, because of the eternal nature of the decision, a Christian man has no greater moment of responsibility than that of leading a boy to accept Jesus as his personal Savior.

Leading a boy to the Lord is primarily a spiritual task. God uses the human witness, but salvation is wholly of God through the Holy Spirit. Therefore, any attempt to challenge a boy to receive Christ must be undertaken with complete dependence upon the Lord and with an understanding of basic spiritual principles. This is not a skill to be practiced as though success depended upon some technique. It depends rather upon the man's own relationship to Christ and his willingness to be used by God. His life and testimony become a channel for the work of the Holy Spirit.

A primary need of the Christian man is to know the Word of God, and thus to understand how the Holy Spirit works to convict boys of sin and draw them to Christ.

THE HOLY SPIRIT'S ROLE

To guard against the danger of attempting to accomplish spiritual work by human means, it is necessary to understand the ministry of the Holy Spirit in salvation. The Gospel of John presents this truth in chapters 3:1-18; 16:7-15. It is clear that the Holy Spirit is the agent in accomplishing the new birth. When a boy comes to Christ, he is drawn by the Holy Spirit and born of the Spirit, who bears witness that he is a child of God. While God uses different means and circumstances to accomplish his work in each person's life, the following principles show how the Holy Spirit works:

1. He works through the Word of God (Romans 10:17). The Bible presents fully the message of salvation and is the basis for all personal evangelism. Leading a boy to Christ requires constant reference to the Scriptures, both in quoting and in actually showing the boy specific verses. If the boy's trust is anchored to the written Word, he has a solid foundation.
2. He works through prayer (Acts 4:31, 33). Prayer is the means God has provided for making his power available. The man who seeks to bring boys to Christ must himself come to the Lord frequently in prayer for their salvation and strengthening. Time spent talking to a boy about God should be paralleled by time spent talking with God about the boy.
3. He works through faithful personal witness (Romans 10:13, 14). The Bible records frequent instances of personal witnessing, some of which resulted in people placing their faith in Christ. Personal telling of the gospel is the foremost means which God uses to implant his Word in human hearts. The Christian man's responsibility is to proclaim faithfully the Lord Jesus Christ.

Though the sharing of the gospel should include a deep sense of urgency, a man who influences boys must realize that a persuasive man can sometimes get young boys to do almost anything. A boy can be led to make a decision to follow Christ as a result of his admiration for a certain man. But that would be to make a lip profession while his heart had not been convicted by the Holy Spirit. A true friend of boys seeks the fruit which God gives, rather than pressing for numbers of professions.

Patterns for personal witness are given in Scripture to guide the soul-winner. (See Brigade Learning Module #207.)

FOLLOWING THROUGH ON DECISIONS THAT ARE MADE
One of the biggest struggles in a boy's spiritual life normally comes right after he has received Christ as his Savior. This is the moment when Satan wages his fiercest warfare. Satan uses two primary methods: (1) He tries to intimidate through some other person, unsaved parents, or scoffing friends; or (2) he seeks to distract the new believer and create doubts as to what God has done for him through the renewed influence of worldly habits and acquaintances.

A Christian man can help a new convert best by two means. First, he should reemphasize what took place when the boy came to know Christ, recalling again such Scripture passages as John 1:10-12; 3:16; 2 Corinthians 5:17; or Romans 5:8. God's Word is the basis for assurance of salvation. In addition, the man should acquaint him with the principles and means of Christian growth, stressing the importance of Bible study, prayer, personal witnessing, and fellowship with other Christians.

The man's own continuing friendship and interest will itself be an encouragement to a new Christian. The long-term involvement of a mature Christian with a younger one, as exemplified by the relationship of Timothy and Paul, seems to be God's pattern for growth. This work of "making disciples" is at the heart of the Great Commission, "Go therefore and make disciples of all nations" (Matthew 28:19, 20).

Though a new Christian must rely on the Holy Spirit rather than on other people for spiritual strength, it is important for him to be linked in close relationships with other Christians. His involvement with Christian fellows his own age and Christian men at a local level is essential for his Christian growth. A boy who is not participating in a local church should therefore be urged to do so.

GROWING ON

A boy will inevitably face various problems in his growth to Christian manhood, even with a solid relationship with Christ and a healthy spiritual environment. The success with which these problems are met, however, often determines the vitality of a boy's Christian life and ultimately affects his usefulness in service for the Lord. A boy's ability to call on spiritual resources when he needs help and the availability of a concerned man often mean the difference between success and failure. Suggestions for helping boys in this way are part of the Christian Service Brigade training program.

A frequent question of Christian youth is how to know God's will for their lives. God guides believers when they live by faith in his direction and seek through prayer and faithful study of the Word to know him and his will. An intimate relation with God carries the promise of his guidance throughout life. A Christian man who is following the will of God in his life can be a vivid demonstration to a boy of the value of yieldedness to the Lord. When a boy has confidence in a man, he may come for counsel regarding God's will. This is an opportunity to help the youth analyze his problem and arrive at a solution, in the context of prayerful consideration of biblical principles.

MORE INFORMATION AVAILABLE

The Christian Service Brigade maintains a national headquarters in Wheaton, Illinois, and publishes manuals, books, and training programs for the establishment of groups within churches of all denominations. Most people are not aware that it is basically an evangelistic outreach for boys within the community. In most groups, half of the boys attending are nonchurched. The action-packed program draws boys from outside the group as well as church related families.

Christian Service Brigade exists to make a difference in the lives of boys. Through the fruitful labor of committed men, a church can reach boys for Christ. The Brigade program can be an important part of any church's evangelistic thrust within its community.

For further information on Christian Service Brigade, write the Rev. Paul Heidebrecht, Vice President, at Box 150, Wheaton, IL 60187; or telephone (312) 665-0630.

THE EVANGELISTIC EVENT
SONLIFE MINISTRIES
DANN SPADER, DIRECTOR

YOUTH EVANGELISM

Now it came to pass that a group existed who called themselves fishermen. And lo, there were many fish in the waters all around. In fact the whole area was surrounded by streams and lakes filled with fish. And the fish were hungry.

Week after week, month after month, and year after year, those who called themselves fishermen met in meetings and talked about their call to fish, the abundance of fish, and how they might go about fishing. Year after year they carefully defined what fishing means, defended fishing as an occupation, and declared that fishing is always to be a primary task of fishermen.

These fishermen built large, beautiful buildings for local fishing headquarters. The plea was that everyone should be a fisherman and every fisherman should fish. One thing they didn't do, however; they didn't fish.

In addition to meeting regularly, they organized a board to send out fishermen to other places where there were many fish. The board was formed by those who had the great vision and courage to speak about fishing, to define fishing, to promote the idea of fishing in faraway streams and lakes where many other fish of different colors lived. Also the board hired staffs and appointed committees and held many meetings to define fishing, to defend fishing, to decide what new streams should be thought about. But the staff and committee members did not fish.

Large, elaborate, and expensive training centers were built whose original and primary purpose was to teach fishermen how to fish. Over the years courses were offered on the needs of the fish, the nature of the fish, how to define fish, the psychological reactions of fish, and how to approach and feed fish. Those who taught had doctorates in "fishology." But the teachers did not fish. They only taught fishing.

Further, the fishermen built large printing houses to publish fishing guides. Presses were kept busy day and night to produce materials solely devoted to fishing methods, equipment, and programs, to arrange and encourage meetings, to talk about fishing. A speakers' bureau was also provided to schedule special speakers on the subject of fishing.

After one stirring meeting on "The Necessity of Fishing," one young fellow left the meeting and went fishing. The next day he reported that he had caught two outstanding fish. He was honored for his excellent catch and scheduled to visit all the big meetings possible to tell how he did it. So he quit his fishing in order to have time to tell about the experience to the other fishermen. He was also placed on the Fishermen's General Board as a person having considerable experience.

Now it's true that many of the fishermen sacrificed and put up with all kinds of difficulties. Some lived near the water and bore the smell of dead fish. They received the ridicule of some who made fun of their fishermen's clubs and the fact that they claimed to be fishermen yet never fished. They wondered about those who felt it was little use to attend and talk about fishing. After all, were they not following the Master who said, "Follow me, and I will make you fishers of men" (Matthew 4:19)?

Imagine how hurt some were when one day a person suggested that those who don't fish were not really fishermen, no matter how much they claimed to be. Yet it did sound correct. Is a person a fisherman if year after year he never catches a fish? Is one following if he isn't fishing?[1]

Youth evangelism? How do we do it effectively? How do we keep from just talking about it and not really helping it happen? Can we *help* our young people reach their friends? How do we produce an evangelism that stems from a proper inner motivation rather than a guilt-associated surface activity? Can we use today's youth culture to naturally reach young people for Jesus Christ?

As I begin to think about this broad subject of youth evangelism, these plus many other questions come to my mind. In this chapter I'd like to step back and first ask a critical question: "Is a ministry to young people even valid? And if so—why?" From there I'd like to look at one practical and workable approach in reaching young people for Jesus Christ within the local church setting.

THE NEED

PRACTICALLY

Is a ministry to young people that important? And if so—why? It has been my own personal experience as I have worked with hundreds of churches that *unless* this question is adequately addressed, youth evangelism will *never* happen—or if it does happen it will only die off and never be maintained throughout the years!

George Gallup, Jr., in his recent book, *The Search for America's Faith*, states, "The future of the church will rise or fall on its success with its young people. . . ."[2] Gallup went on to say that, contrary to many views about teens today, the "studies continue to underline the yearning, attention and enthusiasm that young people are putting into their religious pursuits. Teenagers reveal an abiding interest in spiritual questions and *high levels* [emphasis mine] of personal involvement."[3] "Sixty-two percent said that during a twenty-four hour period, God and religion had been on their mind."[4] "Seventy-five percent of those who responded noted that religious beliefs would [in ten years] be fairly or very important in their lives."[5]

Gallup went on to say that "teenagers claim a deep relationship to God . . . a higher proportion of those polled believe in a personal God than do their parents. Four in ten say that religion plays a very important role in their lives. . . ."[6] "They are disappointed that the churches do not have many youth programs."[7] Gallup warns, "If the church does not respond, young people will find an agency, movement, or experience that does."[8] He then states that over 27 million people within the last few years, most under the age of thirty, have turned to cults of one form or another. "Clearly the deep spiritual hunger of young people is not being met by the established church."[9] If the mainline churches are serious about the complaints and cries of youth, they will find themselves entering into a whole new period of program, attention, and care of the youth around them.[10]

When Mr. Gallup concludes by saying that, "The arriving generation is more than hinting, it is screaming to be used in some demanding cause,"[11] he is obviously laying out a challenge to the church of America.

But the challenge is picked up by others also. Dennis Miller of Church Youth Development states from his studies that six out of the nine major parachurch movements have been started by individuals college age or younger. David Howard of Inter-Varsity responds, "I'm surprised that figure is so low. In almost every instance of a missionary thrust, youth have been the instruments through whom God works. I am convinced the youth of our churches are the 'sleeping giants' yet to be tapped and mobilized for Jesus Christ."[12]

Statistics from many sources reconfirm this potential. Consistently 85 to 90 percent of all those who receive Christ do so before their nineteenth birthday.[13] Of the 27 million teens in America, the harvest field is ripe and ready. As J. McQuilkin found in his research, "The junior-age children from Christian homes and the high school age youngsters from non-Christian homes respond more readily to the gospel than any other age groups."[14]

Not only is there an incredible harvest, but studies consistently show that "the churches' basic expectations concerning the seriousness of youth are much too low."[15] Something needs to be done. Youth not only are in a key time of their life to respond to the gospel of Jesus Christ, but are "screaming" for a cause to which they can commit their lives.

It would seem obvious then that the church would be actively mobilized in reaching the youth of today. Yet the opposite seems true.

According to Dennis Miller, "The average local church allocates only 2 percent of its budget to youth ministry while secular companies selling everything from makeup to pornographic magazines are focusing up to 70 percent of their advertising budgets on the teenage market."[16]

It is only in the last few years that aggressive evangelistic-oriented youth ministry has begun to develop on a larger scale within the local church. Most evangelistic-oriented youth ministry was done through parachurch youth ministries such as Youth For Christ, Young Life, Campus Crusade, etc., but within the last ten or fifteen years, the local church has begun to move forward in an attempt to effectively reach youth.

Now more than ever the local church is recognizing the need to reach young people. As Jay Kesler of Youth For Christ states, "Our current generation of lost young people are more lost than they ever used to be."[17] Overall, "our current generation of young people do not even have a memory of Christianity." Parents of the sixties declared God to be dead. Parents of teens today have the memory of a churchgoing Christianity—but teens of today don't even have that memory. As a result, multitudes of teens today never have, and probably never will step inside the doors of a church. Thus, now more than ever the church needs to be reawakened to the responsibility of taking the message of Jesus Christ *to* the students. We no longer can be content with just Christian nurture in our youth programming. We must aggressively seek to reach and win young people to the person of Jesus Christ.

BIBLICALLY
Recognizing the need practically, we now need to ask: Is a youth ministry valid biblically? For years, churches got along without aggressive youth evangelism; why do we need it now? Is there a biblical foundation for ministry specifically directed toward young people? Let's look at three areas in which I see the

Scriptures addressing the validity of youth ministry in the local church. First, some direct admonitions. Second, some principles for ministry. Third, the need in today's culture.

First, some direct admonitions. At this point, I want to be careful not to overstate the issue or read into the biblical text on the validity of youth ministry. I don't want to stretch the text like a well-known youth speaker at a major conference who stated, "It is clear that the Bible states that the greatest calling of ministry is youth work!"

However, Scripture is not silent in this area, either. The Great Commission challenges us to "make disciples of all nations."[18] The Bible is not written only to adults. In 1 John we read the contrary, that Scripture is for all of us—children, young men, and adults.[19] Every generation is requested to reach its own generation for Christ and to "pass the torch" to the next generation.[20] Unfortunately, we often have low expectations of the potential of our young people. We're like the pastor who said, "If we could only lock all the teens in a closet when they turn twelve and then let them out when they turn twenty, we'd be so much better off." We really don't believe that young people are capable of reaching their peers; we advocate just nurturing them along until they become adults, when they can become effective in ministry. Yet the Great Commission was written to all believers, young and old. Contrary to some who would hold that it was addressed only to the twelve, it was designed as God's command to us to reach our generations for Jesus Christ—our Judea, Samaria, and the uttermost parts of the earth. This also applies to reaching the teen subculture, which in turn can reach its world for the cause of Christ. The church of Jesus Christ cannot ignore this large segment of today's culture.

Second, if we'd go to the Gospel of John, chapter 21, we'd find another direct command by Jesus to tend and care for the young lambs.[21] In this passage we have three definite commands: "Feed my lambs" in verse 15; "Tend my sheep" in verse 16; and "Feed my sheep" in verse 17. While it is clear that there are two categories of sheep mentioned (in verse 15, and in verses 16 and 17), some would argue that there might be a case for stating that three ages of sheep are referred to. Hendriksen states, "It is probably that in speaking of lambs (verse 15), sheep (verse 16), and dear sheep (or dear little sheep; note the diminutive), this may not have reference to age or physical size, but may be due to Christ's tender affection for His own. He had in mind three different groups within the church; for example, little children, adults, and young people."[22]

Hendriksen then goes on to argue that this is probably not the most likely translation even though it might have some validity. Nevertheless, Tenney, in his commentary, makes this statement: "All classes of believers are clearly represented by the two groupings, whether the small lambs or the grown sheep."[23]

Either way, we see the command to care for those in the body of Christ, both young and old. No one age group should necessarily have priority or extra validity. God is concerned for all of his flock.

Second, some principles from Scripture. Throughout Scripture we find general principles which can be fulfilled very pragmatically in an effective ministry to young people. Let's look at some of the principles.

1. Christ's love for the children. We never find Jesus too busy for the children. He took them into his arms (Mark 10:16); he set a child in the midst of a crowd for a lesson to adults (Mark 9:36, 37); he used children's games to illustrate lessons for adults (Matthew 11:16, 17; Luke 11:13). He strongly warned against causing a child to stumble or go astray (Matthew 18:5, 6). In Isaiah 40:11 we see God as the perfect Shepherd stating that the "lambs are close to the heart of God" (NIV).

2. Our children and young people are a gift from God. God gives us our children as a gift from himself, not to abuse or ignore, but to teach, love, and admonish in the Lord. God teaches us about his great fatherly love as we minister to those whom God has given to us, either physically or by becoming a "substitute" parent to needy children. We are adopted as sons of God, and God becomes our heavenly Father. God reveals his love to us and we become a part of the family of God. Today over 50 percent of teens are from broken homes. As we seek to model and imitate God's love to us, it will cause us to reach out and in love seek to "adopt" those who need to experience that love. Through that reflecting of God's character, it would be our desire to see these young people become a part of God's family.

3. Young people are open to the things of God. The Scriptures tell us that God "desires none to perish but all to come to repentance." In a report published by Campus Crusade for Christ, statistics demonstrated that 80 percent of all those who received Jesus Christ did so before their eighteenth birthday, and 15 percent of the remaining 20 percent did so because of the seed sown in their life prior to their eighteenth birthday.[24] Church growth experts argue that we should concentrate our greatest efforts in areas which are responding to the gospel of Jesus Christ.

4. The church is described as the "family of God." During the late nineteenth century when families began to move off the farm and into the city, family life began to deteriorate. Dad went off to work all day. The children often worked somewhere else or spent their time in school. The automobile and TV added even more separation of family life. Divorce began to tear families apart; now almost 50 percent of all teens come from broken homes.[25] The relatives live far away and the extended family is almost nil. Now more than ever teens need the family of God. That family needs to reach out to them and say, "We love you; we care." Perhaps the only family life many teens will experience will be within the family of God. "Young people now more than ever need the church; and the church, now more than ever, needs the vitality and zeal of the young."[26]

5. The Scriptures consistently remind us of our responsibility to teach the young. In Exodus 12:1-24 the rite of the Passover is described. While observing this rite, the children would ask about its meaning, thus providing a natural opportunity to teach them truth (12:25-27). In Exodus 13:11-13 we find the dedication of all firstborn to the Lord, again providing an opportunity to teach the children (13:14-16). In Deuteronomy 6:1-9 we find the words of Moses to the people as he admonishes them to obey the Lord with all their heart, soul, and might. He emphasizes their responsibility to teach their children throughout life's experiences. Deuteronomy 11:18-21 reemphasizes the responsibility to continually be communicating to our children God's presence in all of life. Proverbs 22:6 admonishes us to "train up a child in the way he should go and when he is old he will not depart from it." Cam Abel, in writing an article on youth ministry, translated this verse,

"Dedicate to the Lord and create a taste for the things of the Lord in a child in accordance with his age level, and even when he becomes mature, he will not depart from his spiritual training."[27]

Also in Ephesians 6:4, fathers are admonished not to "exasperate their children." Gene Getz, in commenting on this passage, stated, "note that the word translated 'children' in this passage does not refer to 'small children.' Paul is speaking of children who were no doubt teens or older children who were mature enough to be responsible for their actions."[28] God is concerned that the youth grow in knowledge of the things of God; therefore, it becomes our responsibility to see this desire of God's heart fulfilled.

CULTURALLY
Being aware of the practical and biblical need, let's now look at the need culturally.

Teenagers, as we think of them now, are a relatively new phenomenon in our culture. Francis Schaeffer stated, "The youth culture has changed more within the last twenty years than it changed from the Renaissance to the 60s." We need to trace briefly the history of this teen generation. Prior to the 1900s there was no noticeable gap between childhood and adulthood. Families were closely knit, working together, learning together, and living in the same area for years. Children would learn their father's trade. A child never had to question what he was going to do or where he was going to go as he grew up. Life was relatively stable, in comparison with today's life and standards. But by the end of the nineteenth century, several factors came on the scene and changed all of this. Teens began to become a brand new subculture. Listed below are some of the factors that helped to create this whole new segment of our society.

1. *Urbanization.* In the eighteenth and nineteenth centuries, farming was the most important American occupation, but as industry began to develop and new machinery on the farm improved, young men began to leave the farms. In 1870, sixty out of every one hundred Americans worked on the farm, whereas by 1960 only six out of one hundred Americans worked on farms. On the farm the family was central.

Everyone worked together to keep the farm going. When families would move to town, the fathers would be gone all day working in a factory. The children had free time with little responsibility. The family began to lose its centrality and teens began to have lots of free time on their hands.

2. *Mobility.* The automobile increased our opportunity to get around. Today it is suggested that one in three American families move each year—uprooting friendships, jobs, schools, and communities. The extended family very rarely existed. Even members of the nuclear family began to see less and less of each other. Parents became less of an influence in the lives of their teens. Thus teens began to turn more toward their peers.

3. *The women go to work.* During World War II women by the hundreds of thousands worked in factories. This was a sign of patriotism to support the war effort. After the war, many returned to the home, only to find idle time on their hands, with all the new time-saving devices. Many returned to work, even demanding their rights to do so. By 1978, 45 percent of all of America's work force consisted of women. Children were often left with relatives, neighbors, or baby-sitters. Child care centers took over the parental care for many children. Often the family members would only see each other around the supper table before the teens would rush off in cars to school activities.

4. *Increased education.* By the turn of the century, more and more American youth were attending high school, increasing from 202,963 in 1890 to 1.8 million in 1920.[29] After the depression of the thirties and the war of the forties, teens en masse began to attend high school—over 10 million by 1950. The 1950s, influenced by the automobile, television, extended schooling, and the writings and interests of psychologists such as Hall and Erickson, began to spark the development of a whole new subculture—teenagers. Gradually, as Americans began to move out of the Industrial Age into the Technological Age, the need for additional education began to stretch out this transition between childhood and adulthood. During the sixties and seventies, teens moved into college, creating the generation gap and new subculture. Teens became a misplaced group of people; they were neither adults nor children. They were not trained enough to go into the work force; thus they were

shipped off to schools and left to identify primarily with their peers rather than with their families. Knowledge began to explode, doubling every seven years. Change became the norm. Teens could not look to the past because it seemed so outdated. The future seemed so uncertain, so they began to live for the here and now—becoming labeled the "now" generation. Their focus later turned inward to create what is now recognized as the "me" generation. Twenty-seven million teenagers, trapped in their own subculture. Not children, but not allowed to be adults, either. A new cultural phenomenon! Do we ignore it? How do we respond as a church? How would Jesus respond to this need? Stuart Briscoe touches the heart of the need when he writes:

THE UPRIGHT AND THE UPTIGHT

How would you describe them?
"The beautiful people?"
"Dirty, long-haired, unwashed, good-for-nothing
    communist-inspired louts?"
"Peace-loving, socially responsible, politically aware
    members of society?"
"Rebellious, thankless, self-centered hooligans?"
"Sex-obsessed, pleasure-loving, work-shy, drug-addicted
    layabouts?"
"Dangerous, destructive anarchists?"
"Normal, healthy, red-blooded, hard-working kids?"
There are more of them than ever before.
    Healthier because of the balance of their diets.
    Wealthier because of the balance of payments.
They travel more
    see more
    earn more
    spend more
    demand more
    receive more.
Publicized
Criticized
Idolized
Pressurized

Analyzed
Shouted at
Shot at
Spouted at
Spat at
They are pandered to,
    planned for,
    pleaded with and
    preached about.
Cheering, jeering
Swinging, singing
Learning, burning
Hippies, Yippies
Nudity, crudity
Turning on, putting on
Dropping out, making out
Pot, pop and pill
Hairy, scary
Drug scene
Teen scene
Obscene
The whirling world of YOUTH.
Meanwhile back at the Church . . .
Preachers preach
Sermons carefully, prayerfully prepared.
Expositional
Exegetical
Dispensational
Devotional
Inspirational
Indigestible
Information leads to
Illustration leads to
Invitation leads to
Integration into
Congregation
    (Membership is increased)
Deacons deac.
Business-like and Christ-like men
Running a well-oiled operation.

Budget met.
Baptistry wet
Regularly.
   (Membership is satisfied)
Tithers tithe
Large tenths in tiny envelopes.
Faithfully, cheerfully giving
Abundantly out of abundance
Ensuring
   (Membership is comfortable)
Choristers chorus
Impeccably gowned and groomed
With an excess of crescendos and sopranos
Rousing, rising anthems.
   (Membership is inspired)
Well dressed
Well pressed
Well blessed
   (Membership is dismissed)
The placid world of CHURCH.
Two worlds on one planet
The woolly weird Youth World
   The calm, cool Church World.
The weak and wild world.
   The redeemed, respectable world.
The "out of sight" world.
   The "out of touch" world.
And never the two shall meet . . .
But they must![30]

The need of reaching young people is there—practically,
biblically, and culturally. How then do we develop our ministry to
respond to that need?

Twenty-five to thirty years ago God raised up parachurch
organizations to meet the immediate needs of young people:
organizations such as Youth For Christ, Young Life, Campus
Crusade for Christ, and others. Thousands of teens have been
reached, nurtured, and mobilized for Jesus Christ.

But now the church *must* be mobilized! Campuses are closing
to these parachurch organizations. Financial concerns continue to

plague these organizations, keeping them from being able to meet all the needs. Campus Crusade, Youth For Christ, and Young Life have all admitted the need to see local churches take the lead in effective youth ministry.

How can the local church begin to reach young people? In the next few pages I'd like to suggest one practical and workable approach to reaching these people. With Sonlife Ministries we have developed a number of model ministries which are aggressively using the evangelistic big event. Our statistics show us that the regular development of this outreach has within two years doubled the size of these youth ministries in both big and small churches.

THE EVANGELISTIC EVENT

As we practically discuss how to do evangelism through the evangelistic big event, some important statements need to be made.

Statement Number 1: There are many ways to reach young people, and the evangelistic big event is only one way. Across the country, some of the most effective youth ministries are using this method to reach young people. With Sonlife Ministries, many churches are consistently using this method. Statistically, these churches have doubled the size of their youth ministries as they have regularly applied these principles. The evangelistic big event has proven itself culturally effective, and is being used by many churches, big or small.

Statement Number 2: When used properly, the big event is just a part of the total youth ministry. Not only do we need to win young people to Jesus Christ, but the youth ministry must concentrate on building them up in their faith and then equipping them to train others.

Statement Number 3: The evangelistic big event is a tool designed to help your students become effective in reaching their friends for Christ. It is not an end in itself. It will only be effective as your students personally are involved in a loving way in the lives of their non-Christian friends.

What, then, is the evangelistic big event? We need to begin with a definition. *It is a regular, special event designed to reach the non-Christian.* By "regular" we mean it is a once-a-month, once-aquarter, or once every two weeks activity. It needs to be seen as something which is more than a one-time activity. By being regular, it allows students to be continually working and praying toward leading their friends to Christ. If this big event is something we do just occasionally, it becomes difficult for our students to work *consistently* toward bringing their friends.

By "special" event we mean that it needs to be advertised for everyone in your group—all regular students as well as fringe or new contact students. You want as many there as possible. You advertise it up big and talk it up big. You do the best you can with the resources you have to make it as good as possible. It can't be just thrown together. You seek to make it very special in the minds of your students.

When we say "designed" we mean that it has a definite purpose with definite goals in mind. First, it is not for the Christian kid but is designed to reach the secular student. You want all the Christians there, but they are to come to help create a good atmosphere, reach out to the newcomers, and bring their own friends. The Christians are to come to give. It's in giving that they will really experience the joy of the outreach.

Also, this outreach is designed to break down barriers that the typical secular student has about Jesus Christ, barriers such as: Christianity is not relevant; Christians can't have fun; Christians are weird; Christianity is dull; etc. There is only one barrier that can't be broken down and that is the stumbling block of the Cross.

When we say we want to reach the non-Christian we mean that the major purpose for this activity is just that. We evaluate on this basis: "Did new people come? Were they exposed to Christ in a positive way? Did they either accept Christ or come closer to accepting Christ?" The bottom line is, over a period of time, are we reaching the non-Christian for Christ? If ever it is important to count numbers, it is so at the outreach. Our outreach should be our largest event with many new students being exposed to Christ.

Why is outreach so important? First, to reach the masses. Statistics tell us that eight out of ten people will never accept Christ if they aren't exposed to Christ prior to their eighteenth birthday. High schoolers are extremely receptive to the gospel. We know that without Christ students would go to hell. That is a subject we don't like to talk about. Yet Jesus spoke more about hell than he did about heaven. It is not an option for us to share Jesus Christ and practice outreach. It is a mandate!

Second, we run outreaches to train our ministry team (key students). As our ministry team is involved in helping us plan the outreach, invite their friends, put the program together, and help create an atmosphere in which Christ is presented in a positive way, they are given the chance to minister.

After the outreach, students will ask questions such as: Did we demonstrate Christ's love? Were there new people there? Was it a positive experience? Did any respond to Jesus Christ? Who will continue to help them grow? These types of questions help our key students learn what ministry is all about. Thus, the outreach becomes an excellent tool to train our key students.

Third, outreach helps the growing Christian students. It gives them an opportunity to bring their friends and expose them to Christ. As our growing students see their friends accept Christ, it helps them grow in their own personal relationship. Philemon 6 states, "I pray that you will be active in sharing your faith so that you may come to a full knowledge of an understanding of Jesus Christ." As our students are working to share Christ with other students, they experience depth and growth in their own life. As a new Christian or an older Christian sees his friends accept Christ, he takes on the responsibility of spiritual parenting. This builds growth in character as he seeks to help his friend grow.

Fourth, good outreaches create an excitement in the whole youth group. If a youth group consists of ten students and fourteen come to an outreach, it creates a great deal of excitement. Something is happening! Our youth group is on the move! If 100 students come to a church regularly, and 150 students come to the outreach, it creates a sense of excitement about where the whole youth group is headed. I have often said it becomes one of the best ways to create a healthy youth group image. It becomes the positive image builder. The students get excited about the youth group as a whole. All types of studies of teenagers demonstrate that how they view (their image of) their group greatly determines the extent to which they identify with that youth group and with the cause of Jesus Christ. If they are excited about the youth group, they will be more apt to identify with Jesus Christ. If they are negative about their youth group, they will tend to transfer those negative feelings over to the person of Jesus Christ and to Christianity.

What makes a good *outreach?* I want to suggest five criteria in establishing a group outreach:

It needs to have many parts to it. When I first began to conduct outreaches, I would have only one major activity such as volleyball. Our students loved volleyball, and I think the best place to begin is to go to your students and ask them what they would bring their friends to. That first outreach went fine, as long as the volleyball game went well. But I soon found that there were many students who didn't like volleyball; or even, at times, the volleyball game didn't go well. If a student didn't like volleyball, or if we had a bad evening, the new students would go away feeling the activity was a flop. We began to discover that if an outreach had many parts it was more likely to be a success. I want to suggest three major parts:

1. *The activity.* During this time, it is best to have a high-energy time of mingling. This consists of one or several games. Again, having many different kinds of games is usually more successful. That way, if one of the games flops and four are successful it still can be a good activity period. With junior highers we need a lot of activity. With high schoolers we still seek to create a lot of activity with a lot of enthusiasm. With college-age individuals we need less activity and more of a low-key type of interaction.
2. *The meeting period.* This is a time when Jesus Christ is presented in a relevant way. During this period the message of Christ can be communicated through many means: movies, media, drama, role plays, skits, slide shows, etc. Our whole desire during the meeting period is to expose students to Jesus Christ in a positive way. It has been our experience that it is best to pick one major theme and seek to develop that theme clearly throughout the various avenues of communication. For example, if at one outreach the theme was family relationships, the meeting period could deal with how to get along with the rest of your family. The skits, the media, the

drama, the slide shows, could all focus on this theme. The message could show biblical principles of how to relate more effectively within the family.

3. *The interaction time.* This is the time after the meeting when light refreshments are offered. This allows for your ministry team or your key students to divide and conquer. This is a time for your students to go up to new people and get to know them better and perhaps share their own testimony or share what Christ means to them. It is also an excellent opportunity to personally present the claims of Christ to students that are interested and receptive. It has been our experience that this interaction time can be one of the most important parts of the whole evening, especially if the meeting period was done well. The interaction time becomes the basis of effectively drawing in the net.

It needs to be as good as possible. It is very important to make outreaches as sharp as possible. If the students in the youth group work hard to bring their friends, and the outreach bombs, we've damaged the witness of our students. If the students bring their friends and it goes over very well, it enhances the witness of our teens, thus helping them to be successful in reaching their friends for Christ. Remember, this big event is a tool to help your students share Christ with their friends. Therefore, as leadership, our job is to work hard to make it as sharp as possible. Also, we want to expose new students to Jesus Christ in a positive way. Therefore, we need to put extra energy into making this outreach as sharp as we possibly can.

A good outreach needs a good name. When I first began outreaches, we called them "Gym Night." This did not help create any sense of identity or excitement about the outreach. When we developed a better name, this improved the image of the activity. As we continued these outreaches and continued to grow, the title became the focus of our youth group. The secular student is able to identify more with a group if it has a good name. It can also be used on logos, book covers, or even placed on jackets and sweaters, thus helping to give the group a sense of identity. Many different types of names have been used, such as: "Sonlife," "Joy Explosion," "Great Escape," "The Riot," "The Thing," "Body Works," "Student Works," etc. I know of one Evangelical Free church who called their outreaches, "Free for All."

A good outreach is one that is bathed in prayer. Before each of our outreaches, we would challenge our students to spend five to ten minutes praying for that event. As our students began to bathe the outreach in prayer they would come with more of a mindset of service. Rather than coming to get, they would come to give. Also, as they prayed for that outreach it created a broad base of prayer. The Scriptures strongly advocate that the task of evangelism is a spiritual undertaking. Prayer is essential to seeing evangelism take place. Many groups have organized telephone prayer chains for their outreaches. Others have signed students in advance to fifteen-minute slots in which to pray for the outreach, thus creating a prayer chain before the activity.

A good outreach is one that has good evaluation done afterward. After each outreach, questions need to be asked, such as: "Were the games good? Which games were the best? Did new students come? Were people exposed to Jesus Christ? Did we get their names and addresses? Did they accept Christ? How was the message? Was it too long? Too short? What could we do better? Who is going to call them for the next outreach?"

These types of questions create an environment of excellence. If ever in our ministries we are striving to excel it needs to be at outreaches. We are seeking to present Jesus Christ in an environment that is attractive and appealing to the secular student. Tough evaluation at the end of each outreach helps develop that excellence in our future outreaches.

As we conduct training for youth leaders across the country, I find I am constantly asked two questions in terms of the evangelistic big event. The first question is, "When do we get started?" And then, second, "How do we begin?" I think the time to begin is when you have a group of students coming to you expressing an inward desire to reach their friends for Christ. This is the time to begin. How do you get started? Go to your students and ask them what type of activity you could offer to which they would bring their friends. Of course, we know that we would never do anything that would be questionable morally or ethically; but our students are the best source of helping us determine what type of event with which to start. Be creative. There are many different types of big events that could be conducted. There are as many different events as there are different people. Pull together your key students; be creative with them. Have fun organizing that big event. Make it creative; make it enjoyable.

Sonlife Ministries is designed to provide training for the youth worker within the local church. If you are interested in knowing more in detail how to design and develop outreaches, we have different types of training available. We have a two-day Sonlife Strategy Seminar that is designed to help you develop the total youth ministry within your church. We also have one-day Youth Discipleship Institutes which are designed to help you and your young people come up with creative outreaches which are specifically designed for your own group. It is my conviction that every youth group is different, and what works in one youth group will not necessarily work in the next group. Therefore, our Youth Discipleship Institutes are designed to help you and your leadership creatively plan the best outreaches for your own youth group. If you want more information about this training you can write us at: Sonlife Ministries, Moody Bible Institute, 820 N. LaSalle Drive, Chicago, IL 60610.

NOTES

1. Adapted from John M. Drescher, "A Plea for Fishing," from *Pulpit Digest*, July/August 1978.
2. George Gallup, Jr., and David Poling, *The Search for America's Faith*, (Nashville, Tenn.: Abingdon Press, 1980), p. 114.
3. *Ibid.*, p. 16.
4. *Ibid.*, p. 21.
5. *Ibid.*, p. 21.
6. *Ibid.*, p. 16.
7. *Ibid.*, p. 16.
8. *Ibid.*, p. 17.
9. *Ibid.*, p. 17.
10. *Ibid.*, p. 33.
11. *Ibid.*, p. 34.
12. David Howard, Personal interview on Feb. 3, 1983.
13. Roy G. Irving and Roy B. Zuck, *Youth and the Church* (Chicago: Moody Press, 1968), p. 14.
14. *Ibid.*, p. 14.
15. *Ibid.*, p. 15.
16. J. Dennis Miller, from proposal to develop resource ministries submitted to Moody Bible Institute on June 15, 1981.
17. "Family Portrait," article presented by Jay Kesler at Save the Family Conference, March 2-4, 1982, in Arlington Heights, Ill.
18. Matthew 28:18-20.
19. Matthew 28:18-20.
20. 1 John 2:12-14.
21. John 21:15-18.
22. William Hendriksen, *Gospel of John* (Grand Rapids: Baker Book House, 1970), p. 498.

23. Merrill Tenney, *John: The Gospel of Belief* (Grand Rapids: Eerdmans Publishing, 1948), p. 293.
24. *Insight Newsletter,* Campus Crusade for Christ, Nov. 1981.
25. "Working Mothers and Their Children," Department of Labor Report, 1978, p. 42.
26. Howard Hendricks, message given at National Conference on High School Discipleship, Aug. 1981.
27. Cam Abel, paper presented to church leadership of Harmony Bible Church, New London, Iowa, July 1982.
28. Gen Getz, "Christian Children and Obedience," message given at Fellowship Bible Church, Nov. 30, 1975.
29. David Roadcup, *Ministering to Youth, A Strategy for the 80s* (Cincinnati, Ohio: Standard Publishing, 1980), pp. 22, 23.
30. Stuart Briscoe, *Where Was the Church When the Youth Exploded?* (Grand Rapids: Zondervan Publishing, 1972), pp. 9-11.

Dr. Dann Spader, coordinator of Sonlife Ministries at Moody Bible Institute, has been working for the last fourteen years with young people. He served for over nine years as youth pastor, and has worked the last five years as coordinator of Sonlife Ministries.

Sonlife Ministries is an organization geared to the development of discipling youth ministries across the United States and Canada. Its vision is that of seeing 10,000 youth groups over the next ten years committed to discipleship and evangelism. Sonlife Ministries is working with churches across the United States and in Canada. Its training focuses upon helping the youth leadership expand their vision and develop skills in the area of youth work. Besides offering several levels of training, Sonlife Ministries also provides personalized consulting to churches. The three levels of training offered are designed for youth pastors, youth leaders, and key student leaders. In 1983, over 3,000 lay and student leaders, along with over 600 youth pastors, attended various aspects of the training.

Besides having a number of tapes and one-day training institutes available, Sonlife Ministries has week-long advanced seminars for those completing various aspects of the training of Sonlife Ministries. Some of the training is also available on videotape for rental by individual churches. For more information, write Sonlife Ministries, Moody Bible Institute, 820 North LaSalle Drive, Chicago, IL 60610, or call (312) 329-4406.

LEADING GIRLS TO CHRIST
PIONEER GIRLS
MRS. VIRGINIA PATTERSON, PRESIDENT

THE Pioneer Clubs for girls began in 1939 in response to expressed needs of a group of junior high schoolers who wanted a place where they could study the Bible, learn new things, develop skills, and have fun with their friends. Because one club was successful, other clubs began. As a result, a club format of informal activities, singing, and participative Bible study developed. Churches soon realized that a club program could attract young people from the surrounding community, and then these young people would become involved in the Christian education ministries within the churches as well.

As Pioneer Clubs began to grow and move across the United States and Canada, church and club leaders felt a need for summer camps to supplement and support the clubs' programs. In 1940 a national camping program under the direct guidance of Pioneer Clubs was organized.

HOW WAS SUCH
SUCCESSFUL GROWTH POSSIBLE?

Our growth, we believe, is based upon a continuous study and updating on how children and young people learn and grow. For example, a club leader of first and second graders needs to know that at this stage of growth, large muscles are developing. Physical activities should require the use of these muscles in games and activities such as running and jumping. This age group isn't capable of doing activities which require small muscle skills. Because younger children think more concretely, abstract concepts should not be taught until the junior high school level. Therefore, Bible studies on the life of Christ which show Jesus as a friend could be used with third and fourth grade children to whom friends are very important.

In other words, Pioneer Girls prepared a program of both activities and spiritual growth based upon the maturation level of the child, rather than on the false idea that simply "force-feeding" a lot of religious concepts would produce a spiritual response.

We know that junior high schoolers can understand parables, symbolism, and abstract concepts such as the work of the Holy Spirit. The understanding of the stages of spiritual growth and the development of faith aids in the teaching of values so necessary in the lives of children. Even first graders can understand sin because they know right from wrong and have experienced punishment and obedience. Junior high schoolers are more idealistic and often make commitments to Christ based upon their idealism and desire to live up to standards, even though these standards may be established by their peers. This is where a club leader can successfully teach and model biblical standards of living to young children.

From our study of children, ongoing research is conducted on what the needs and interests of young people are at any given time in our present culture. Curriculum materials have been developed to meet these needs and interests. The materials are tested, evaluated, continually revised, and updated in order to continue to meet the children's needs.

We believe this awareness of children's needs and interests has made our program expand so rapidly and be so successful across the nation.

WHAT IS THE MOTIVATION OF PIONEER GIRLS?

Our motivation for developing club and camping programs has been to establish Christ's Great Commission of preaching the gospel and discipling believers. We have chosen to concentrate our evangelism primarily with children and young people because values are formed at an early age. Research studies have confirmed the biblical principle, "Train up a child in the way he should go: and when he is old, he will not depart from it" (Proverbs 22:6).

Our reasons for carrying out evangelism and discipleship in a club and camp context is based on a philosophy that the most effective learning takes place in informal settings where the child is actively involved in the learning process. We have developed lesson plans which emphasize the importance and role of adult leaders.

Throughout the growing years of a child, meaningful relationships with significant adults are necessary. The relationships provide a child with role models to imitate and persons with whom to identify. A child also learns values as he or she observes and participates with adults in a variety of situations. Interaction with adults shows young people how to be "adult" as well as how character is developed.

Club and camp provide laboratory-type settings that create an environment which allows relationships to develop and encourages commitment to Christ in a secure, accepting atmosphere.

HOW WELL HAS PIONEER GIRLS SUCCEEDED?

From our rather simple beginnings, Pioneer Girls Organizations have grown from one club of junior high schoolers in 1939 to more than 2,600 churches representing some 6,500 Pioneer Clubs in the United States and Canada in 1982. Twenty-six Camp Cherith camps have been established in North America, allowing Pioneer Club members to extend their club experience in the local churches out into a camp setting during the summer months.

The program of clubs and camps has been adapted and translated into the languages and cultures of twenty foreign countries.

A complete program manual is available from our national headquarters which describes how a church may begin a program and reach out evangelistically to the girls within their own community. Simply write to Mrs. Virginia Patterson, National President, Pioneer Clubs, Inc., P.O. Box 788, Wheaton, IL 60187.

PUTTING EVANGELISM INTO YOUR LIFE STYLE
THE NAVIGATORS
BILL THRELKELD

IN sharing your faith with others, remember that it's your faith you're trying to share, not someone else's.

It's not something you heard about, not just something you read about—even though you might have read it in your Bible. Do you really know who Jesus is? If you do, sharing his gospel with someone else will be greatly simplified. It's not what information you know, but *whom* you know, and how well you know him.

It would be totally ridiculous for me to start to introduce my wife to someone and then forget her name. I know her too well for that. I can go to a foreign country and taste some exotic food and tell you right away whether my wife would like it. I can hear a song and tell you the same thing. I know the things she likes and the things she doesn't like. I know her that well. We have a relationship. I don't just know about her, but I experience life with her.

That's the way it should be in our relationship with Jesus—

living in him daily, and he in us, moment by moment. If we know him that fully, we'll be ready to talk about him with others.

Beyond that, one attitude you must have—and if it isn't there you'll need to ask God to give it to you—is a real concern for the souls of people. This is a Christlike attitude. When Jesus looked on the multitudes he was moved with compassion. Why? Because he saw that they were scared. They had no shepherd: they were drifting, they were lost.

When I was first thinking about evangelism I asked myself these questions: If when I drive home from work today and pass a house on fire, and I stop and hear someone screaming inside, would I be willing to go in there to try to pull him out? Most of us would try something, somehow.

But when someone is spiritually lost and going to hell, does it affect me in the same way?

As he was speaking one day, a pastor took off his glasses and marked a cross on the lenses with a grease pencil. Then he put them back on and said to his hearers, "You look different. Everywhere I look now I see the cross of Jesus Christ. I see the price that was paid for you."

God gave up Christ on the cross because he loved the world—everybody in it. If we don't let this fact grip us to the depths of our souls, I fear our evangelism will become mechanical—just something we do every Tuesday night, or whenever.

The right heart motivation in evangelism is love—a loving response to the loving God. We love because he first loved us. Yes, obedience is a factor too—witnessing to others because we are commanded to. But why should we want to obey? Surely the love factor must be there.

If you asked me to summarize the Bible's theme, I would say love. We know from 1 John 4 that God is love. And when Jesus was asked to tell the greatest commandment he gave a two-part answer with love in both parts: Love God and love your fellowman. Love was the motivation for God giving his only begotten Son. We need not ask why God gave us his Son. He's already told us. It's because he loves us.

Since we are in his image, following in his footsteps, we also must love. This love will cause us to be motivated. Witnessing will become an issue of life style for us. Our gospel glasses will be on; our motivation will be right; we will recognize the value of a soul.

As for obedience, 2 Timothy 4:5 is a striking illustration. Here Paul told Timothy to "do the work of an evangelist." I presume that if Timothy had possessed the gift of evangelism, Paul would have said, "Exercise the gift of evangelism that is in you." Or, more likely, Timothy would already be exercising the gift and Paul would simply encourage him to continue.

But Paul instead told him to do an evangelist's work, to be an evangelist. The issue for Timothy was to be obediently sharing the gospel, whether or not he was gifted in the subject.

So the right way to witness is in love and obedience, and to share your own faith in Christ. There is also a right time to share.

Some years ago when I was in the military, a man was assigned to me for training who was arrogant, egotistical, and argumentative. He was an agnostic, and proudly so. I was praying for him, and asking God to show me how to deal with this fellow. I said, "Lord, I don't have the foggiest notion what to do with him. But you know, and I'm asking you to tell me what to do." The answer was clear: Tell him nothing. Live the Christian life and love him, but tell him nothing about Christ unless he asks.

Weeks went by. I was conducting a seminar and was also responsible for teaching him how to conduct it. He had been through the course before as a student, and now was watching me to learn how to teach it.

One day he said, "You conduct your seminar differently."

I said, "Yes, I agree with you." I said no more.

Later he said, "You have a different relationship with these men than most other instructors have."

I answered, "I think that's true. In fact, I intend for that to happen."

He kept probing until I said, "Bob, there's no way you can understand it. Not now, not in your situation."

He's a very intelligent man, and he gave me a strange look. The truth of 1 Corinthians 2:14 was in my mind: "The man without the Spirit does not accept the things that come from the Spirit of God, for they are foolishness to him, and he cannot understand them."

"I'm serious about that," I said. "This is a spiritual matter and it has to be spiritually discerned. And in your situation you can't understand that. But I can explain it—if you really desire to understand it. Would you like me to?"

He said yes. I was privileged then not only to lead him to Christ, but also to disciple him afterward. He later told me how quickly he would have rejected what I said if I had spoken about Christ in those early weeks. He asked me why I waited, and I said God had told me to.

The Holy Spirit is our power source for knowing when to speak and what to say. If you don't rely on the Spirit, you'll find evangelism becoming mechanical. You'll become disillusioned. You'll become disheartened. You won't see what you expect to see. People may respond, but it won't be real.

I once went through a gospel tract with a fellow, and when we came to the prayer at the end I asked him if he could pray this prayer and really mean it. He looked at the prayer and said yes.

Then it was just as if I heard the Lord say to me, "Hold it." I quickly prayed for direction, and the issue of sin came forcefully to mind.

I said to the fellow, "We need to go over another issue or two," and we looked again at sin. We looked up the list of sins in Galatians 5. He knew stealing was sin, and lying. But when I explained fornication to him, he said he didn't know it was a sin.

When I asked him if he was willing to give it up, he said, "Not on your life."

"Well, are you willing to pray and ask God to help you give it up?"

"No, you don't understand. I really like that."

"Well, are you willing to pray and ask God to change your heart so that you'll want to give it up?"

"I'm not willing to give it up for anybody," he said.

"Are you willing to go to hell over it?"

He said, "I guess I am."

He had been ready to pray the prayer just as the Holy Spirit stopped me. I would have let him get away with a cheap gospel with no repentance. He was responding to a mechanical thrust, no more believing in it than he would believe in the man in the moon.

Eight months later I saw him in an airport terminal. By this time he had become willing and repentant, and he had made a decision for Jesus Christ.

Yes, the secret is capitalizing on the Holy Spirit's power. Recognize that you're in a spiritual war. This is not fun and games, or simply a manner of methodology. It's God against the devil.

Prayer is required to tap this spiritual power. One thing that has changed my life is to pray while I'm in conversation with someone I'm witnessing to: "Lord, show me where to start . . . what would you have me to do? What would you have me say? What Scripture passages would you have me use? How would you have me answer his questions?"

If there's a rule, it's to find out what God wants you to do and to say. Maybe it's nothing. Or maybe you should take a strong initiative. Perhaps rather than speak, you should help the person with something, or ask him to help you.

Once I was driving on Interstate 65 in Alabama after an afternoon rain and I saw a car off the road on the opposite side of the highway, with two young women standing there. Now the Lord knows I don't like to change a tire. The first time my father showed me how to do it, I decided I didn't like it, and I still don't. But I prayed and slowed down.

I stopped my car and walked over the median and got to them just in time. They were about to drop the car off the jack because they didn't have the jack in the slot in the bumper.

So we straightened that out and I changed the tire. They thanked me and asked me if they could pay for my trouble. I said, "No, not with money. But I gave you fifteen minutes out of my life and I would appreciate it if you would give me fifteen minutes out of your life to tell you something I consider very important."

I knew God wanted me to talk to them. I knew it was a possibility when I first slowed the car down and I prayed, "Lord, do you really want me to do this?" His answer was yes. So I knew to stop and help, whether or not I like to change tires.

I guess there's no way I could really tell you how to do this, except to give you the perspective from my life. For me the secret is to continually pray, "Lord, what would you have me to do?"

As you pray, learn to plead with God: "O God, please!" I learned this from my daughter when she was small. She was very disobedient, and I said, "Joy, what does Ephesians 6:1 say?"

She said, "I don't want to tell you." I asked her to tell me anyway.

"Well, it says, 'Children, obey your parents in the Lord, for this is right.' "

"Yes, that's exactly right; and what did you do?"

"I know, Daddy, I disobeyed."

"What are you supposed to do when you disobey?"

"I know, Daddy, I know what I'm supposed to do."

So I let her spend some time alone with the Lord to work that out. When I put her to bed that night she volunteered to pray. She took a deep breath: "God, I'm sorry. Help me not to do it anymore!"

It was such a plea. I thought, here's someone pleading from the depths of her heart. When is the last time I pleaded with God?

Most of us don't plead. In fact, a lot of us don't even ask. But earnest prayer like this brings answers.

I've asked the Lord to give me a real empathy for people, to help me feel how they feel. I believe God has helped me do that, and he's continuing to help me so I can identify more closely with people.

It's important to meet people at their point of interest, just as Jesus did with the woman at the well. It helps in this to be widely read. I try to read in several subject areas, and I make it a point to read the newspaper. Once I met a fellow who was interested in track. I had read that day about regional track championships that were being held locally. I knew a few names of the expected top finishers. He was excited as we began talking about this. We developed a strong rapport and I was able to share the gospel with him.

Have you ever gone up to the trashman and thanked him for picking up your garbage? I did that last week. He didn't have time to listen to the gospel, but at least the door has been opened.

That's life-style evangelism. Think and pray about it every morning when you walk out your front door. Let it be a way of life for you, whatever you do.

Manuals and lesson books on life-style evangelism are available from The Navigators, and interested persons may obtain a catalog by simply writing to The Navigators, P.O. Box 6000, Colorado Springs, CO 80934.

REACHING TEENS
THROUGH PROGRAM
FATHER MICHAEL G. FOLEY

GOOD NEWS: A STARTLING DEVELOPMENT

The immense energy with which the gospel burst upon the world was startling even to the early disciples. Each of their lives was consumed with the single-minded purpose of proclaiming God's kingdom and showing how that Good News might penetrate and transform the lives of individuals and whole communities. They were called to trust completely in his Word and promise and to give themselves over to his transforming Spirit. God's revolution had begun.

The person and the message of Jesus provided the foundation upon which such a life of faith, hope, and love would be developed. Christ's own role as prophet, priest, and servant king came to life in the mission of his people as they proclaimed and taught God's Word, celebrated the sacred mysteries, and dedicated themselves in compassionate service to others.

Today we share that same mission. The same wellspring of energy that is the presence of the Holy Spirit continues to offer refreshment, wisdom, and strength. This is what we hope to share with the young. This is not merely the task of highly developed youth evangelization movements. It is the responsibility of each local parish community to offer to our youth the Good News of Jesus. What I hope to share with you are some of the equally startling yet simple ways that our ordinary parishes can invite their youth into the great Christian adventure.

"WHERE ARE THE KIDS?"

In 1976, the United States Catholic Conference published a small booklet with the provocative title "Where Are the 6.6 Million?" Using baptismal records as a base, they compared the potential number of elementary and high school age Roman Catholic youth with the actual number involved in formal religious education in either our schools or parish programs. Six and a half million youth were not involved in formal religious education in 1974. That was a sobering piece of information. At the same time they noted that over 8.5 million youth were receiving formal religious education during this one year alone. So many young people were missing, but the numbers involved were equally astounding. Moreover these figures did not include nonacademic youth ministries.

Imagine what would happen if the hearts of those young people who are already involved in our parish and school ministries could be touched in a significant way by the Good News that is the Lord's gift. Perhaps these young people could be the bridge to reach the uninvolved.

One of the problems that the Catholic Church faces, especially here in the Northeast, is not lack of numbers of youth but, on the contrary, too many youth to handle effectively in the way we organize our ministries. Even in a medium-sized diocese such as Worcester, Massachusetts, where the parishes are of reasonable size, it is not unusual to have high school religious education programs that number from 200 to 500 youth. It is a strange paradox. In some ways our abundance can leave us overwhelmed and we can be satisfied with the goal of survival. Extraordinary opportunities for evangelization and care for the young are missed because there are so many young people. We can become satisfied with far less than what God wants to give. But how can we tap this exceptional opportunity to reach our own young people?

WHAT IS AN EVANGELIZING CATECHESIS?

In the past several years, with the renewed efforts of catechesis called for by the *National Catechetical Directory* and by Pope John Paul II in *Catechesi Tradendae,* there has been a concerted effort to incorporate the elements of evangelization into already-existing opportunities for catechesis.

Evangelization seeks to *arouse the beginnings of faith that center around an experience of interior change and conversion.* Disciples of Jesus who follow him and desire to love God and one another as they have been loved themselves, will need to recognize their sinfulness and undergo a real conversion, "a profound change of the whole person by which one begins to consider, judge, and arrange his life according to the holiness and love of God."

Conversion is always present in the dynamics of true growth in faith. The process of conversion is ongoing and is the constant reference point from which deeper religious learning and commitment will emerge. A need, a hunger for God and his Word arises within the context of our basic human need for security, affection, growth, and intellectual development. Through the power of the Holy Spirit and the Word and example of believers, the gospel invitation is extended.

The purpose of *catechesis* is *to make a person's faith become living, conscious, and active through the light of instruction.* Sharing faith life, experiencing liturgical worship, taking part in Christian service, and participating in religious instruction are all essential components of the catechetical experience. Although initiation, education, and formation of individuals and the faith community pertain expecially to catechesis, every pastoral activity has a catechetical dimension.

The source of catechesis, which is also its content, is found in God's Word, fully revealed in Jesus Christ. As people exercise their faith under the guidance of the teaching church and the inspiration of the Spirit, they become more capable of revealing God's Word in their own lives. Religious education is intended to help people become more aware of the signs of God's saving activity and self-communication in the world through the process of catechesis.

We study Scripture, liturgical symbolism, creedal formulations, and church history to understand the powerful and concrete witness of our Christian heritage. A true understanding and interpretation of this heritage should inspire us to lead moral lives, consistent with our Christian beliefs and values. Such conviction also requires that we seek to correct conditions in society and the church which hinder authentic human development and the flourishing of Christian values.

In theory, when people are engaged in the process of catechesis, it is presumed that they have already experienced some degree of evangelization and conversion to Jesus Christ. However, most of our young people have been baptized as small children. In many cases, while they have psychological, emotional, and cultural identification with the church, there is little explicit commitment of their lives to Jesus. Even after many years of systematic catechesis and in-depth preparation for the sacraments, they can leave with mere knowledge of formulas and experience of rituals. In such cases, obviously something needs to be changed.

Pope John Paul II in *Catechesi Tradendae* called for such a change when he observed that, "Catechesis must often concern itself not only with nourishing and teaching the faith, but also with arousing it unceasingly with the help of grace, with opening the heart, with converting, and with preparing total adherence to Jesus Christ on the part of those who are still on the threshold of faith. This concern will in part decide the tone, the language and the method of catechesis" (#19).

Father Francis D. Kelly, of the National Catholic Education Association, has suggested an attempt to unify and energize catechesis by centering it on the person of Jesus and orienting it toward conversion. He calls this approach *an evangelizing catechesis*. He sees this approach as consolidating the best of the past by enabling us to harness the spirit, energy, and dynamism of the biblical, educational, and liturgical renewals of the twentieth century. More importantly, this evangelizing catechesis can put these great resources at the disposal of the Spirit's work of developing the faith life of the young.

But how realistic is such an evangelizing catechesis? Can it, in fact, be incorporated into the very structure of present parish life and the existing youth culture? Are the numbers too great? Are the hearts too hard? My own skepticism has been profoundly challenged by two personal experiences.

THE REASON FOR MY HOPE

In 1970, I had the good fortune of serving as a deacon in St. Paul's parish, Mbaga, Kenya. Here was a community of more than twenty thousand active Christians living in a parish that covered about two hundred square miles. There were two parish priests, eight African sisters, and a trained catechist on staff.

Surely I could have made a list of at least twenty sociological reasons why such a community should not work. But when I read in the Acts of the Apostles of the incredible power in the early church that engulfed the people of Jerusalem, I feel that I really know what happened because I experienced it in the people of St. Paul's. All my excuses about size, mobility, and lack of communication being insurmountable barriers to the gospel were dissipated. Why did it work there? The answer was simple. There was clearly one center for this community and it was the Lord Jesus.

Although physically scattered, we were bonded intimately together. People would spend as many as three years living together in the mission prior to baptism. Each week more than fifty smaller communities would gather in the local villages for prayer, study, and ministry. We would personally visit three or four of these small communities each week. We were welcomed warmly, as were the hundreds of visitors that came to the mission each week. Our shared faith in Jesus Christ, especially as it was experienced in the celebration of Eucharist, gave us unity and was at the heart of all that this community did.

What happened was that everything was transformed. The ordinary and the routine were invigorated. When we learned about God we fell in love, and that love turned to service for one another.

The young were easily and naturally welcomed into this church. Expectations were clear, and training was vigorous, but always in an atmosphere of genuine love. We had our problems, just like the early church did. But there was no question that this was a community of faith touched by the Spirit of God.

The second experience happened about seven years ago when our ministry began to work with prisoners at the local jail. The average age of the men confined there was early twenties, with not a few teenagers. My fears turned to awe as the weekend retreats progressed. I can still hear a young man named Jim, serving time for kidnapping and attempted rape, speak of the love of God he had experienced, his sorrow for what he had done, and his newfound freedom, even in the midst of prison. I saw a young man we called T.P. experience an incredible emotional healing which released a long-lost gift of song. To paraphrase Pope Paul VI, I experienced firsthand that hidden energy of the Good News which is able to have a powerful effect on the human conscience. In this small community of broken men, the incredible transforming force of the gospel was unleashed. Moreover, it was done with ordinary people using the simplest of methods.

My experience in jail raised a disturbing paradox for me. Why should these criminals, these outcasts of society, be so responsive to the gospel and so many of our apparently "good" people, especially the young, be so uninspired or even bored?

Paul's letter to the Hebrews says that "the word of God is alive and active, sharper than any two-edged sword." Sometimes in our classes and gatherings it appeared that we were using a wet noodle rather than a two-edged sword.

Have we really underestimated God's gift? Are we too easily satisfied with survival? Will it even be possible to survive if the gift is not used as fully as God expects?

Each community really needs to answer these questions for itself. My own belief is that young people have a far more radical need for God, and a readiness to respond to the Good News, than we usually recognize. A profound, although often inarticulate, awareness of the radical vulnerability of being human is just below the apparently secure surface of most young people's lives. It strikes me as symptomatic that seventeen-year-olds should make courses on death and dying a popular school elective; that the suicide rate among teenagers has increased 250 percent in one generation; or that a growing body of evidence points to dramatic negative psychological undercurrents being caused by fear of nuclear destruction. Those fortunate enough to share those sacred and personal moments with youth, as they peel back and probe what really matters in their lives, know of the profound need that is there. I believe there is a real urgency within the lives of young people today, an urgency to which the gospel must effectively speak. However, we must be careful that the urgency of the need not lead to a compulsive and overbearing response on the part of the adults. Rather we must take the time to let patience, compassion, and wisdom temper our enthusiasm and clarify our expectations.

JESUS WAS A TEENAGER, TOO!

What does a spiritually healthy Christian teenager look like? How do teenagers fit into God's plan of salvation? All of us in ministry with the young work out of some set of expectations, either unconsciously or consciously. It is important to have a clear understanding of our expectations because they will profoundly influence what we do and how effective we might be. Some people develop their expectations upon psychological or sociological models. While these can be helpful, personally I prefer the simple, yet profound model for youthful expectations found in Scripture, especially as it is seen in the life of Jesus himself. If, indeed, Jesus is "like us in all things but sin" then we might find in him not only a model of mature adult living, but also a model for appreciating maturity in a teenager.

But Scripture seems to say so little about the teenage Jesus. The Gospel of Luke provides us with a somewhat troubling account of a twelve-year-old Jesus who has avoided returning home to Nazareth in order to do what he will later cryptically call "his Father's business." Mary and Joseph are not terribly impressed with the excuse of their pseudo-runaway. They are still recovering from the trauma of the imagined loss of their precious child. "Father's business" or not, he returns to Nazareth with his parents and is obedient to them. Luke then goes on to summarize the next eighteen years, what we call youth and young adulthood, with but one sentence: "Jesus grew in wisdom, stature, and grace before God and man." Luke's words are few, but they hold a wealth of revealed truth.

First, according to Luke, Jesus went through a process of growth. While that seems obvious, adults often have difficulties dealing with youth because they presume that teenagers are really adults like themselves, simply packaged in less mature bodies. A teenager's less-than-adult response to a situation becomes a source of aggravation and even scandal. That Jesus was a teenager and went through a similar process of growth might give adults pause for thought.

It was a common practice of the biographers and novelists of antiquity to emphasize the harmonious physical and intellectual development of their heroes. Luke seems to follow this practice. The word Luke uses, *Prokopo*, is an ancient Greek nautical term that referred to making headway even in the midst of storms. Our contemporary idea of "making progress" has its roots in this concept. While the concept of growth involves a clear positive direction of progressive change, it does set some limits to our expectations. Growth will ultimately be dependent on God. It will take time. It will move through various stages of development. It will demand patience on the part of those who would like to assist in the developmental process to allow the change to evolve. In the word's ancient roots we also find a hint of pain and struggle that will accompany this growth.

Luke goes on to present to us three specific areas of growth that took place in the life of the young Jesus. Jesus grew in wisdom, grace, and stature. We might consider these three as the goals of adolescent growth or the criteria for recognizing the presence of God's Spirit in the young. Our role in relationship to the young is to nurture, support, and challenge their growth in these areas. We must be cautioned, however, that while we might mediate these goals, they are essentially dependent upon God's gift.

The remainder of this presentation will concern itself with practical ways that the parish community can support the harmonious growth of adolescence in these three areas. We will look at growth in grace in terms of conversion and community; growth in wisdom as content and contemplation; and growth in stature in terms of commitment and the Cross.

GROWING IN GRACE: CONVERSION AND COMMUNITY

Recently I was talking with Ann, a new graduate from one of our Catholic high schools. She had experienced one of our young adult retreat weekends called T.E.C., Teens Encounter Christ. She held up her Bible and said, "There is just so much here. I can't believe it. Why didn't anybody tell me about this before?" Now, I am very familiar with the school and the teachers where Ann attended. Ann, indeed, had some very good courses on the Bible, and she knows a great deal about God and her religion. However, obviously something was missing. Maybe she was not really ready to appreciate what she was being offered before. But maybe these courses presumed too much. Perhaps Ann never had an explicit opportunity to build what she was learning on a personal acceptance of Jesus as her Lord and connect what she studied with what she was experiencing in her heart.

Luke says that Jesus grew in grace, or *charis*. The richness of this word defies easy definition. It is used in the New Testament to designate the saving will of God, both in itself and in its effect. It is the saving will of God that enables the Christian to hear the Good News, to believe it, to become one with Jesus, and to live in union with him according to his ideals. It captures the sense of ecstatic joy that filled the Wise Men at the sight of the Bethlehem star, and the wonder and awe that moved the followers of Jesus. It refers to the divine spark that reaches in and draws a person beyond herself so that she can be one with God and one with other people. Was this the spark that Ann's weekend retreat had provided her an opportunity to recognize?

THE GRACE OF CONVERSION

Since we cannot by our own power give this "grace" or set this spark, our goal with youth must rest within the realm of our responsibility. The goal we set for ourselves was: *To provide to our youth a clear, personal, and authentic presentation of the fundamentals of the gospel, communicated in language they can understand, with an opportunity for them to respond to it personally and freely.*

Such a goal makes some very explicit demands upon us. First, we must have a sound and precise knowledge of the *kerygma*, the fundamentals of the gospel. We must clearly know what is the "Good News" we have to offer. We must not confuse our own priorities with God's priorities. Second, in order to communicate in language, including different forms of image, methods, and experience that they can understand, we really need to know our own young people in a personal and concrete way. We must be able to interpret how this is "Good News" for them today. This was precisely the task of the early evangelists as they proclaimed the gospel to very different communities.

In preparing people for ministry with the young we take them through a three-step process called "Getting in Touch." We begin by helping them remember what it was like when they were teenagers. We help them recall what they did, what they felt, and how others responded to them. We presume that as people remember they become gentler.

Humor often takes the place of anger. Sometimes they might uncover an unhealed wound. It is important that they begin to experience healing before they go further.

After they have a pretty good sense of themselves, we try to help them go through some activities in order to get to know their own young people personally. Who are the young people they want to serve? What is their high school like? What really bothers them? What do they do after school? What do they want out of life?

It is only after they have really come to know a specific group of young people that we introduce them to more theoretical and academic information about youth. At this point they can read critically, calling upon a real knowledge based on personal and lived experience.

Finally, it is not enough to present the gospel; we need also to create an atmosphere in which youth will have the opportunity to respond personally and freely to this proclamation. Our methods become ones that treat youth in a patient, gentle, and respectful way. We scrupulously guard the freedom of the adolescent and are careful not to manipulate their developing sensibilities and vulnerabilities.

We know that conversion cannot be programmed but that we can offer opportunities for conversion. Moreover, we have come to realize that because of the dramatic growth dimension of young lives, conversion is seldom a one experience event. As youth mature and their language and experiences deepen they need again and again to be invited to new depths of experiencing God's love and the call to conversion.

Within an evangelizing catechesis this means that there must be a continual interplay between arousing the beginnings of faith and the effort to help that faith become "living, conscious, and active through instruction." We might use the imagery of a song with a recurring melody or refrain to express this relationship. The verses of the song are the ever-deepening instruction in the faith. The melody or refrain, which penetrates all of the instruction, is a constant invitation to reclaim the foundation upon which all the rest depends, the fundamental experience of God's love, the call to repentance and acceptance of Jesus as one's personal Lord and God.

We have also found that God works more powerfully in the young the more the experience of an evangelizing catechesis is integrated into the full life of the community. The divine spark that draws people closer to God also makes them hunger to be one with other people. This is especially evident in the experience of the sacraments. In fact, the celebration of the sacraments of Eucharist and reconciliation are the two best opportunities we have found for evangelizing the young.

It is amazing. When most young people are asked what was the most important part of a retreat weekend, they often speak of a special intimacy with God and the other young people experienced at Mass or a heavy burden lifted or a powerful healing experienced during confession. Should this surprise us? After all, in the celebration of these sacraments we are laying claim to the most fundamental of Jesus' redemptive promises as they are mediated through his church.

In reconciliation we are called to recognize our sin, experience sorrow, turn back toward God, and accept his healing and transforming forgiveness. In Eucharist we stand and approach the altar, in what some might call an altar call, and say, "Yes, I accept the very life of Jesus Christ as the source of my life." We have found that when these sacraments are celebrated in a way that respects our evangelical goal stated above, that God works in extraordinary ways, both personally and communally, with the young. This entire experience is heightened when young people are given active roles in the preparation and enactment of these celebrations.

The sacrament of confirmation has become a powerful religious event on which young people can focus their spiritual growth. As youth enter the ninth grade they are invited to participate in a minimum of two years of preparation for this sacrament. During this preparation they are asked to reaffirm their faith and accept more deeply the transforming power of the Holy Spirit so that what they believe can be better lived. Most youth are juniors or seniors in high school before receiving the sacrament. What this preparation does provide is an explicit opportunity for youth to review their baptismal commitment in the light of their maturing years.

Years of personal contact with these youth have shown me that they experience a far deeper relationship with God and the church than they can articulate. Too often their inability to speak well is interpreted as lack of faith. It is critical in this preparation that there be many opportunities and different forms of activity that help youth express outwardly what is being experienced in their hearts. Whether this takes place by writing, art forms, or group experience, etc., the very attempt at expression helps clarify the experience and encourages others to share more deeply.

THE GRACE OF COMMUNITY

A parish with a healthy evangelical relationship with the young will be characterized by its capacity for welcome and participation. Young people tend to be natural outsiders in most adult communities, not by choice but by the inability of adults to welcome and integrate them into full community life. We are welcomed primarily by being accepted and valued, but not simply on adult terms. As adults we must be ready to be open to what youth have to offer and need, be ready to affirm the positive qualities of their way of life, and patiently try to understand that which is foreign to us. Preaching will touch life issues that are important to them. Like the apostles at the first Pentecost, we can learn to speak in tongues that are understandable even to youth and young adults.

Some of our parishes have found it very effective to develop their religious education classes as small base communities. Over a three-year period of preparation for confirmation, a group of eight to ten youth will have the same teacher. Often they meet in the home of the teacher or in the parish house. A very natural and profound process of welcome usually occurs as anxiety and distrust are replaced by personal affection and confidence. Such a way of organizing provides entry into the community through a nonparental adult. It also provides for a less formal atmosphere and opportunities for both adults and youth to deal with the personal needs of each other. These teachers have often become interpreters and advocates for the young among the rest of the adult community, and they provide a source of continuity for the young.

It is critical that such adults be emotionally and spiritually healthy. They must love the young, know their faith, and be committed to the Christian life style. Their personal example and witness will model what they teach. It is also quite easy to integrate into this setting opportunities for personal and intimate prayer and reflection so that the invitation from God might be recognized and accepted.

It is important also that young people develop a sense of community that goes beyond the local parish. Our appreciation of ourselves as a transcultural, worldwide, universal church community can be a source of wonder, awe, and inspiration to the young. To be part of a church community that reaches back through 6,000 years of Jewish Christian tradition and into every corner and culture of the world provides more than fascination. It is a very concrete step in the realization of our destiny as set by Jesus, "that they may be one."

It has been a profound and moving experience to take young people on pilgrimage to Rome and the Holy Land. Since this is not possible for everybody, we also have been able to introduce our youth to the incredible variety of religious expressions that are found locally. In the diocese of Worcester there are at least thirteen major strains of Roman Catholicism, ranging from Trappist monks to Catholic workers, Eastern Rites, and charismatic renewal, just to name a few. Young people respond to this variety with an awareness that there probably is a place well suited to them in this church.

What we are as community is both awesome and fragile. Some youth might perceive a universal church as distant, unfeeling, and authoritarian. They might also be turned off by our all too obvious and specific failings within the parish itself. But I have confidence that as they get to really know us, they will also grow to love us.

Finally, one of the best ways we can welcome our youth into our community is by offering them opportunities to participate more fully by using their gifts and talents in service. We will share more about this point when we deal with commitment.

GROWING IN WISDOM: CONTENT AND CONTEMPLATION

The second quality that we expect to see emerging in the lives of young Christians is wisdom. True wisdom, *sophia,* comes from God. It gives to us "a heart capable of discerning good from evil" (1 Kings 3:9). This is in contrast to a false wisdom by which we acquire by our own power "the knowledge of good and evil" (Genesis 3:5). True wisdom is a divine gift, mysterious and hidden, revealed by the Spirit of God to those who are open to him (1 Corinthians 2ff.). It involves first a revelation of the mystery of God, and second, counsels of practical ethics and matters of daily Christian living.

WISDOM THROUGH CONTENT

Clearly there is a specific content, a body of wisdom, that is part of our Christian tradition. It is a content that goes beyond the *kerygma.* Clearly it is part of the responsibility of the adult community to share this fuller expression of the "Good News" with the young. However, when we begin to make decisions about how much and in what way we are to communicate this material, we sometimes run into problems. There is so much to learn and so little time. It is easy to panic and become compulsive. We can imagine a fifteen-year-old with a funnel in the top of his head having 6,000 years of history, experience, and teaching being pumped in mercilessly. Again, expectations are critical for setting reasonable goals when it comes to content.

There is an old Jewish saying that describes the four kinds of pupils of the wise teacher. There is the "sponge" who absorbs everything without distinction. There is the "funnel" who lets the words of the teacher in one end and then out the other. There is the "strainer" who lets the good wine pass and retains sediment. Finally, there is the "sieve" who lets out the bran dust and retains the fine flower. Only the "sieve" is a true student, one who is expected to gather the best from the teacher's words and then add to this richness from his own experience.

Sharing the content of faith with the young is subject to some clear limitations. There is the limit set by the historical condition and personal capacity of the minister of the Word, the teacher or catechist. The key to good content is clearly a good teacher. Good teachers have always been able to overcome the dullness and boredom of any subject and "turn-on" students. Effective teachers need to be properly prepared and supported. We assume that adults who share the gospel with youth are, indeed, believers themselves who have experienced a profound, personal experience of Jesus in their lives. Even when that is the case, it is not enough. They must also have developed their own capacity for wisdom.

Prior to teaching, volunteer catechists are required to attend a forty-hour training program that reviews the basic elements of Christian revelation and church teaching. Along with this they are provided with resources to adapt this material to the capacity and needs of the young people they serve. For the more adventurous, a 120-hour training program for those ministering with high school age or young adults is offered. In eight years more than two hundred people have participated in this latter program. An array of other learning programs and spiritual growth opportunities are offered throughout the year so that the adults too might continue to be challenged and grow.

Well-prepared catechists are able to center the entire preparation of their lesson plans around the person of Jesus. Young people should be able to meet Jesus in every class. When the catechist prepares with both Jesus and specific youth in mind, something special occurs. They reflect on what Jesus said about this material and how he taught it. Moreover, they can ask more specifically what they think he would like to say to these particular young people. What would he do so that he could speak to their hearts? When we give room for the Holy Spirit to work we should not be surprised when something happens. A lesson prepared around the mind and heart of Jesus is seldom boring.

A second limit is found in the young people themselves. We must be aware of the personal capacity of each person as well as the developmental limits of each stage of growth. We can easily forget the practical advice of St. Paul to feed children in the faith "milk, not solid food" because they are not ready for it (1 Corinthians 3:1, 2). On the other hand, we must be careful not to underestimate the movement of God or the intellectual and spiritual skills of the young. The development of "peer ministry" in which youth share a role in the teaching process with younger children and with their contemporaries has opened up a source of dramatic impact on the young church. The witness value is exceptional and young people often share the more formal role as teacher themselves. As we learn to demand and challenge, not out of compulsive fear, but based upon the realistic capacity of specific youth, the growth in wisdom accelerates.

Finally we need to be aware of the limits of the expression of the gospel and the tradition themselves. They too, in spite of their divine origins, were experienced and expressed within a particular context and a specific historical perspective. While all elements of our heritage are precious, some truths are, in fact, more essential than others. We refer to this distinction as the "hierarchy of truths." In preparing the curriculum for an evangelizing catechesis, a real effort must be given to choosing what will be taught so that it can be a foundation for future learning.

Religious learning need not be limited to a formal religion class. Content is most effective when it is seen as having a bearing on real life. There are many opportunities to challenge young people to learn more about their faith and to interpret their activities with Christian eyes. The way a sports program or a service activity is handled can make it an excellent opportunity for learning how God fits into our everyday life.

WISDOM THROUGH CONTEMPLATION

Even if the standards for catechesis suggested by Pope John Paul II are followed—that it be systematic, dealing with essentials, sufficiently complete, and an integral Christian initiation—there is another needed dimension. We might call it the contemplative.

All catechesis points to prayer and worship. It should lead people to a sense of the sacred and to a recognition of God's presence in their lives (National Catechetical Directory 145). If wisdom gives us a "heart capable of discovering good and evil" we need a real effort to bring the knowledge of the mind to dwell with the heart. Admittedly, trying to nurture the development of spirituality in a young person is a humbling experience. Prayer and spiritual relationships begin only with God's invitation. We can assume a role somewhat akin to a tour director. We can guide people on a journey to see the sights. We can help explain what we see. But we cannot make them have a good time.

Young people need to pray. Our fast-paced world can often make their lives frantic and fragmented. An element of stability and sanity can be introduced into their lives through experiencing silence, solitude, and a life consciously centered on God. In contrast to compulsive learning, contemplative learning allows time to get to know the God we are hearing about. There is time to feel what it means to be loved by God and called to repentance and transformation. There is the opportunity to begin to personally apply the teachings of the gospel and the church to my life.

Prayer and time for God need to be introduced into all aspects and occasions of Christian gathering with the young. There is a wisdom of how we function as physical/spiritual beings that can be learned and applied to the way we live. We encourage young people to learn about the history and forms of prayer, to experiment with various ways of prayer, and to meet and share with other people who have grown wise in their experience of prayer and intimacy with God.

GROWING IN STATURE: COMMITMENT AND THE CROSS

If God, as the author of all creation, rules over all growth, then even physical growth is a tangible sign of his presence and activity. Luke says that Jesus grew in stature, *haylakia*. In contrast to the other two qualities of youthful growth, stature is much simpler. It can refer to growing older, physically larger and stronger, emotionally more mature; and to developing the personal qualities and powers that are our own special gifts from God. This external growth can also, by way of analogy, mirror a profound interior spiritual change that is taking place. There is a sense of maturing strength of the whole person both externally and internally.

The key for Jesus' own maturing was "obedience." After Jesus is found in the temple, he will go back to Nazareth with Mary and Joseph to their ordinary life and he will be obedient to them. Obedience means far more than simple submitting to the power of another. Its deepest meaning is to listen to another. We listen not just with our ears but with all of our senses. To listen and to obey is to learn by example. Obedience will be central to the way Jesus himself teaches. At the heart of Jesus' way of teaching is the call to "follow him." Jesus will teach not only by his words and actions but above all by the example of his own life. To "follow" Jesus conveys the strong sense that we are to pay close attention to the way he lives and then imitate his way of living. To the rich young man, he invites, "Do what I have done" (Mark 10:17-21). Even more explicitly at the washing of the feet at the Last Supper he tells his apostles, "I have set an example for you, so that you will do just what I have done for you" (John 13:15).

While Jesus learned a great deal by "listening to" Mary and Joseph, the real source of his own growth is his Father. At one point Jesus reflects on an ancient Hebrew proverb: "I tell you the truth, the Son can do nothing on his own; he does only what he sees his Father doing. For the Father loves the Son and shows him all that he himself is doing" (John 5:19, 20).

A true child of God would watch and imitate the working of God in all the life around and within himself. He would learn not only the trade of the carpenter from an earthly father, but the ways of creative love from a heavenly Father. The witness of others, the witness of creation, and the witness of the Scriptures provided the example to be imitated.

Young people today need to grow in this same way. An evangelical catechesis would hope to help youth grow strong by providing the example and support of a believing community; a challenge to know their own hearts and develop their own gifts; and opportunities to use in practical and useful ways their gifts and knowledge about the ways of God and his people in service to the community and the world. This is hard work. It is at the heart of the challenge of discipleship which demands dying to self, picking up our cross each day, and following in the footsteps of Jesus.

If we take seriously the Body of Christ imagery presented by St. Paul, we will realize that the useful, creative, and productive participation of young people is necessary for healthy Christian community. It is not enough to prepare youth to be the "church of the future." We will be overlooking one of God's most precious gifts if we do not recognize and accept our youth as the "young church today."

Our culture continues to delay the transition from youth to adulthood to ever older ages. Sometimes we want to protect young people too much, but our delay tactics often just keep them from growing strong. In many ways we have been quite successful by instilling a sense of social awareness in our youth. Many of our young people have developed a sense of duty to do their part for charity, peace, and justice. However, often they do not know where to begin.

In 1976 when we gathered hundreds of youth for a "Share Your Gifts '76" project, the most commonly introduced concern was, "I see people in need but I don't know what to do." Disciples need to develop disciplines of service. To care effectively in a world where self-interest and power appear to rule will require not only interior strength but practical skills.

Many of the problems faced by contemporary society are long-term and multigenerational. The "now" generation will have nothing to offer. Only those faithful ones, working out of a great vision and serving as part of a community will be able to bring the healing and hope that Jesus promises. It is the Cross of Jesus that reveals the demands and dimensions of real sacrificial and redemptive love. Whether it develops in our appreciation of Eucharist or awareness of Right to Life issues, the Cross opens to us an experience of being loved beyond measure. Here is the source of our real strength, for "if God is for us who can be against us?" Over the years our youth ministry has worked out a model for helping our youth learn the way of Christian service.

LEARNING A WAY OF CHRISTIAN SERVICE

The context for any real Christian service must be a prayer-filled life that seeks the will of the Lord and desires to see people with the sensitivity and compassion of Jesus himself. There are eight steps in developing a strong and sensitive Christian servant consciousness.

1. Start where you are.
2. Take time to see the needs.

3. Assess your own personal gifts.
4. Set reasonable goals and make a personal commitment.
5. Pray and reflect about what you are about to do.
6. Act.
7. Accept responsibility for and evaluate what you have done.
8. Pray in thanksgiving for what has been done.

START WHERE YOU ARE

If we are ever going to learn to live Christian service as a way of
life rather than simply as a project to be done once in a while, we
must begin to live that life on a day-to-day basis. Very often we
will miss the obvious hurts and needs that are found in our own
friends and in our homes, schools, and parishes. The servant
Christian is one who is sensitive and responsive to the people who
touch his life. If we cannot respond to these immediate and
personal needs, it is unlikely that we will have either the depth or
the commitment necessary to help strangers. We must examine
the quality of our own personal relationships and accept our
responsibility to help those close to us. *It is important to
recognize the contradiction we show when we try to help others in
a service project while at the same time we are insensitive and
perhaps even destructive in the way we treat each other at home,
school, parish, etc.*

TAKE TIME TO SEE THE NEEDS

Whether we are looking at the community in general or are
concerned about a particular group in the community, we must
begin by clearly observing what are the actual needs of the people
and the community. This is the time for personal contact, study,
and reflection. Any project must be initiated only after the actual
needs of the people involved have been thoroughly observed,
studied, and prayed about.

Personal contact and interviews. Talk both with the people who
might receive our service and with others who are already
serving these people. For example, if you are planning a project
with the elderly, sit down and talk with some older people before
you start. Also talk to individuals who work with the
neighborhood council for the aging or in nursing homes, etc.
Check out what is already being done and learn from it.

Scripture and tradition. The Bible and the tradition of the church are very rich in wisdom and insight into the value of the person and the demands and possibilities of caring for others. The proclamations on love and justice encourage us in the necessity of our helping actions. We should study the teachings on the aged and the young and the way God has been present in the sufferings of the poor and the handicapped and any other people in need. How did Jesus minister to these people? How was he sensitive to their personal worth and self-respect? We should try to approach these people in the prayerful attitude of the Lord himself.

Study and reflection. A great deal can be learned from a more formal study of the needs of a particular group. Studies on the elderly, youth, ecology, etc., can open up practical and more complex dimensions of the people we are trying to serve. The social sciences, other religious traditions, philosophy, etc., offer a wealth of insights into the practical steps for effective care for others.

ASSESS YOUR OWN PERSONAL GIFTS

After we have very clearly in mind what the needs actually are, we must very honestly ask the question, "Can I really do what needs to be done?" "Do I have the necessary gifts and skills to meet these specific needs?" It is important that we be very honest in evaluating what gifts we do have so that we can accept responsibility for them. By recognizing the gifts we do not have, we might also avoid the unnecessary pain to ourselves or others which comes from trying to accomplish something we are ill-equipped to handle. We need not feel guilty because we do not have all the gifts to meet all the needs of every person and situation. It is in the whole Body of Christ working together that the many gifts are evident. The need for getting the help of others or of taking a minor role in a particular service should become very evident at this time. *Nice feelings about helping others are not enough.* If we are more concerned about the persons we help and the actual good we do, then we will take this step of personal assessment very seriously and with real truthfulness.

SET REASONABLE GOALS AND
MAKE A PERSONAL COMMITMENT

What we will do and how we will do it are the next questions to be answered. Beware of concern without commitment. To actually pin ourselves down to a specific work, with a specific commitment of time and a specific plan of action, is a critical step in effective Christian service. To work effectively in service demands personal sacrifice so that we can actually become the gift. It is best to be quite formal in our commitment even to writing out what we hope to accomplish and what we are willing to personally offer so that it might happen. Beware also of the "Messiah complex" in which I have all the answers and will do it all myself. Be very realistic in making commitments.

PRAY AND REFLECT ABOUT WHAT WE WILL DO
While the entire attitude of preparing for Christian service should be prayer-filled and constantly seeking the will of the Father, at this point in the preparation it has special importance. Any real Christian service must be done *in the name of the Lord*. The first disciples realized this and saw that the power by which they cared for others always had Jesus as the source. Sometimes a project can get way out of hand and very unrealistic and insensitive during the period of preparation. Sometimes the motives for doing a service become very mixed. This is a good opportunity to get everything in perspective, to remove the impulsiveness and duplicity from our motives and to seek a sense of real peace, so that this too might be brought to those we will help. It is also the time to ask the Lord for forgiveness and his help with some of our own baggage which might keep us from being open and responsive. If we know personally the people we will be serving, it is also important to pray for their particular needs.

ACT
All the good intentions and well-prepared plans in the world do not help people. We have to actually begin to serve in a very personal and concrete way. Many people will want to jump ahead before they have taken sufficient time to prepare. To serve someone effectively demands both preparation and action. It is also critical to remember that the way we serve must exemplify the message we are trying to share. Our model of service is Jesus himself. We must be very wary of doing something to people simply to get the job done. We are always trying to respond to the personal needs of the person being aided.

We should also proceed with great hope and expectation in our service. Expect the Lord to be present in our activity and to be the source of our sensitivity and strength.

ACCEPT RESPONSIBILITY FOR AND
EVALUATE WHAT YOU HAVE DONE

Sometimes when people help others and they finish their particular task they consider everything over and done with. Christian service can never end with the completion of the project. We must take the time to really evaluate the effectiveness, sensitivity, and quality of our service. Sometimes we are very successful and help the people involved in a most significant way. It is extremely important to see the good that is done. In it we can recognize how powerfully the Lord can work through each of us.

Often we find that we have also received a great deal from the people we sought to help. It is important to realize that when we deal with people in this personal, Christian way of Jesus we are often recipients of the richness and the gifts of others.

Finally, we often make mistakes, both simple and serious, in our care for others. Sometimes we do not live up to our commitments or we are insensitive to the people we are trying to help. Sometimes we get in over our heads and do not know what to do. Sometimes we find ourselves in embarrassing situations when something unforeseen goes wrong. It is essential that we look at what we have done with real truthfulness. Sometimes our failures are a real call to change the way or the motivation for our actions. Whatever has happened, however, will be rich in learning if we look closely at what we have done. We can learn even more if we share with one another what has taken place and how well we have served. By sharing with others we receive the encouragement for future service; we learn from each other's success and failure; we receive solace and support; and we begin to recognize the many different ways that the Lord works through his Body.

PRAY IN THANKSGIVING FOR WHAT HAS BEEN DONE

The Lord has promised great joy and happiness for those who serve in his name. It is important that we claim that joy and happiness. In a prayerful thanksgiving we once again recognize that all is gift and that the Lord was present even in our failures. This thanksgiving is not simply something tacked on the end. It is the gathering together of mind, heart, and body and recognizing concretely that all is done through the power and love of God himself.

Over the years hundreds of young people have journeyed through these steps. Many of them work closely with our diocesan ministries. In fact, our ministry could not function effectively without these young people who have grown strong in their service to others. But we are quite demanding. Our peer ministers participate in at least three training weekends each year. They are challenged not only to work hard but to live in accordance with the call of Jesus and as an active member of the church. Some are teachers, some counselors, some help with cooking and cleaning, some lead group dynamics, and some lead us in prayer. As these young people have grown they have reached out beyond our small ministry and have sought to do the work of the Lord in many new and exciting ways. In many cases their strength has taken them far beyond ourselves.

CONCLUSION: THE BEGINNING

As young people begin to develop a servant consciousness, use their gifts in the care of others, and learn new skills for social justice, they have really embarked on a new cycle of growth. In the Gospel of Luke, after Jesus sent his disciples out to preach the kingdom and heal the sick for the first time on their own, they came back ready to go deeper into his mystery. "Who do you say that I am?" is the question placed before them. A deeper response of faith was called for. Peter's response echoed what they felt in their hearts.

As our youth return from mission they must hear the Good News melody again for themselves so that it might penetrate deeper and more completely transform the newly growing parts of their lives. If they are welcomed back into a graceful community they will continue their growth as joyful, hopeful, wonder-filled young adults. If their community is wise they will become compassionate listeners, practical, truthful, and penetrating in their understanding of life and people. If their community is characterized by strength they will learn to blend gentleness with power and to be self-accepting yet self-critical. Qualities of boldness, endurance, and dependability will emerge.

What we have offered to them comes back again to us. The qualities and gifts of the Spirit which we hope to see emerging in their lives are the same fruits we hope to find in ourselves.

The church of Jesus Christ is at its heart evangelical. It is a mission community that finds no rest in itself but will only find its completion in the fullness of the kingdom. The young are attracted to what is vibrant and alive, to what is bold and dynamic, to the adventurous and the challenging. Are these not qualities that should characterize our parish life? With the active participation of the young these qualities can continue to burn brightly.

THE REVEREND MICHAEL GERARD FOLEY

Michael Foley was born on September 22, 1945, in Chicago Heights, Illinois. His family soon moved to Worcester, Massachusetts, where he has spent most of his life.

Michael became involved in the youth apostolate in 1959 when he became a member of the Catholic Youth Council in the Ascension parish in Worcester. He served as an officer in the parish youth group for four years. As a sophomore in high school he was part of a youth panel that gave a workshop at the National CYO Convention in Buffalo. Two years later he coordinated a second youth workshop at the Chicago convention. In 1962-63 he served as president of the Worcester diocesan Youth Council, and from 1962-67 worked as a part-time youth minister out of the Diocesan Youth Department in Worcester under Monsignor John P. Martin.

In 1963, after graduating from St. John's high school in Shrewsbury, he entered Holy Cross College in Worcester. Michael graduated with honors in 1967 with an A.B. degree in Philosophy. In 1963-64 he served as New England Representative to the National Youth Advisory Board. He was also keynote speaker at the New England CYO and Young Adult convention in 1965. During 1966-67 he was responsible for establishing and directing the Search and Retreat Program for the Diocese of Worcester.

Upon graduation from Holy Cross College, Michael entered the seminary and began four years at North American College and Gregorian University in Rome, Italy. During that time he participated in a variety of special programs, including summer spent at the Hebrew Union Biblical and Archaeological School in Jerusalem and a travel/study program in Comparative Religions in northern India. His Deaconate Internship (June-October, 1970) was spent serving the people of Saint Paul's Parish, Mbaga, Kenya, East Central Africa. From 1969 to 1971 he worked as coordinator of the junior/senior high school religious education program at Marymount International School in Rome. He also developed a retreat program for youth of U.S. Army personnel in Germany. Michael was ordained to the priesthood in Saint Peter's Basilica in 1970 and received his STL with honors from Gregorian University in 1971.

Through the summer of 1971, Father Foley served as full-time chaplain at Saint Vincent's Hospital in Worcester, Massachusetts. He then spent from 1971-73 as associate pastor of Our Lady of Fatima Parish in Worcester's inner city and chaplain for the Memorial and Doctors Hospitals. He has served as Treasurer for the Lincoln/Belmont Neighborhood Council, Secretary of the Worcester Diocesan Senate of Priests, Diocesan Delegate to the New England Conference of Priests' Senates and the National Federation of Priests' Councils, Vice President of the Central Massachusetts Interfaith Clergy Association, and diocesan representative and treasurer of the Board of Directors of Central Massachusetts Interfaith Center for Draft Information.

From 1973 to 1976 Michael served as Diocesan Consultant for Adolescent Catechesis in the Office of Religious Education of the Diocese of Worcester. In 1976 he became Coordinator of the Interdepartmental Youth Ministry Team. As Coordinator of Youth Ministry he functions as administrator of the Catholic Youth Department and Assistant Director of the Office of Religious Education.

Besides his diocesan responsibilities Father Foley has given workshops, retreats, and seminars throughout the United States, including Los Angeles, New York, Chicago, St. Louis, Memphis, Boston, St. Paul, Milwaukee, Charlotte, North Carolina, and New Orleans. He has been a frequent keynote and focus speaker at New England Youth Ministry and Religious Education diocesan and regional conventions. In 1985 he will be giving workshops in both Youth and Young Adult Ministries at the N.C.E.A. Convention in St. Louis, Missouri.

Father Foley was a member of the Advisory Board for Young Adult Ministry of the United States Catholic Conference since its inception in 1975 until 1980. In this capacity he has served on the design teams for two National Young Adult Convocations, the Aura: Training for Young Adult Ministry, and has served as liaison with the National Center for Youth Adult Ministry at Merimack College. In 1977 he was the author and presenter of the position paper on young adult ministry at the Symposium on the Parish and the Educational Mission of the Church, sponsored by the U.S.C.C. He has also written articles and reviews on both youth and young adult ministries for the U.S.C.C., N.C.E.A., and Paulist Press. Most recently he has authored the chapter on Young Adult Ministry in *Gathering God's People: Signs of a Successful Parish*, published by Our Sunday Visitor. At the 1979 National Young Adult Convocation in Los Angeles, Father Foley was named as one of the ten outstanding leaders in Young Adult Ministry.